How to Promote Your Music Successfully on the Internet

The Musician's Guide to Effective Music Promotion on the Internet

2011 Edition

by David Nevue
http://www.davidnevue.com

Brought to You By...

The Music Biz Academy

http://www.musicbizacademy.com

The Music Biz Academy Bookstore

http://www.musicbizacademy.com/bookstore

Recommends These Additional Resources for the Serious Musician...

Music is Your Business
The Complete Guide to Starting a Record Company
How to Be Your Own Booking Agent
The Guerrilla Music Marketing Handbook
The Indie Bible

Get them at http://www.musicbizacademy.com/bookstore

Published by Midnight Rain Productions, P.O. Box 21831, Eugene, OR 97402. Brought to you by *The Music Biz Academy* - http://www.musicbizacademy.com.

Table of Contents

First Things First -
Stuff to Read Before You Start Exploring

Thank you for purchasing the 2011 edition of "How to Promote Your Music Successfully on the Internet!"

Do you want to be an Internet marketing expert? Do you want to promote your music to millions of listeners and find new and interesting ways to advance your music career using the Internet? Since you've purchased this book, I presume you do. However, it's very natural for you to be skeptical about how truly useful this book might be. You may be one of those musicians whose attitude is that they've "heard it all before" or, you may be in the opposite situation, feeling completely overwhelmed by the Internet and having no idea where to start. Maybe you're somewhere in-between. Regardless of where you are in your music career, this book is probably unlike any you've read before on this particular subject. Why? Because unlike most other books about promoting your music on the Internet, this book is a *personal account*, written by an independent musician, like you, who has actually done the work and been successful at it. How successful? I started promoting my music on the Internet in 1995 and by 2001, just six years later, I was able to quit my day job. I've been doing music full time ever since.

I'm sure you have questions you hope this book will answer. Two such questions might be "Is it really possible for me to sell my music on the Internet and make much money doing it?" and "Can I really use the Internet to advance my music career?" The short answer to both questions is "Yes." I have proven it can be done with my own music. My objective with this book is to outline the strategies I myself have used to market my music, advance my career, and bring in significant income, all by taking advantage of the Internet.

Before getting into the guts of this book, however, you should probably know who it is you're getting advice from and why you should listen to anything I have to say. My name is David Nevue. I'm an independent musician (a pianist and composer) and I've been promoting my music on the Internet since 1995. It's been a very long, interesting road. Let me tell you a little bit about my background...

A Brief History

In 1993, I started working at Symantec Corporation, the makers of Norton Antivirus, Norton Internet Security and other software. I was working there when the Internet first came into public view. I can still remember the first time I saw a web browser while on the job. Back then, I had no idea the extent to which the Internet would change the world. How could I? In 1993, a web browser was a mere curiosity, a toy to pass the time between customer support calls.

It didn't take long, however, for me to realize that the Internet could be a great way to create exposure for my music. I had recorded two albums of my original solo piano music and had been selling them to friends, family and fans at the few local gigs I played (I only played a few shows a year at that point). Like most musicians, I dreamed of doing music full time. So, in 1995, I did what most musicians still do today. I put up a web page, added some sound samples (*.wav files in those days), and hoped people would find me. My first year selling music online I sold just two CDs. It was a rather disappointing start. I wasn't satisfied with that at all, so being the rather determined individual I am, I put my energy into testing new and creative ways to market my music. I knew I was on to something when I started selling four or five CDs a week. That gave me the idea to write this book, the first edition of which came out in November of 1997.

In the years that followed, I continued to build on that early success. I expanded my Internet business to include not only sales of my CDs, but also sheet music (transcriptions of my own piano compositions), music downloads, books (like this one), information and advertising. By the year 2000, I was making as much money running my Internet-based music business as I was working at Symantec. In November of 2001, after saving up a year's salary as a safety net, I achieved my longtime dream; I quit my day job at Symantec to work on my business full-time. Needless to say, that was a major turning point in my life. I have enjoyed the freedom that has come with that accomplishment, spending the extra time on my music, growing my business and being with my family. Life has never been better or more fulfilling.

So, to answer the questions that may still be lingering in your mind, yes, you can make money selling music on the Internet. I've done it, and if you put the effort into it, you can do it too. The next obvious question you probably have is, "How much money can I make?"

Will You Make Millions?

Let's get real for a moment. Promoting your music successfully on the Internet is *hard work*. Don't ever forget that. I've spent *years* doing this. The Internet is not a shortcut to success – it's simply another tool, one that can be very effective in the hands of someone who knows how to use it. Still, it's important to have realistic expectations before investing your time and money marketing your music online. You're going to face some very heated competition. There are literally *hundreds of thousands* of musicians out there who already have web pages on the Internet (as of this writing there are over 360,000 albums registered with CDBaby.com alone). How can you compete with all those artists? That's just the tip of the iceberg. Once you embark upon your promotional journey, you are in a very real sense competing with every other web page out there. How can you possibly stand out in *that* crowd? Pretty daunting, isn't it? It's worse than being a needle in a haystack.

According to the Nielsen Netratings web site, there are over 234 million people actively using the Internet (see http://blog.nielsen.com/nielsenwire/online_mobile/top-u-s-web-brands-and-site-usage-december-2009/). A Georgia Tech survey of *actual buyers* provided some very interesting statistics: 70% of all buyers searched for the item they bought, 16% searched for a topic *related* to what they bought, and 4% searched for the name of another product which led them to the final product they purchased. Adding it up, 90% of all buyers used the Internet as a modern-day, digital Yellow Pages. So the question is, what does this tell you about selling your music on the Net?

Quite simply, it means that creating a web page to sell your music is *not enough*. That's something I discovered very early on. Even if you get your web site listed in the search engines, you're not likely to see a significant traffic increase. Think about it. If 90% of the buyers out there already know what they are looking for and are searching the Internet for that particular item, how will they find *you*, someone whose music they have likely never heard of? If they aren't looking for you, they won't find you. So, what ARE they looking for? Therein lies the key. More on that later.

Here's the slap-in-the-face reality: In my experience, the *average* musician sells between two and five CDs a year from their web site. Those selling digital music downloads on iTunes *might* make a hundred bucks a year on top of that. Can you do better than that? Yes, you can do much, *much* better, selling not only CDs and digital music downloads, but sheet music and other merchandise. But you'll only find success if you have a quality product people care about and market it properly. Let me be up front with you. To succeed on the Internet, you must prepare yourself for the long haul (I'm talking years) and prepare to work hard. Success on the Internet won't come overnight.

As you read this book, keep the following questions in the back of your mind. They hold the key to successful online music promotion:

- *What is unique about my music?*
- *What general style of music are my fans most interested in?*
- *What other artists do my fans compare my music to?*
- *What other artist would the "average person on the street" say my music sounds like?* and most importantly….
- *Who is my target customer?*
- *What is my target customer searching for on the Internet?*
- *Where does my target customer spend their leisure time on the Internet?*
- *Where does my target customer go to find and listen to new music on the Internet?*
- *How can I use that information to bring that target customer to my web site?*

Within the pages of this book I will show you what marketing ideas worked for me and steer you away from those that didn't. Although I cannot make any guarantees about how well these ideas will work for you, if you put the ideas in this book into practice, you should see some improvement in the overall income you're generating from the Internet. For me, the improvement was immediately noticeable and over time it has become quite dramatic.

So, to answer the question I posed at the beginning of this section, no, you are not likely to make *millions* on the Internet doing just music. But you can bring in a *good, steady income*. In 2010, I was able to generate an average income of over $6,000 per month just from sales of my music via the Internet. That income came from CD sales, digital music downloads and sheet music sales. *In addition* to that, I earned income from concert tours, performances and fees (all self-booked, promoted and arranged online), CDs sold at those performances, music licensing, music royalties, Internet radio subscriptions (I created an Internet radio station just to promote my music), advertisement revenue and, of course, sales of this book. With all those different revenue streams going, I make a very nice living, and every single thing I do is related to the music business I love. How great is that? What a blessing!

Of course, money isn't everything. There's still the question of using the Internet to advance your music career, and that's something the Internet can help you do also. I've been able to generate a lot of publicity for my music online. As a result, not only do I sell a lot of music, but I often receive requests to have my music used in independent film and media projects. I've negotiated three distribution deals overseas as a result of someone finding my music online. One company is using my music on an internationally distributed DVD series that raises funds for various charities. NBC contacted me to inquire about using my music in a made-for-TV film. Photographers are regularly (almost weekly) asking to license my music for use on their web sites, slide shows, and DVD presentations. The Wall Street Journal took notice of my efforts, including me on their "New Media Power List" of people "being catapulted into positions of enormous influence" (July 29, 2006 edition). Finally, I'm playing a lot more gigs in a lot more places as a direct result of marketing my music online and as you know, the more you play live, the more doors get opened up for you. You, like me, can use the Internet to *create opportunities* for your music, and the more opportunities you create, the more likely you are to gain new fans, sell more music, book larger paying gigs, and of course, make those contacts you want to make within the music industry.

A Note on Gigs and Touring: One of the most unexpected "surprises" I've had as a result of promoting my music online is the ease with which I can now set up and book my own concert tours across the country. This isn't something I expected to happen. In fact, only a few years ago I was quoted as saying "I will never tour - I have no desire to tour." But after the success I've had promoting my music online, the demand from my fans for live shows became something I could no longer ignore. I realized that by not touring, I was leaving money (and potentially new customers) on the table. I now book three to four tours a year using my *fan base* as my only significant booking resource. It's exciting!

I know many reading this book may be of the mind that they will never tour or perform live. Well, as the old adage goes, never say never. You CAN be successful promoting and selling your music online without performing live – I did that very thing for years. But if you do find success, you may discover that booking concerts is not only easy to do, it's a serious revenue generator. I'll be devoting an entire chapter to the topic of booking your own concerts and tours later.

Getting Signed

I get email almost every day from musicians looking to be signed by a major record label. Perhaps you too, have aspirations of "making it big" in the music business. If there is one thing I've learned over the years, it's that record labels aren't looking for fly-by-night musicians and songwriters to turn into stars (American Idol and a few other copycat TV shows being the exception). They are looking for musicians who are already *doing the work.* They are looking for artists who have created a huge fan base, sold tens of thousands of CDs (or hundreds of thousands of downloads) and played sold-out shows all *on their own.* What I'm saying, in a roundabout way, is this: if you want to make it big and get signed to a major label, the best way to do that is to forget about being signed to a major label and do the work yourself. Get out there, play your music, build your fan base, and sell your music. Your goal should *not* be to "get signed," but to bring yourself to a point to where you no longer *need* the backing of a record label. Once you reach that point, and you have a marketable name and product, *then* you might find some A&R people knocking on your door. Maybe. But keep this in mind: over the next few years, record labels, as we know them, may not exist. Very few labels actually develop artists anymore. They develop *product.* Are you a product? Or are you an artist? In this modern era, you cannot rely on a record label to "discover" you. If you want your music to be found by new fans, YOU must be the record label. YOU are the record label.

My intent with these comments isn't to discourage you, but to *empower* you. You don't need a contract with a major label to have a successful music career. If you are seeking only *fame* and the satisfaction of seeing your face in People magazine someday, then yes, you'll probably need the backing of big money to help you do that. But if you just want to do music full-time and be the quintessential artist, that's something you can do all on your own. The Internet can help you reach that goal. I'm living proof of that.

My goal with this book is quite simple. I want to teach other musicians to use the Internet the way I have, not only to bring in more income, but to gain significant exposure for their music. I will show you how to target an audience *most likely* to buy your music. I will show you how to convert visitors to your web site into sales, and how to increase your fan base. I will show you how to sell more CDs, how to sell music downloads, and how and where to distribute your music online. Basically, I'm going to use this book to pass on pretty much everything I know about marketing music on the Internet. Whatever your end goal is, if it involves using the Internet to promote your music, this book will help you do that.

But Will it Really Work for ME?

One of the most common questions I get is…

> "You're a solo piano artist, but my music is (*insert your own musical genre here*) and I live in (*insert your country of residence here*). Will your marketing ideas work for me?"

Let me assure you that the style of music doesn't really matter. What matters isn't so much *what* you're selling as it is *who* you're selling to and knowing how to target that particular audience. Finding your audience is what this book will help you do.

There are really only two basic requirements for creating music people will buy. First, your music must be the sort that someone, somewhere, would be drawn to purchase if they had the opportunity to hear it. Second, your recordings must be *quality* recordings. Obviously, you'll have a tougher time selling music that sounds terrible than something that sounds polished and professional. So, while I'm not prepared to say this book will help you sell your music if it's poorly written, performed, produced and recorded, if your music is quality music that someone, somewhere can feel and relate to, then you have something you can market online.

As to your location, your country of residence, that doesn't really matter either. The Internet is global. I could sell my music from anywhere on the planet so long as I had a good, solid Internet connection with unrestricted access to the rest of the world.

How to Use This Book Effectively

There are several points I would like to emphasize before going further:

1) Within this book, I will not dwell on topics like purchasing a computer, setting up an Internet connection, how to write HTML or build your web site from scratch. Yes, I will give you the basics (see *Getting Started* section), and I will point you to locations where you can find more information, but for complete details on these topics, please research other materials. I will make the assumption that you already have a computer with Internet access. This book will focus mostly on successful music marketing techniques.

2) If you already have a web site, you may be tempted to skip the *Getting Started* section. Please don't. Although this section is geared toward newer Internet users, I will, along the way, discuss some marketing issues which may be of interest to you.

3) I won't spend ten pages saying what I could say in two paragraphs. The reason this book isn't 400 pages long is that it doesn't need to be. My goal is to give you the information and advice you need, quickly and to the point. It's up to you to take it from there and find success.

4) Once you put the ideas in this book into effect, you should begin to see marked improvement in the number of visitors to your web site as well as an increase in your mailing list sign-ups and sales. The results you see, however, will depend greatly on the quality of your product, how attractive your package is and, of course, how well you market your music and target your web site. Successful marketing on the Internet takes an incredible amount of persistence, trial and error, business savvy and *time*. It's taken me years to get to this point, and I'm still learning, so don't expect to be able to put all the ideas in this book into effect over a weekend.

5) Take the ideas you learn and sit down and write an online marketing plan. Set small goals to accomplish over the next several months. Don't try to do it all at once. Start small, and create a strong foundation to build your future on.

6) Take notes! There's a ton of helpful material within these pages. If something I say strikes your fancy, *highlight it immediately*. That will make your life easier when you want to refer back to those specific comments later.

7) Throughout this book I make references to hundreds of web sites. These sites are changing all the time and although I try to keep on top of them, it is possible that one or more of these web addresses may go out of date. If you happen to find a link that is no longer valid, please let me know! You can contact me at dnevue@rainmusic.com . Please put "Suggestion for your music promotion book" in the subject line so it will get my attention and I'll know your message isn't spam.

8) Lastly, you'll notice that I make reference to many different products and services throughout this book. The reason I recommend the products and services I do is because they appeal to me personally and I have found them useful. In other words, no one is paying me to advertise or pump up the variety of services mentioned in this book. Every opinion expressed in this book is free of payola. It's just my opinion.

The Glossary of Universal Terms:

Casting the Characters: Topics I'll be Talking About... a LOT!

One of the cool things about the Internet is that everything is connected to everything else. It's part of what makes the Internet such a powerful marketing and communications tool. However, it's also one of the reasons the Internet is such a difficult subject to teach. To teach one aspect of the Internet, you frequently need to make reference to several other aspects of the Internet that haven't been discussed yet in full detail. In that sense, learning about the Internet is like learning a new language. It's a convoluted web of terminology that can get your head spinning… much like a book or film that has so many characters that it's hard to keep track of who's who.

I want to do everything I can to make sure you and I are on the same page throughout this book, so before I go further, I want to briefly introduce you to a few of the "main players" that I will be discussing. Now, it may be that you are already familiar with all of these terms. If so, move on to the next chapter. But if you have no clue what "Social Media" is, for example, then this is your crib sheet. If I reference a term later in this book and you aren't sure or don't remember what it is I'm talking about, you can quickly flip back to this section to brush up on your terminology. I will, of course, be discussing each of these in great detail throughout the book. But here's a short summary of common terms and phrases listed in alphabetical order:

Blog (or blogging): "Blog" is short for "web log," which is a sort of web-based diary entry. In your blog, you can discuss any and all topics and share your thoughts with anyone who cares to read them. Blogging is a very popular pastime for a lot of people. Blog postings fill the search engines and there are entire web sites that are nothing more than blog directories or links to blogs. Blogging is something you can do on your own web site to keep your web site content fresh, current, and new.

Digital Music Downloads: Digital versions of your original songs or your entire CD. In other words, people purchase and download the digital version of your album or song(s) direct to their computers or device (an iPhone, for example) without having to buy a physical CD. As of this writing, digital music accounts for about 25% of all music purchases worldwide, and 40% of all music purchases in the U.S. Digital music has become such a force in today's music business that many artists are abandoning the production of physical CDs altogether and are going straight to digital.

Facebook.com: The most popular social networking web site on the Internet, bar none. You can use it to quickly connect with friends (from your past or present), coworkers, family, and fans of your music. Checking Facebook is an ongoing daily routine for lots of folks. It has become a grown up version of email and is one of the most immediate ways to connect with your fans.

Flash: *Flash* is one of the most popular web design technologies in use today. Flash makes use of high-powered animation and pictures to put what is essentially a moving short film on your web site. Many sites use Flash for their entire design, which can be cool, but can also be a great source of irritation to visitors. Flash-styled design can enhance your web site, or detract from it. I'll be going into detail about that later.

Keywords or Key Phrases: Specific words and/or phrases that relate to your web site content. Assuming you have a web site, what words or phrases do you think people will type into a search engine (such as Google) that *should* result in their finding your web page? Those words, whatever they are, are your strategic keywords or key phrases. Your name, or band name, is obviously a "key phrase." When someone types your name in Google, you want your web site to be the first result returned.

Host, Hosting or **Web Site Host**: A web site "host" is a company that rents out computer space for the purpose of serving up a web site. When you create the files that make up your web site pages, you need a place to upload those pages to so the world at large can see them. You sign up with a hosting company, upload your files to the computer space they provide, and you're good to go. Each web site host has a unique DNS "address." You purchase a domain name (ie. www.yourwebsitename.com) and point that domain name to that web host's DNS address. Then, when someone types your domain name into their browser, through the magic of the Internet, the viewer is directed to the proper computer web server to see your pages. Sounds complicated, but it will be explained in more detail in this book.

HTML: The text-based "code" behind most web pages you view in your browser. When you design web pages, you are, generally speaking, manipulating HTML. A lot of folks who don't know a thing about designing web sites are intimidated by this word. Don't be. You don't need to know HTML to design web pages in this day and age. It's helpful, but not necessary. So if this is something that worries you, fret not.

iTunes: Software installed on every Mac computer (and a great many PCs) that gives music fans a quick way to preview, purchase and download their favorite music in a digital format. As of this writing (Dec. 2010), about 66% of all digital music sales worldwide happen through iTunes. The second largest digital music store, at just 13% of the market, is Amazon.com.

MP3: The audio format most commonly used for music on the Internet. When someone refers to an MP3 file, they are talking about a digital audio file that can be played in most media players.

MySpace.com: MySpace was, until recently, the most popular social networking site on the web (it was eclipsed by Facebook by 2009). MySpace is very heavy on music sharing and strongly reflects a youth culture. MySpace is losing market share very quickly as people jump to Facebook, and although MySpace continues to try and reinvent itself, it appears to be a sinking ship. Even so, for the moment, MySpace still presents opportunities to promote your music, gain fans and build your mailing list.

PayPal.com: A convenient way to purchase items or transfer money online. Set up a PayPal account and you can hook it right into either your bank account, or your credit card account. Then when you shop online at a store that accepts PayPal, you have a faster and easier method of paying. On the flip side, when you're selling your music from your web site, you'll want to be able to accept PayPal as a method of payment.

Podcast: A podcast is basically a portable radio program, one that you can download, sync up to your computer, iPod, or media player, and listen to at your own convenience. It's rather like a DVR for Internet radio. If you have a favorite podcast, you can subscribe to it and when you sync your computer and/or iPod to it, the program will automatically transfer the latest episodes to your device.

Ringtones: You know those cute little noises your cell phone makes when a phone call comes in? You know, the "ring?" That's a ringtone. You can make your music available as a ringtone for people to purchase and put on their own cell phones, so that when they receive a call, your music alerts them to it. Pretty cool!

Social Media, Social Marketing and Social Networking: There are countless web sites built around social networks; "meeting places" where groups of people talk, chat, share opinions, and gossip with one another on an almost continuous basis. Marketing your music at these social water coolers is an absolute must. In this book, I will cover the most important of those, which include (but are not limited to) Facebook, Twitter, MySpace and YouTube.

Technorati.com: Arguably the largest blog tracker on the Internet. If you get turned on to blogging, Technorati is a great tool to use to search for other bloggers talking about the same things you are. You'll find other blogs to review in your blog, people to interview, and even inspiration for subjects to write about and express your own opinions on.

Twitter.com: A hugely popular social network based on the concept of tracking "What I'm Doing Right Now…" You "follow" people or people "follow" you, and people can keep track of what you're doing and/or thinking about throughout the day. It sounds silly and a bit 'big-brother'-ish, but it's a great marketing tool.

Viral: To say something is "viral," in Internet terms, means that something you have created has taken a promotional life of its own. If you create a video and it goes "viral," it means that your video is so interesting that people feel compelled to share it with other people. One person shares your post with six of their friends, who each love it and share it with six more, who each share with six others, and so on. Within a week, you're a semi-celebrity and hundreds of thousands of people know who you are. At least, that's the aim. One of the best things that can happen to you, promotionally speaking, is if your blog, music, or video goes "viral."

Vlog: "Vlog" is short for video blog, which is a blog recorded to video rather than written. Vlogs are a great way to engage your fans, or make new ones, if you do them well.

Widget: A web "widget" is a portable chunk of code that can be installed into virtually any web page and still function. Common examples, which I'll reference many times in this book, are widget music players. Once you load up the music player with your songs, you can cut and paste the code for the widget into any web site where you'd like to display it. That way you can use the same music player on your web site, Facebook page, MySpace page, in your blog, and so on. The widget concept is designed to simplify your coding. You do it once and paste it everywhere.

YouTube.com: A treasure trove of videos of varying quality, style, and content. You'll find video commentaries (vlogs), music videos, silly videos, stunts, and bizarre stuff – everything and anything you can imagine. Millions post their videos on YouTube. It's a great place to market your music which I will, of course, be expounding upon in this book.

With that behind us, let's get started....

Getting Started:
Where to Begin When You Have Nothing!

What You Need, What it Costs, and How to Get by with Less!

The nice thing about doing business on the Internet is that you can start with very little cash up front. If you already have a computer and Internet access, you can get going for as little as $50. Below is a short list of items you will need to get started on the Internet, along with estimated costs:

The 'Right' Computer System

Most any computer system you purchase today will come with built-in Internet connectibility. You can easily purchase an Internet-ready computer for less than $700, but expect to pay $1200-$1300 for a system that comes with all of the most up-to-date goodies. If you are buying new and for the first time, you may want to consider purchasing your system locally. That way, if you encounter difficulties, you can take your system right to the dealer for repair. I recommend you avoid buying a computer from office supply mega-stores like OfficeMax or Staples. You'll get better support from a small, localized computer professional who cares about you as an individual customer. Purchasing a computer from a Best Buy store is a respectable option as well, as their "Geek Squad" staff is readily available to help you with any difficulties you might have. The point is, wherever you purchase your computer, make sure it's from a location that can provide *direct support* to you should you need it.

There are basically two ways to go when looking for a computer system: you can buy one with Microsoft Windows pre-installed or go the Macintosh route. Many musicians prefer the Macintosh operating system as the Mac is known for its friendly, easy-to-use interface and innovative design. Personally, I prefer the Windows environment, but that's just what I'm used to. Either way, once you have a system, getting onto the Net will be a relatively simple process. Today's high-speed systems come pre-configured with all the hardware and software you need.

If you don't mind buying via mail order, and if you, like me, prefer the Windows operating system, let me recommend you check out Vision Computers (http://www.visioncomputers.com). Every Vision-built desktop system comes with a three year parts and labor warranty (which is virtually unheard of), and their 24/7 *lifetime* support is known for its excellence. However you go about it, when you are ready to buy your computer make sure you find out what kind of warranty you are getting. For a new system, your warranty should cover labor for at *least* one year and parts for at least three.

A Fast Internet Service Provider

Once you have a computer system, the next thing you'll need is an Internet connection. Most systems you buy today come with two or three ISP (Internet Service Provider) choices preconfigured for you (MSN or

AOL are common examples). However, I would avoid using either of these services as they tend to be slow and unreliable. The easiest, most painless way to get hooked up with an Internet connection (if you don't already have one), is to contact your local cable company. They'll get it all set up for you and you won't have to worry about a thing.

The only real disadvantage to going with your cable company is that you are going to pay a premium rate for the service. If you do a little research, you'll find rates that will be a lot less expensive. However, the trade off may be the level of service you can expect with a third party. Cable companies, generally speaking, have lightning fast connections. And, for the most part, if you need help with anything you can call and get assistance fairly quickly.

I use my local cable company, Comcast (http://www.comcast.com) and I have been very happy with their service. It's $29.99/month for their high-speed Internet-only service, but the connection is blazing fast and I can't remember the last time the connection was down or not working properly. When I have had issues, I've called Comcast and had someone on the phone with me very quickly.

A trustworthy alternative you might look into is Verizon. Verizon offers high-speed Internet at prices starting at just $19.99 per month (see http://www.verizon.com/dsl). As tempting as it is to switch to Verizon at that price, I've stayed with Comcast as I've been very happy with their service. However you choose to go, get a *fast* connection. If you're doing serious business on the Internet, you'll need the speed.

If you want other options, you can look in your local phone book Yellow Pages under "Internet." Your local providers will be listed there. If you still have difficulty finding an Internet service provider, try searching "The List" at http://www.thelist.com or Broadband Reports DSL search at http://www.dslreports.com/search . The latter service is great, as you can see reviews of your local services as posted by customers.

A Note of Caution! You MUST have a personal firewall to prevent unwanted tampering on your system. When using a cable modem, DSL or wireless connection, you are *continuously* connected to the Internet and thus vulnerable to hacking. Windows comes with a firewall built in, but if you just can't bring yourself to trust Microsoft (and you probably shouldn't), check out the free ZoneAlarm firewall software at http://www.download.com/ZoneAlarm/3000-10435_4-10039884.html .

My Firewall/Antivirus Recommendation: If you can afford to spend a bit to protect your computer investment, I recommend (and use) Kaspersky Internet Security. See http://usa.kaspersky.com/products-services/home-computer-security/internet-security273 .

For more recommended reading on this topic, see *ISPs* in the *Quick Reference Guide* near the back of this book.

Just Browsing

The next item you'll need is a web browser. I really doubt I need to say much about this since, if you are reading this book, chances are about 99.5% that you already have one. If not, a web browser is the tool that allows you to view web sites on the Internet. If you want to stick to the tried and tested browsers, you have three basic choices: The first is Internet Explorer, which comes pre-installed with the Windows operating system. You can download the latest version (or any updates) from Microsoft's web site at http://www.microsoft.com/windows/internet-explorer/default.aspx . Your second choice is Mozilla Firefox, a competitor to Internet Explorer, and my favorite. Firefox can be downloaded from Mozilla's web site at http://www.mozilla.com/firefox . Your third choice is Safari, from Apple, available at http://www.apple.com/safari . Safari is the default browser for the Mac but is also available for Windows. Most PC users opt for either Internet Explorer or Firefox, but there are dozens of other web browsers available. For a list, see http://browsers.evolt.org .

Finding the Perfect Web Host - A Place to Call Home

You'll need a place to call 'home' on the Internet, a place to put your web pages so others can view them. A web hosting service will allow you to put your web site on their servers for a monthly fee. You are essentially renting the space from them. To assist you in finding a web host, check out the Top Hosts web site at http://www.tophosts.com . This site allows you to search and compare web host services by price and other criteria. Many web hosting guides like Top Hosts are available on the Internet. For a list, see *Web Hosts* in the *Quick Reference Guide* at the end of this book.

The fee for web hosting varies, but generally lies between $4 and $20 dollars a month depending on the options you need. The more space, features and bandwidth you want, the more it will cost you. You may also be asked to pay a one-time setup fee which can run anywhere from $10 to $50.

The company I currently use for hosting is PowWeb at http://www.powweb.com . Hosting plans start at just $3.88 per month, and you're just one click away from being able to chat with someone on PowWeb's support team who will gladly help you.

Other hosts recommended to me by readers have included Site5 (http://www.site5.com) , LunarPages (http://www.LunarPages.com) , Surpass Hosting (http://www.surpasshosting.com/) and for really cheap hosting, SiteFlip (http://www.siteflip.com) . I haven't tried any of these, but on the surface, everything looks very reasonable. Finally, I'm sure most readers are familiar with GoDaddy.com (http://www.godaddy.com), a hosting company that's been around forever and has developed a solid reputation as a host.

You will also find companies online that can provide you with not only hosting, but an "instant" web site through template-driven web building tools. I'll be discussing those in the next chapter.

Note: Make sure the web host you select supports MP3 file streaming. You're going to need that. I'll explain more in a later chapter.

The Pros and Cons of 'Free' Web Hosts

If you've done any searching for a web host, you probably already know there are many so-called "free" web hosting services available. You'll find a few listed at http://www.free-webhosts.com . Generally speaking, if the hosting is free, you're giving up something in return. You'll have limited space and bandwidth for sure, and in many cases the "free" web host will display their advertisements on your web site. Some free services don't even give you your own domain name, but instead make your site an extension of their own. For example, rather than having a web site at the web address of "yoursitename.com," the address would be http://www.yourwebhost.com/yoursitename . That's a long and difficult address for your visitors to remember. So just know that if you go with a free web host, there are trade-offs, sometimes pretty serious ones. You are much better off in the long run if you purchase your own easy-to-remember domain name and set up an account with a professional hosting company. Don't treat your music career like a cheap date. Spend the $5 bucks per month necessary for professional hosting. The reasons will become more evident as you read further along in this book.

Claim Your Domain

In addition to a place to host your web site, you'll need to register a domain name (such as yoursitename.com) to serve as your web site address. I use DirectNIC (http://www.directnic.com) to register and manage all of my domain names. The cost of their service is $15.00 per year, per domain, and while you can find cheaper registration services, you'll be hard pressed to find one that's easier to use. I highly recommend their service.

You can search DirectNIC to see if your desired domain name (your web site address) is available right from the home page. If the name you want is already taken, DirectNIC will make some suggestions based on your initial search. As you explore your options, do your best to choose a web site address that's *easy to remember*. Keep in mind, as you search, that you'll be repeating this web site address to not only your fans, but to important contacts you make. Avoid the use of hyphens (such as my-musicplace.com) or oddball naming conventions and spelling (such as 4starmuzik.com). Keep your name simple and its spelling obvious. Finally, if at all possible, use a dot.com (*.com) extension. Although .net, .us, .org, .biz, and other extensions are available, the .com extension has become synonymous with the Internet and will be the easiest for your fans, contacts, and visitors to remember.

Once you have selected and registered your domain name, you'll need to tell your domain name registration service where to direct traffic for that domain name. In other words, when someone types "yourwebsiteaddress.com" into their web browser, to what server should they be directed? To set this up, simply find out from your web host what your primary and secondary domain name server (DNS) information is. It will either be an IP address (i.e., 12.345.67.8) or a hostname (ns1.hostname.com). More than likely this information was emailed to you when you signed up for your hosting service. Take this information, go to your domain registration service (again, I use DirectNIC.com), login to your account, and add your DNS information to your nameserver (or they might call it DNS) configuration. The process sounds more complicated than it is. Once you get started, the techno-speak above will make more sense.

TIP: If you find domain name registration and configuration difficult, talk to your web host provider. Most providers will take care of the entire registration process for you at no extra cost. You just pay the cost of the actual registration.

FTP Client Software Recommendations

FTP is an acronym for "File Transfer Protocol." The basic function of FTP client software is to upload and download files to and from your web host's server. Once you have your web page designed (I'll discuss web page design software in the next chapter), the HTML document and graphic files that make up that page need to be transferred from your computer to your web host's server via an FTP client. FTP client file utilities are readily available on the Internet. I recommend any of the following FTP client tools:

CoreFTP:	http://www.coreftp.com/
CuteFTP:	http://www.cuteftp.com/cuteftp/
WS_FTP:	http://www.ipswitchft.com/Products/Ws_Ftp_Pro/Index.aspx?redirect=h_index
Fetch (for the Mac):	http://www.fetchsoftworks.com/

Personally, I use CoreFTP. It's free and works just great.

Your web hosting service can help you set up your FTP client so you can upload files to their server. The process is very simple, and only requires you to fill in two or three fields with configuration information your web host will provide. Once it's set up, you can upload or download your files to your host service with the click of a button. For a few FTP tutorials, simply go to YouTube.com and search for "FTP Tutorial."

Email: Your New Best Friend

Electronic mail (email) makes it easy for your customers to contact you. Most services, including web hosts, ISPs and online services, will provide you with a free email address to go along with your web site. If you'd rather, you can use one of the many free web-based email services on the Net, such as Yahoo! Mail (http://mail.yahoo.com) or Google's Gmail (http://gmail.google.com). The one big advantage of going this route is that you can check your email with ease from any computer with an Internet connection. For a quick study on all the services available to you, check out the Free Email Address Directory at http://www.emailaddresses.com .

In Summary...

The tools mentioned above are all you should need to get started on the Internet. You will use these tools just about every day as you run your online business. If you are a beginner and new to this kind of technology, some of what I described above may sound a bit complicated, but it's really not. If you take the time, you can learn all this stuff pretty quickly, and soon you won't even think about it - you'll do it all automatically. If you find you need more assistance with any of the above, free tutorials are available online for every aspect of connecting to the Internet. To find help with a particular topic, just go to Google at http://www.google.com and search for the specific item you need help with, for example; "ftp tutorial." It won't take you long to find a number of useful resources.

To sum up:

1) **Buy a computer:** I recommend buying locally from an established company that you can get direct service with. If you purchase a computer from BestBuy, hire the Best Buy Geek Squad to remove all the presales junk that companies like HP and Sony preload onto your new computer. That way you start with a clean system.

2) **Find an Internet Service Provider (ISP):** Get hooked up to the Internet with a *fast* connection. I recommend the digital cable services offered by Comcast (http://www.comcast.com).

3) **Get to know your web browser:** Internet Explorer more than likely came preinstalled on your computer, but do check out Firefox (http://www.mozilla.com/firefox) as Firefox is my preference.

4) **Find someone to host your web site:** I have been very satisfied with PowWeb hosting (http://www.powweb.com) . If you need help with anything, you can get immediate support via their chat tools.

5) **Register your desired web site address:** DirectNIC.com is my registrar of choice.

6) **Download and configure your file transfer tools:** CoreFTP all the way.

7) **Set up your email account:** Start by asking your web host about available options. I use Yahoo! Mail (http://mail.yahoo.com). I also recommend Google's Gmail service (http://mail.google.com).

If you find all of this is just too confusing and you feel that learning it is beyond you, let me encourage you to *take up the challenge*, dive in and educate yourself. If you want to find success promoting your music online, you'll need to learn this stuff at some point. There's no better time than NOW.

With that covered, let's talk about the process of designing a web site....

Planning Your Web Site - Inspiration, Creation and Consideration

---

Design Considerations for the Design Challenged!

If you're going to market your music successfully on the Internet, you need an "official" web site of your own. Sure, you can put your music on iTunes, CD Baby and Amazon.com and yes, you'll probably sell tunes through those venues. However, if you want to be successful long-term and *build a following* you can count on to buy your music again and again for years to come, you need a web site "home;" a place your fans can visit to keep up with your latest releases, news, concert dates, and so on.

The purpose of this chapter is to get you thinking about your web site design options; how to get started, where to find ideas and inspiration, and to generally cover the basic elements of creating your web site. Later in this book, I will teach you how to organize your web site into a powerful sales tool for your music. For the moment, though, let's just focus on getting your web site up and running.

What about making a MySpace/Facebook/CD Baby/ReverbNation/Etc page your "official" web site?
Rather than creating an actual web site, some artists opt to sign up for a service like MySpace, Facebook, CD Baby and/or ReverbNation and make those their "home" on the Internet. Having a page on MySpace or one of these other social music services is fine, but you don't want to make such places your home of homes on the Internet. Why? Because sooner or later these web sites will become yesterday's news. MySpace (http://www.myspace.com) is the perfect example. Once hugely popular, MySpace is no longer the hip place to be. People are moving from MySpace to Facebook in droves, as Facebook is the happening place to be right now. However, you can be sure that Facebook's cool factor will diminish over time as well. Like MySpace, Facebook's popularity will fade, and something new and exciting will come along to replace it. It's inevitable. People are easily enticed to chase after the "next big thing." For this reason, you *never* want to put your primary web residence on a third-party web site or service that is subject to changes in the culture, times and technology. You're better off having your own web site and your own web address, something you'll have control of long after MySpace, Facebook, or your service of choice is relegated to the Internet dustbin. If at all possible, take the time to learn how to create your own unique web site.

You have a number of options for creating a web site of your own. You can design one yourself, hire a professional to design it, or go with a template-based web site option. Let's start with the template-based design options as those are the quickest to get up and running.

Web Site "Design by Template"

If you have no idea how to design a web site and don't want to take the time (or make the effort) to learn, there are hosting communities you can join that will provide you with the closest thing you can find to an "instant" web site. For about twenty bucks a month, you get a pre-designed web site with hosting included. All you do is sign up, select the web site "template" you prefer from the choices provided, and then add the text and/or images you want to display on your web page. In this way, you can create a web site of your own without having to understand, or even touch, "code." If you decide you don't like the template design you chose, with the click of a button you can switch to another template, instantly changing the look of your entire web site. It's fast, it's relatively simple, and it's a pretty inexpensive option.

Here are a few examples of some of the better "design by template" services available:

HostBaby (http://www.hostbaby.com) : If you want a web site and you want it quickly, HostBaby.com will give you everything you need to get a basic "band" web site online in about an hour. Features include a concert calendar, email list mailer, audio streaming, guestbook and blog. The cost to you will be $20/month (No setup fee, first month free).

Bandzoogle (http://www.bandzoogle.com) : Bandzoogle offers snazzy, ready-to-go templates and a full range of features including a mailing list, music player, forum, blog, event calendar, photo gallery and you can sell both digital music and physical CDs and merchandise through PayPal. Bandzoogle's standard plan starts at $14.95/month with a "pro" plan that gives you a bit more for just $19.95/month. Bandzoogle offers 30 days free if you'd like to try it out. View some of their fabulous web site templates at http://bandzoogle.com/sample-band-sites.cfm .

BandVista (http://www.bandvista.com) : Another point and click web site builder designed for musicians. Hundreds of templates, MP3 player, image gallery, mail list management, calendar, guestbook and more. Prices start at $14.95/month.

ReverbNation: (http://www.reverbnation.com/) : ReverbNation is a fabulous service for musicians with gobs of features, including Site Builder, their template-based design system. ReverbNation's Site Builder easily integrates with all their music promotion tools, widgets and so on. Check out ReverbNation's list of tools to promote and sell your music and you'll be impressed.

Wix: (http://www.wix.com/) : Create stylish Flash-based web sites with the Wix Web Site Builder, all point and click without having to know or understand Flash. Many music-based Flash templates are pre-made for you. Flash is generally not the best way to go when it comes to search engine optimization, and it could create some other limitations for you. I'll discuss those issues in a bit. Even so, check out Wix to see what they offer.

Homestead (http://www.homestead.com) : While not designed specifically for musicians, Homestead offers an easy solution that will enable you to put a terrific looking web site online quickly. Choose from 2,000 attractive pre-made site web designs (or have one custom made). The basic package starts at just $4.99/month. Updating your site is quick and easy with a template-based, point-and-click design interface.

Viviti (http://viviti.com) : Viviti is one of the least expensive – and simplest – options for creating a template-based web site. As with Homestead above, the service isn't geared specifically for musicians, but looking at some of their featured web sites, it's obvious that a least a couple of musicians have taken advantage of their service to create nice, functional web sites. A basic site with Viviti is free, and while you probably won't want to stick with that (it's ad-supported and quite limited), it gives you a chance to test out the service before you commit. Viviti's basic plan is just $10/month, a price that includes hosting and your own domain. Visit http://viviti.com/featured_sites to see some of their featured sites and the kinds of layouts you can create with Viviti – all without knowing any "code."

Template-driven services like the above offer some great-looking designs and the speed and ease with which you can get a web site up and running makes them a tempting option. However, these pre-made template-style web sites do have serious disadvantages that you need to consider. First, your design isn't unique, meaning other people will choose the same exact design you do. Secondly, template-driven web sites aren't usually very flexible. If you want to deviate from the pre-made design, customize the layout and/or add new features for your fans, you may find it difficult or even impossible to do. Finally and most importantly, what happens if you ever, in the future, decide you want to change web hosts? Can you take your design with you? Or, do you lose everything and have to start all over again from scratch? That's an important question to ponder, and it's something you should ask the service before signing up.

Personally, I prefer to have total control over everything. Call me a control freak – that's OK – I freely admit it! In the end, I believe the flexibility and freedom of having your own web site is of great benefit. While services like those mentioned above are great for getting up and running with a web site quickly, if you get serious about promoting your music online I think you'll find that you, too, will desire more and more control of your content. That being the case, I recommend against going with any of these "instant," cookie-cutter style solutions for the long term.

If you like the concept of having a template-driven web site, but you want more control over the design and want to be able to customize the look and feel of your pages, you might consider taking the blog approach…

Blogging Your Web Site

To refresh your memory, a blog (short for web log), on its most *basic* level, is an online diary; a page where you can write your thoughts down, post articles, write reviews and so on. Professional bloggers have turned the concept of blogging into an art form and because of this, blog tools have become very versatile. If you have the tools and the know-how, you can customize your blog to the point to where it can pretty much serve as your web site. Not only can you post your thoughts, articles and commentary, you can add on all kinds of widget-based functions like music players, concert calendars, mailing list sign-up forms and more. Finally, unlike most of the template-driven options above, you can install the blog software on virtually any web server. That means you're not tied to a particular host and/or service. If you ever want to change web hosts, you can do so without losing your work.

Why might you want to use a blog for your web site? One of the most attractive features is that once you have your blog/site design in place, updating the content is a breeze. Have a thought? Write it, post it, and you're done. The blogging software automatically creates new web pages for you. Once it's built, the maintenance on a blog-based web site is pretty low key.

I'm going to talk about blogging in detail later in the book, so I don't want to delve too much into the topic here, but if the concept of creating a blog and using that as your web site appeals to you, start researching Wordpress (see both http://www.Wordpress.com and http://www.Wordpress.org). The templates that come with Wordpress make it easy to just choose a design and start writing. Creating a basic blog is a simple process, just as simple as any of the template-driven hosting options above. The difference is that, with a blog, you can customize the look and feel of it to your heart's content with few limitations. Wordpress has a feature called "pages" which allows you to create actual web pages. You can add a "Bio" page, for example, and a link to that page would be added automatically to your blog's sidebar. Using the pages feature, you can create an entire web site. Combine that feature with some of the e-commerce options I'll be discussing later for selling your music merchandise, and you're pretty much good to go.

The downside? Though you can design a blog to look pretty much however you want it to look, the customization process (depending on how far you want to take it) can be tricky to learn. It's not a three-step process, that's for sure. If you want to deviate very far from the basic pre-made templates (and you will) you'll need to spend some time educating yourself about CSS, PHP and more. Take a look at the Wordpress Codex page at http://codex.wordpress.org/Blog_Design_and_Layout and you'll see what you're in for.

So now you begin to see the trade off. The more control you want over your web site design, the more time you need to invest in learning how web sites work. If you want a web site that looks original, that doesn't look like a cookie-cutter template and is uniquely *you*, at some point it would benefit you to invest some time educating yourself about how to design a web site.

Now, before you fall completely into despair, let me tell you that there is hope! There is another option; a way to create your own web site without having to learn the underlying code.

Curing the Common Code: How to Build a Web Site Without Being Nerdy

Having talked about some of the template-based options, let's now talk about what I do, personally.

I'm a control freak, so I want complete control over my web site. I also want flexibility, so that I can add new features to my site at any time in the future. The problem is, I'm not a programmer or a techno-geek. I like software that is easy to use. I'm a visual, point-and-click kind of guy. I want to manipulate my web pages based on what I "see," and not based on code. I want to use web site development software that looks and feels more like a word processor than it does something from the Matrix.

Are you with me? Good! So let's talk about HTML. Just for a minute. Bear with me.

HTML is the text-based "code" behind most web pages you view in your browser. When you design traditional web pages, you are, generally speaking, manipulating HTML code. Now, if you already know about HTML, then you're probably all set when it comes to web design. You probably already know plenty about it and have a favorite software package you like to use for that purpose. Awesome for you!

However, let's say you *don't* know a thing about HTML, but you want to design your own web site. What's a person like you to do? You do what I did; you purchase a WYSIWYG web site editor.

WYSIWYG (Pronounced "Wizzy-wig") is short for "What You See is What You Get."

It works like a desktop publishing program. Think Microsoft Word on steroids. It lets you see the web page as you're making it, and rather than typing code, you're typing the words you want, placing the text where you want it on the page, then inserting your images and moving them around as needed. Yes, the HTML is there, but it's all in the background, behind the scenes. You don't actually see it, touch it, or worry about it - unless you want to.

Sound good? This is exactly how I design my web sites. Are my web sites brilliant displays of engineering? No, they aren't. But do they sell product? Oh yes, most definitely. My web site designs are simple, classy, and to the point. They do the job.

My favorite of the WYSIWYG editors is Namo WebEditor. I've been using Namo for many years and I love it. You can download a free trial version of the software from Namo's web site at http://www.namo.com .

Many other WYSIWYG software choices are available as well. One of my readers recommended an editor called Site Spinner (http://www.virtualmechanics.com/products/spinner). I haven't used this one, but it looks great. Site Spinner offers a free trial version of their software.

Another option is CoffeeCup Software's Visual Site Designer (http://www.coffeecup.com/designer/). Coffee Cup also offers a free trial version of the software to play with. I've always liked Coffee Cup's software, so this one is worth checking out. Plus, there are a few dozen really nice web site templates you can purchase from CoffeeCup to go along with the software.

Another well received WYSIWYG editor is StudioLine Web, available at http://www.studioline.net/EN/products/overview-web/default.htm . This one looks really good.

A free, open-source WYSIWYG editor called Nvu is available at http://net2.com/nvu/ .

Another free WYSIWYG editor that looks promising for beginners is PageBreeze at http://www.pagebreeze.com/ . This one comes with lots of templates (and access to hundreds more) that make getting started with your web site design much easier.

For reviews of other editors (if you want to find more) see "25 Useful WYSIWYG Editors Reviewed" at http://www.smashingmagazine.com/2008/05/06/25-wysiwyg-editors-reviewed/ . You can do further research at http://webdesign.about.com/od/htmleditors/ as well as Google's vast list of editors at http://directory.google.com/Top/Computers/Software/Internet/Authoring/HTML/WYSIWYG_Editors/ .

If you're still unsure which way to go, just search Google for "wysiwyg html editor reviews" and you'll find lots of information to sort through. Do some serious investigation here, because finding the right editor will simplify your work and prevent frustration later.

How to Jump Start Your Web Site Design

So how do you start? One of the things I love about WYSIWYG editors is that you don't have to start from scratch. Many of the editors listed above come with dozens of pre-made designs that you can customize to your liking. If the designs that come with the software don't appeal to you, you can find thousands of web site templates available online, many of them free. Here are just a few examples:

Free Web Site Templates:	http://www.freewebsitetemplates.com/
Boxed Art:	http://www.boxedart.com/
4Templates:	http://www.4templates.com/
Design Galaxy:	http://www.designgalaxy.net/
Deonix Design:	http://www.deonixdesign.com/

Template Monster:	http://www.templatemonster.com/
Free Site Templates:	http://www.freesitetemplates.com/
Elated Pagekits:	http://www.elated.com/pagekits/
CoffeeCup Templates:	https://www.coffeecup.com/store/themes/visual-site-designer/
Ice Templates:	http://www.icetemplates.com/
Full Moon Graphics:	http://www.fullmoongraphics.com/
A+ Templates:	http://www.aplustemplates.com/
Basic Templates:	http://www.basictemplates.biz/servlet/StoreFront
The Template Store:	http://www.thetemplatestore.com/
Web Zone Templates:	http://www.webzonetemplates.com/

I haven't listed these sites in any particular order. Check them out to see if the design styles appeal to you. Between them, you have a huge selection of templates to choose from. Some are free, some charge a fee. Download and open one of these pre-made templates into your WYSIWYG web page editor and you are well on your way to designing your own web site. Start moving graphics around, adding images and text. Just play. That's how you learn to use the software and once you get the concept down, you can start creating your own pages and designs.

Give some of the WYSIWYG editors I mentioned a try. You'll find creating web sites this way is much easier than learning code, and you'll also find that, as you experiment, you may actually start understanding the code behind what you're doing. That is exactly how I learned HTML; by creating web sites visually first.

Before you go about designing your web site, there are some basic technical things you will need to know:

Graphic Types: There are two types of graphic image files that are most commonly used in web design; *.gif and *.jpg files. Unless you're doing something really unusual, all your images will be saved in one format or the other. Which format is best? Well, here's the general rule: for photos, pictures, intricate illustrations and artwork that you scan, use *.jpg files. For text logos, small graphics or line-based graphics use *.gif files.

HTML: If you're using a WYSIWYG editor, you don't even have to worry about seeing the HTML "code." As you become more skilled as a web page designer, however, I guarantee you'll find understanding HTML useful. It's cool, because you can create your page visually in the editor, then view the code to see what your changes look like at a code level. Again, that's exactly how I learned HTML.

If you don't know a thing about HTML and want to learn more about it, let me recommend the interactive HTML tutorial for beginners at http://davesite.com/webstation/html/ .

See Also: HTML Clinic: http://www.htmlclinic.com/
HTML Goodies: http://www.htmlgoodies.com/tutorials/getting_started/
HTML Center: http://www.htmlcenter.com/

Your 'Home' Page: Incidentally, your web site 'Home' page should be saved as index.html (or index.htm, it doesn't matter). Once you've designed your home page, use your FTP client (discussed last chapter) to upload it to the root directory provided to you by your web host. Then, when you type your web site address into your web browser, your index.html file will be displayed by default.

During the process of designing, you may find you need to do something a little different with your page headings and/or your menu and navigational structure. For those situations, you may find these web sites useful:

ButtonGenerator:	http://www.buttongenerator.com/
FlashButtons:	http://www.flashbuttons.com/
CoolText:	http://www.cooltext.com/
Flaming Text:	http://www.flamingtext.com/start.html

If you need stock photos or stock art to add some life to your pages, check out http://www.iStockphoto.com. I just love browsing around that site.

Finally, if you have difficulty finding what you're looking for, whether it be page template sets or a particular image, check out http://www.freegraphics.com/ . That's a good place to start.

How Much Is Too Much?

There are all kinds of fancy things you can do with your site graphically. However, I find it best to keep your web site design simple and to the point. The more graphics you have on your web page, the longer your page will take to load in your visitor's browser. Some people think the more *stuff* they have flashing and spinning on their web site, the cooler it is. But it's not cool at all. It looks really unprofessional.

The truth is, in terms of web design, *less* is better. Pages load faster, and your site is easier to navigate. Whatever you do, make sure the text on your web site is *easy to read.* There is nothing wrong with using a solid color or even just white for your web site background. Want a classy web site? Just find a simple graphic theme that uses a few small images and repeat that theme throughout your web site.

For a **Fantastic Tutorial on Web Design**, I recommend you read "Web Designs from Scratch" at http://www.webdesignfromscratch.com/ . The site includes some great articles and tutorials that will teach you everything you need to know about basic web site design – what to do and what not to do – and it will flat out inspire you. Read it and learn.

Article of Note: Visitors judge your web site in the blink of an eye. See http://news.bbc.co.uk/1/hi/technology/4616700.stm

Those are some ideas to get you started with your basic web site design. Later in this book, I'll show you how to design a web site that is *sales friendly,* and how you can implement a few strategies to significantly increase your chances of selling your music to your web site visitors.

Make It So! How to Make Your Site "Live"!

In the *Getting Started* section, I talked briefly about FTP client software. This is what you will use to upload your image, sound (see next chapter), and HTML files to your web host's server. Once you've decided on a hosting service, that service will provide you with the username and password necessary to gain access (via an FTP client) to your web site's file directory. This file directory looks just like what you see when you open up Windows Explorer. Using your FTP client software, you connect, navigate to the desired directory, then simply select and upload your files. Once you've done this, those files are visible to the world on the Internet.

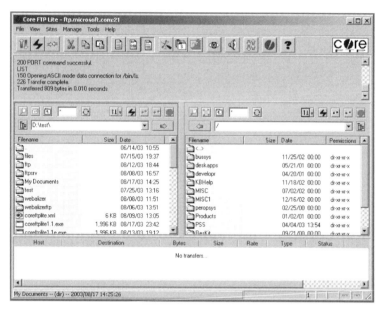

You will find useful step-by-step tutorials for virtually any FTP Client on YouTube. Just visit http://www.youtube.com and search for "ftp tutorial" and then the name of your preferred FTP software.

If It Doesn't Flow, Hire a Pro...

At this point, I've given you several options for creating your own web site. I really encourage you to explore them. If you're a beginner, I'm sure this all seems pretty overwhelming. Running a business online (and that is what you're doing if you are selling and promoting music online) takes a lot of work. However, it's very rewarding. If you spend just a little time on this, I think you'll find a path that works for you.

If all else fails, you can always hire a professional. The appearance of your web site is *very* important to success, so if you have any doubts at all about your design capabilities, or if you just can't get your head around it, find someone who can do the job for you and make you look good. At the very least, a design professional may be able to help get you started and you can take it from there.

There are literally thousands of Internet-based companies out there ready to design your web site for you. The fees for such services vary greatly. You may find an amateur designer will provide you with great work for $250, while a "pro" might create a very basic site for you and charge $2500. Regardless of the price, there is one thing you must demand from each potential designer: a sample of his or her work. Any professional or amateur designer worth their salt should have several web sites they can refer you to to preview their work. One thing to keep in mind before hiring a professional is that many Internet-based companies are in fact run by one person. Knowing this, ask yourself... do you trust this person? Always, *always* contact past clients of anyone you are considering working with and ask how satisfied they've been with the service. One other note...*for every service someone will sell you, there is someone else who will sell the same service to you for less or for free.* Don't take the first offer that comes along, but do keep in mind *you often get what you pay for*. A cheap designer might give you a cheap design.

There are many places on the Internet where you can search for and make contact with professionals. Not only for web site design, but also general coding, script installation and Wordpress blog customization. Check out Freelancer.com (http://www.freelancer.com). At Freelancer.com you can post your requirements and artists and programmers will bid for your job. You can evaluate each bid, including each bidder's portfolio, before committing to anything. If you see something you like, you can hire them on the spot. Similar options are available at the Elance Agency (http://www.elance.com/p/websites/index.html) ScriptLance.com (http://www.scriptlance.com) and HostBaby.com (http://www.hostbaby.com/wddb).

If you'd like to see some of my personal web site designer recommendations, check out the "Graphic & Web Design Services" listed in the *Internet Resources for the Independent Musician* section near the end of this book.

Also, don't forget to make use of your fan base. Chances are you have a dedicated fan that knows something about web design and has some skill at it. They might jump at the chance to help you get your web site up and running. You might offer them free CDs, MP3s or concert tickets in exchange for their services.

Planning Your Web Site

Are You Inspired? How to Find Ideas for Your Web Site Design.

Whether or not you hire a professional to design your web site, you need to have a web site plan going forward. I would not leave every aspect of your web site plan to a hired hand. A professional designer may be great at laying out pages and images, but have no clue whatsoever about creating a web site that actually sells product. A web site is more than random text, images and data. It has a purpose... to sell your music.

So as you move forward, even if you aren't designing the web site yourself, you need to be the one to develop the overall plan. Yes, your designer can implement the plan, but YOU need to create the plan. So how do you create a plan?

First, you'll need ideas about how to layout your web site. Where can you find ideas? Aside from checking out the aforementioned templates, one of the best ways I know to find design ideas is to simply look at what other musicians have done with their own web pages. A simple way to do this is to search for an artist in your same genre at CDBaby.com. Go to http://www.cdbaby.com and find your genre under the "Genre" listings. Click on that and you'll be presented with a list of the best selling independent artists in your genre. Select an artist that looks interesting. Now, look in the left-hand column of the artists' CD Baby page. Under "Links," most artists will include a link to their 'official' web site. Using this method, you can visit a number of artist's personal web sites to gather ideas. Spend some time on each artist's page and make notes on what you like and don't like about each of them. In particular, pay attention to these bullet points...

- How easy is it to find and buy the artist's CD? Is the purchase process confusing? If yes, what makes it confusing? If no, what makes it simple?
- Is it possible to purchase *downloads* of the artist's songs? Is the process straightforward?
- If you want to listen to an artist's sound samples, is it easy to do?
- Are there customer testimonials that get you excited and interested in this artist's music?

- If you have a question about your order, how easy is it to find the answer?
- What if you wanted to book this artist for a gig? Can you find that information?
- What if you wanted to license this artist's music? Can you find that information?
- How easy is the web site to navigate? Can you get back and forth between important pages easily?
- Do you feel "lost" on the web site, or do you always feel like you know exactly where you are? Why?
- Is the web site easy on the eyes, or confusing and difficult to look at? What makes it that way?
- Does the web site appear to be active and regularly updated? If so, what gives you the impression it's been recently updated?
- Is the web site and/or artist interesting? If yes, what is it that makes the web site and/or artist interesting? If no, what makes them boring or bland?
- Does anything on the web site offend you? Or does it please you?
- Can you relate to the artist? If yes, how does the artist make themselves relatable? If not, why not?

Going through a checklist like this will help you distinguish "good" from "bad" in web site design. As this is the first time you've seen the artist's web site, you can be truly objective. You can have an honest first impression of what turns you on and what turns you off. Whatever notes you take away from this exercise, remember them and *apply them* to your own web site as you create your web site plan. Because in the same way you just critiqued these artist's web sites, people coming to your web site will critique yours. **Every person who visits your web site will critique it**, either consciously or subconsciously, and that critique may be the deciding factor in whether or not they choose to purchase music from you.

Planning Your Online Press Kit

As you begin formulating a plan for the overall layout of your web site, try thinking of your site as an online press kit. Like a press kit, your web site pages should include the following:

- Your name, contact information, and where you are located
- A band or artist photo and/or photo gallery
- A band or artist biography
- Product information (CDs, downloads, DVDs, T-Shirts, posters, whatever)
- Detailed CD/download details (tracks, song descriptions, album notes, sound clips and samples)
- Your upcoming performance schedule
- Booking information
- Press notes, reviews, customer testimonials, awards, links to important related sites
- The latest news about your act
- Links to any other web sites, discussion groups, or social networks you are actively involved with
- How and where to find more information

These are the things your web site should have at a very minimum, and these items ought to be easy for your web site visitors to find. If you hand your business card to a club manager who might want to book you and they look to your web site for information, they ought to be able to find that information quickly and easily. They will also need to be able to contact you directly from your web site.

Keep all this in mind as you plan your web site layout.

Advanced Web Design Considerations

This section, as the title suggests, is for those of you who are a bit more experienced with the web. It includes my thoughts on several topics, including Flash, SSI, web counters, scripts, anti-spamming your web site and site maintenance. This is good reading for everyone, but not necessary for those of you just getting started.

Flash!: Oops, They're Gone.

One of the most popular web design technologies in use today is called *Flash*. Flash makes use of high-powered animation and pictures to put what is essentially a moving short film on your web site. Many sites use Flash on their intro pages and they are very cool to watch – sometimes – but they can also be a great source of irritation. If a visitor is looking for specific information on you and they come to your web site, they don't want to have to sit and watch a Flash presentation before they can continue on to the information they want. That's akin to asking a web site visitor to watch a TV ad before they can actually start checking out your music. That's bad! Flash, when used this way, is an *obstacle* to sales. And not only that, it can take time to load or, in worse case scenarios, not load at all. So obviously, using Flash this way is something to avoid.

You can, of course, add a Flash presentation as an *enhancement* to your web site. To do this, I recommend creating an obvious link to your presentation from your home page. Then, if the visitor *wants* to see your cool Flash presentation, they can view it. They aren't forced to find a way around it.

In addition, there are simple flash elements, such as menu buttons and music players, that you can integrate into your design to enhance it. Those are fine, of course, so long as you make sure that a majority of your web page is text-based, rather than flash or graphic based. I'll explain why that's necessary in the upcoming chapter on search engine optimization.

If you'd like to know more about Flash, check out the easy to read Flash tutorial at http://www.w3schools.com/Flash/default.asp . Then, to dig a bit deeper, visit the "Getting Started" section of the Adobe Flash Developer web site at http://www.adobe.com/devnet/flash/?view=gettingstarted .

Death to Frames!

As it relates to web site design, you may have heard about a layout technique called *Frames*. Frames allow your visitors to view more than one page at a time within a single browser window. The intent of frames, generally speaking, is to simplify web site navigation. In a common scenario, a navigation menu is displayed in the left or top frame of the browser window, while an 'active' page requested by a visitor is displayed in the right frame. You'll find a simple example at http://www.csounds.com/man/manual.htm .

When this technology was first introduced, it spread around the Internet like wildfire. Frames became one of the most prominent web design fads of the late 90's. However, most casual Internet users came to despise them. Have you ever tried to bookmark a framed web site? It's very annoying. The use of frames also makes it difficult for search engines to index your web site properly. For these and other reasons, most designers eventually abandoned their use. Today, it's very rare to find a web site built with frames.

Long Live SSI!

One of the main reasons web designers were attracted to frames initially was because it made managing web site content so much easier. If you had a web site with 100 pages that all used the same navigation menu, rather than creating 100 navigation menus on 100 individual pages, you could create just one menu, place it in a navigation frame, and then use that single frame in conjunction with all the other pages. That way, if you needed to make a change to the navigation menu, you could simply edit the navigation frame one time and your change would be available throughout the entire web site. It's much easier to change one page than a hundred!

There is a much simpler, more attractive way to do this. If you want to create a frame-like site to make managing content on a large site easier, let me recommend you research Server Side Includes (SSI) instead. Server Side Includes are easy to use and will save you a ton of time in terms of updating content. If you have HTML that is exactly the same throughout your web site (like the navigation menu mentioned above), you can create a single HTML file containing this code, and then use SSI to call this single HTML file and insert it into your web pages as they load. Sound complicated? Perhaps the best way to explain the use of SSI is to show you an example:

Navigate your web browser to the Music Biz Academy at http://www.musicbizacademy.com . Now, see the two-line menu near the top? It starts with Home | Blog | Music Promotion | Bookstore | Etc... The HTML for that 'menu' is actually contained in a separate file, a menu.html file that contains nothing other than the two-line menu structure. I use a Server Side Include to call and insert the menu.html information where I want it on this page. To do this, I inserted a single line of code which looks like this:

```
<!--#include virtual="/templates/menu.html" -->
```

This statement, inserted into the HTML of my main index page, calls the menu.html file and displays it in the exact spot I want when the index page loads. The process works a bit like a batch file did in the DOS days if you are familiar with that concept. I've used SSI elsewhere on this index page as well. The navigation you see on the right-hand side (the grey column) is also inserted by use of a Server Side Include.

So, why use SSI? Because these sections of the web page appear on nearly every page of my web site. Now, if I want to update my menu or the right-bar navigation, I can do so by editing one single file rather than several hundred. In essence, I can update all the pages that include those menus in just a minute or two.

As you can see, SSI can be very helpful when designing a web site. For a great tutorial on the use of SSI, see FAQ: SSI at http://www.andreas.com/faq-ssi.html .

Important Note on SSI: in order to use SSI, your web host's server must be configured to support it. If this sounds like a tool you'd like to use, ask your web host if they support the use of SSI. Also find out if any special file extensions are required. Many servers require a *.shtml file extension for any pages that use SSI.

Another option: A few of the WYSIWIG web site editors I mentioned have functions similar to SSI built right into the software. In particular, check out StudioLine Web, available at http://www.studioline.net/EN/products/overview-web/default.htm for this purpose. Read up on the layout editor feature at http://www.studioline.net/EN/products/sl-web/features/layout-editor/default.htm .

Web Counters: The Pros and Cons

Although less common today than in times past, people still do, on occasion, wish to display a web counter on their web site. I really recommend you avoid displaying a visible counter until you are seeing a good deal of traffic coming to your site. If you're doing a lot of traffic, a web counter might help you solicit advertising from your visitors (I'll get into advertising later in this book). If your traffic is low, however, all a counter does is tell your visitor how *unpopular* your site is, which is rather bad for business. So how do you know how much traffic you're doing without a counter, you may ask?

Any quality web host will be able to provide you with a stats management program you can use to view detailed traffic statistics for your site. This service should be free (included in your hosting costs) and will give you access to some great information about your traffic. For example, you'll be able to see what pages on your site are most popular, where your visitors are coming from, how long they are staying and what keywords your visitors are using to find you via the search engines. This service should completely eliminate your need to display a visible counter on your web site.

If your web host service does not offer a stats service you like, there are other options. GoStats (http://gostats.com/) offers a free web counter and stat service. You simply copy and paste the code they provide into the web pages you want to track and you're basically done. You can browse through a number of other free options at http://www.thefreesite.com/freecounters.htm .

IMPORTANT: I haven't talked about designing a web site using "tables" and I won't cover that in this book. However, if this is something you discover and you opt to use tables as part of your design style, it's important for you to realize that you need to place any third-party counters (or any graphic hosted on another web server) *outside* of your tables. Otherwise your web page may not refresh completely until it's finished loading the counter! This can be very serious, for if the site providing your counter goes down, your pages may not load completely. Placing counters outside any tables you create will prevent this.

If you'd like my personal recommendation, rather than using counters I use FastStats, a third-party software program that analyzes web site log files that your web host can make available to you. It's fairly inexpensive, and it's an invaluable tool. You'll find FastStats at http://mach5.com/products/analyzer/index.php . For a similar, but free (and less feature-filled) alternative, check out the "lite" version of WebLog Expert at http://www.weblogexpert.com/lite.htm .

Scripts, Forms, Search, Chat, Guestbooks & More

It seems like every day it gets easier to add cool functionality to your web site. Adding a search engine, guestbook, chat room, or response form to your site can be as simple as copying and pasting HTML. In fact, the process is becoming so easy that adding these features to your site has become almost trivial.

Whenever I'm looking for elements like these to add to one of my web sites, my first stop is always Bravenet.com (http://www.bravenet.com). They have a nice selection of tools and they are all pretty simple to implement. Beyond this, check out the "Webmaster Freebies" section of The Free Site at http://www.thefreesite.com . This directory includes everything from chat and guestbooks to javascripts, banners, polls, graphics, search forms and counters. The Free Site reviews literally hundreds of sites all listed by category.

In the *Scripts, Forms, Site Tools and More* section of the *Quick Reference Guide,* I've listed about two dozen other starting points when searching for cut-and-paste scripts, forms, tricks, and tools. Your options, in terms of advanced web site design, are nearly endless. However, let me remind you once again, *more cool stuff* does not always equal a better web site! Before adding anything "cool" to your web site, ask yourself if that new gadget is really necessary. Does it complicate your site navigation? Does it draw attention *away* from your music? Or does it add real value, giving your visitor another reason to buy?

Finally, keep in mind that when dealing with scripts, your visitor's web browser must be able to support the script to view it. Not all scripts can be viewed in all browsers. There are, for example, Internet Explorer-only scripts that won't work in Firefox. That's a "gotcha" to watch out for.

Incidentally, most WYSIWYG web design software packages come with some cut-and-paste script functionality built in. That's something else to look for when considering web design software to purchase.

If you've found a super cool script and don't know how to get it up and running on your server, you can have most scripts installed for you by posting your requirements at http://www.freelancer.com/ . Freelance programmers will bid for your job. Other script installation services are listed under *Scripts, Forms, Site Tools and More* in the *Quick Reference Guide*.

How to Anti-Spam Your Web Site

One of the negative aspects of doing business on the Internet is that you become subject to spam – those irritating emails from people you don't know advertising everything from stocks, real estate and mortgage loans to (more often than not) certain unmentionable items, products and services of the sensual variety.

The thought that's likely to cross your mind the first time you start receiving this junk is "how did these people get my email address?" Well, that's thanks to a spam-bot, a pesky little critter that crawls the Internet searching for email addresses. If you use your address *anywhere* on the Internet, you can just about guarantee it will be harvested by a spam-bot at some point. Once that happens, your inbox will start filling with annoying emails, most of which you wouldn't want your mother to see.

Spam-bots find your email address all sorts of ways. Through postings you've made in newsgroups, social networks, chat rooms, mailing lists, web forms you've submitted, AOL and MySpace profiles, and even from your web browser. Check out the article, *How Do Spammers Harvest Email Addresses?* at http://www.private.org.il/harvest.html for a detailed discussion of what spam-bots do.

One way to ensure you get spammed is to include your email address on your web site. Eventually, a spam-bot will come along, find that address, and harvest it for the purpose of sending you unwanted mail later. Obviously, this creates a problem. You need to post your email address on your web site so that visitors can contact you, but on the other hand, you don't want to be spammed either. What can you do?

While I don't think you can ever 100% spam-proof yourself, you can make it more difficult for spam-bots to harvest your address from your web site. One of the most common ways to thwart spam-bots is to encode your email address. The simplest way to do that is to replace the "@" sign in your email address with the ASCII character equivalent. For example, instead of using "mailto:myname@myaddress.com" in your web site HTML for an email link, use this: mail to:myname&#064myaddress.com

To a web browser, "&#064" is the same as the "@" sign and it will display it as such to your web site visitor. So even though you use different characters in your text, the browser will still recognize this code as an email link. Spam-bots, on the other hand, tend to key in on the "@" character and in many cases will ignore the "&#064".

While this method of hiding your email address on a web page is hardly fool-proof, it does work in most instances. If you're truly paranoid, you can further encrypt your email address on your web pages. Here are some tools that will help you do that:

Email Protector:	http://www.iconico.com/emailProtector/
Email Munger:	http://www.addressmunger.com/
Stop Spam-Bots:	http://www.safeemail.org/
Automatic Email Protection:	http://www.bronze-age.com/nospam/encode.html

There are hundreds of methods for hiding email addresses from spam-bots, and thousands of web sites that will tell you how to do it. Some of the options offered are very complex and are, in my opinion, more cumbersome than they are worth. Still, email encoding, to some degree, is worth looking into.

Aside from encoding your email address, there are other ways to combat spam as well. You can….

- Set up alias email accounts that filter out the spam and forward only the messages you want.
- Create web site submission forms that force a particular subject line (which can be filtered and forwarded to you at a non-public address) or
- Use software like MailWasher (a fantastic program at http://www.mailwasher.net) to more easily sort through and delete unwanted email before it gets to your inbox.

Personally, I tend to use a combination of these methods. As much as I get around on the Internet, I consider it a near certainty that my email address is going to be harvested by a spam-bot. It's just a part of doing business on the Internet. However, if you encode your email address on your web site when you design it, even using the simplest method, you're likely to reduce the amount of spam you receive from it.

Web Site Maintenance

I think it appropriate before finishing this section to briefly address the concept of web site maintenance. It is of utmost importance to ensure your site is functioning speedily and without any breakdown in site navigation. If a visitor should come to your site and find a number of invalid links, they probably won't come back. After all, who wants to spend time on a site the webmaster cannot even be bothered to keep up-to-date?

There are a number of online site utilities available to help you maintain your site without taking up a lot of your time. One of my favorite services is LinkAlarm (http://www.linkalarm.com) which costs just 1 cent per page (minimum $10.00) to check all the links on your web site on a semi-regular basis and send you a report. It's handy, convenient and detailed. You'll find a large list of links to other site management tools, many free, at http://websitetips.com/tools/ .

Next, I'll address how to create and upload your sound files....

Sound Solutions -
The Technical Stuff Made Easy!

How to Turn Web Site Visitors into Music Listeners

Having covered some web site design basics, I would now like to discuss what should be one of your highest priorities as an online music promoter: creating a means by which your web site visitor can sample your music from your web site. If you want people to buy your music online, you've got to give them a sample of the goods, right? The more of your music visitors can hear up front, the more likely they are to buy it if it appeals to them.

There are dozens of ways you can present your music to your web site visitors. You can provide links to sound clips, embed your music in a flash player or include your music in a flash player that also doubles as a shopping cart system. How you present your music to your visitors *is directly tied* to how you sell your music to them as well. In fact, in the modern age, it's difficult to separate the two.

However, let's begin by focusing on how to create basic links to your music samples. I will address the most common sound file formats, *MP3* and briefly, *Windows Media* and *Apple Quicktime*.

MP3: The Standard for CyberSound

In my mind, MP3 is currently the Internet standard for sound. When it comes to providing audio samples to your web site visitors, the popularity of the MP3 format exceeds all others. As a result, if you go with MP3, you can be confident that anyone visiting your site will be able to listen to your music regardless of which media player they have installed. In terms of sound quality, MP3 is more than sufficient for music samples. It will give your visitors a clear, accurate example of your music.

What about creating sound files in the Windows Media format? Although a few sites like Amazon.com offer music samples in Windows Media, I generally don't recommend Windows Media for independent artists. The reason is simply because there is no need. It's redundant. You're more than covered just using MP3, the dominant Internet standard. The same is true for the Apple AAC format. If you try to support all these formats, you're creating unnecessary work for yourself. Any media player your visitor will have will support MP3, so if you go with that format, you'll support all of your visitors.

Creating MP3 files from your CD is an easy task. Both Windows and the Mac come with software for ripping CDs built in. Here's how to do it:

Creating MP3s using Windows Media Player

These instructions assume you have Windows Media Player version 11, the current (and most common) version used (for Windows XP and Vista) as of this writing. Notes on version 10 and version 12 (for Windows 7) are included at the end of step four. You'll need at least version 10 to rip CDs to MP3 format as versions prior to 10 do not allow ripping CDs to MP3. If you don't have at least version 10, you can download the most current version from Microsoft's web site at http://www.microsoft.com/windows/windowsmedia/default.mspx

1) **First, insert your CD into your computer's CD recorder drive.**

2) **Next, start up Windows Media Player**, then click on the *Rip* tab. Your CD data should come up in the main window. You may need to edit your track and CD information. To do so, just double-click on the track title text to edit it, or alternatively you can right-click on each title to change it. As for the CD information (album name, artist, genre), just right click where it says "Unknown" by each of these to edit and update the information.

3) **Now configure the rip format and audio quality.** Click the *Rip* tab, click on *Format*, and choose MP3. Then click on *Rip* again, click on *Bit Rate*, and choose 128kbps. You'll want to keep the file as small as possible for quick downloading. At 128k, you'll have a smaller file size than the other options and you won't sacrifice much in terms of sound quality. The average person really can't detect much difference between 128k and the higher bit rate settings.

4) **Other configuration options to set...**

   Click on *Rip*, *More Options*, and then go to the *Rip Music* tab in the window that pops up. Make the following changes:

   Rip Music Location: Change this to where you want the created MP3 files to be saved to on your computer.

   File Name: Click on this to change the file naming convention. Always include the artist name and track name in the file name at the very least. Example: David Nevue – This is My Song.mp3

   Note that your format and bit rate can also be set in this window.

   If, by chance, you still have **Version 10** of Windows Media Player, all of these changes can be made under the *Tools/Options* menu and then under the *Rip Music* tab.

   If you have **Version 12** of Windows Media Player (for Windows 7), all of these changes can be made under the *Rip Settings* tab. The rip music location and file name settings are under the *Rip Settings/More Options/Rip Music* tab.

5) **Rip your music:** Click OK to close the options menu and save your changes. You'll then return to the main CD viewing screen (the main RIP tab). Check the boxes next to the songs you want to copy to MP3 and then click the *Start Rip* button on the lower right side (the upper right side in version 10, or the *Start Rip* button near the top of Version 12) to start the process of generating your MP3 files.

Creating MP3s using iTunes

Although Windows Media Player is available for the Mac, most Mac users prefer iTunes. The following instructions apply to Apple iTunes version 10, the current version as of this writing. The instructions are appropriate for both the Mac and PC versions of iTunes.

1) **First, insert your CD into your computer's CD recorder drive.**

2) **Next, start up iTunes**. You may be prompted by iTunes asking you if you want to import the songs. For the moment, say no. Your CD data should come up in the main window. You may need to edit your track and CD information. To do so, click on *Audio CD* under *Devices* on the left side of the window, then click the *File/Get Info* menu to edit the CD information. Then, just click twice on each track title to edit the song titles as needed.

3) **Now configure the rip format.** Go to your *Edit* Menu, click *Preferences*, then the *General* tab. Under that, click the *Import Settings* tab. You'll see several options here:

   Import Using: Set this to MP3 Encoder

   Setting: Good Quality at 128 kbps will be fine for the purpose of offering sample downloads to your web site visitors. You can go higher if you want for better sound quality, but that also means a larger file size, resulting in a longer download time.

   You can look over the other settings while you're here to make sure they are as you want them. The defaults are fine. Now click on the *Advanced* tab.

   iTunes Music Folder Location: Click the *Change* button to indicate where you want iTunes to place the created MP3 files on your computer.

   You can look over the others settings in the *Advanced* tab while you're here if you wish, but they aren't of concern to us now.

4) **Rip your music:** Click OK on the open window to return to the main CD viewing screen. Check the box next to the songs you wish to record to MP3 and click the *Import CD* button on the lower right of your iTunes screen to start the process.

If you don't want to use Windows Media Player or iTunes to create MP3 files from your CD, there are hundreds of MP3 ripping tools to choose from (see http://www.hitsquad.com/smm/cat/CD_RIPPERS/).

Creating Short Audio Clips

Now you need to decide on the length of the sound clips you want to provide your web site visitors. Do you want to allow visitors to listen to your entire song? Or do you want to limit the song sample to one or two minutes? It is my opinion that you ought to give your listener at *least* a two minute sample of your song. 30 seconds or even a minute just isn't long enough for your potential buyer to get into the groove of your music.

If you want to create short clips of your song, you'll need to first import your full length MP3s into an audio file editor. You can then trim them down to the desired length.

The easiest way to create songs clips from your full length MP3s is to use MP3 trimmer software.

For the PC (Windows), I recommend mpTrim, a free software program you can download from http://www.mptrim.com . Just open an MP3 file in mpTrim, indicate how much of the song you want to trim from the end, set your fade time, preview the result, then click on "Save As" to save the change to a new file.

The free version of mpTrim limits you to trimming songs that are no longer than six minutes. You can also trim just one song at a time. If you foresee yourself trimming a lot of files, consider investing in the "Pro" version of mpTrim. mpTrim Pro, which is $69.95, allows you to trim any length of song (up to 1 GB in size) and has some fantastic batch trimming options. You can preset your trim options to a certain length, add a nice fadeout, and then batch trim an entire directory of MP3 files to your presets in about a minute flat. It's outstanding, and will save you a lot of time if you need to trim dozens or even hundreds of MP3 files.

For Mac users, a similar free software option is available called MP3 Trimmer. That can be downloaded from http://www.deepniner.net/mp3trimmer/ and functions much in the same was as mpTrim for the PC above.

If you're a more advanced user, you may want more precise control over your audio file editing. In that case, I recommend Audacity, one of the most popular free audio file editors out there. It's available for both Mac and PC. You can download Audacity from http://audacity.sourceforge.net/ .

Uploading Your Files

Once your MP3 files are ready, use your FTP software to upload your files to your web site. I recommend you create a directory specifically for MP3 files on your host's server and then transfer your newly-created files there.

Optimizing Your MP3 File Names

If you make MP3 files available on your web site (which you should), expect to have them distributed throughout the Internet without your knowledge. This is a rather strange thing, but MP3 files of my songs have mysteriously turned up in all sorts of unexpected places. There are hundreds of "free mp3" directories out there and my songs can be found on a great many of them. I didn't upload my music to any of these places, *they* found ME! I presume sites like these send out little spiders, much like search engines do, to find links to MP3 files, and then import them into their directories. That, or fans have contributed my music to these directories on their own.

If this happens to you, this is not *necessarily* a bad thing. It does potentially mean more exposure for you and your music, and that's a good thing. Even so, I'm sure it doesn't make you feel any better knowing that your music is just floating around out there for people to download for free (although many musicians don't care about this and even *encourage* people to share their music.) But this is one of the reasons I recommend you offer complete downloads of only a few songs from each of your CDs. That, or stick to offering two-minute sound clips for most or all of your songs. That way your entire albums aren't scattered across cyberspace as free downloads without your permission.

To make the most of the possibility that your MP3s will be sucked out of your web site and into some MP3 directory somewhere, be sure you include your artist name as a part of your MP3 file. For example, "artistname_songtitle.mp3". That way if someone downloads your file from an unauthorized source there's no question of who the artist is performing the work. If they like your music, it will be easier for them to find you.

On this topic, you might want to read the following article on optimizing your MP3 file names: http://www.musicsubmit.com/seo/articles/NameOptimization.htm . The article refers to "Kazaa" but the info is really applicable to any file trading/sharing site.

Download or Stream?

Having discussed that, you'll need to make some decisions about how you want to present your music to your visitors on your web site. Do you want your visitors to be able to click your "play" link and *download* your music so they can listen to it on their local computer and/or transfer it to their portable device? Or, would you prefer they *stream* your music without actually downloading the file?

Creating a file download is very easy. If you uploaded your MP3 file to http://www.yoursite.com/mp3/artistname_songtitle.mp3 on your web host's server, for example, just link from your web page directly to that file. It's as simple as that. Your visitor will then be able to download your song to their local computer or portable device and listen at their convenience. How this happens from your visitor's browser depends on what type of computer they have (Mac or PC), as well as which audio software is set as their default for listening to MP3 files. In many cases, the file will just download, but if you have a visitor that has difficulty figuring this out, instruct them as follows: for a PC user, "right-click" the link to the MP3 file and choose "Save Link As…" from the menu that pops up. For a Mac user, instruct them to Ctrl+click the link that points to the mp3 location and choose from the pull down choices ("Download File" for Safari browser, or "Save Link As" for Firefox browser).

The downside to downloading is that it takes *time* and requires *space*. Depending on the size of your file and your visitor's connection speed, they may have to wait a few moments before they can hear your music. Plus some folks (like myself) have an aversion to downloading files onto my computer. When I'm at an artist's web site and I'm given a download option for music, I *might* download one song to see if I like it. The artist has that one song to make an impression on me. But I don't want to sit there and download unnecessary files to my computer. There's enough junk on my system. I'm not saying your music is "junk," but if I have no clue who you are or what your music sounds like, I'm not as inclined to download your music. I don't really want the extra clutter on my system.

So if you offer just the download option, you may only get that one shot to interest a visitor in your music. It's also possible that your visitor may not bother downloading your music at all! That's why I recommend you *stream* your music instead. The streaming option makes it possible for a visitor to click on your song link or play option and hear your music *immediately*, without requiring a formal download. If they like what they hear, they will listen to more of your tracks and hopefully, make the purchase. You can also opt to offer *both* downloads and streams, which is probably the best way to go. Then folks who actually want your downloads can get them, but folks who want to quickly listen to your music without downloading it can do so.

How to Stream MP3s: There are a couple of good ways to offer up streaming MP3 files. The first, and the easiest, is to create a "metafile." The second is to embed your MP3s in a Flash player. I'll cover creating a metafile first, and talk about embedding your music in Flash in a moment.

To create a metafile, simply open up a text editor such as Notepad and type in the web address of your MP3 sound clip. For example, if you uploaded your MP3 file to http://www.yoursite.com/mp3/artistname_songtitle.mp3 , simply insert that web address in your text editor. Now save that text file with an *.m3u extension (such as songtitle.m3u) and, using your FTP software, upload that songtitle.m3u file to the same directory as your MP3 file.

Now, when you create the "play" link for your visitors to click on from your web page, link that directly to the songtitle.m3u file. If you test it, your default Internet audio player should open up songtitle.m3u, which then buffers your MP3 file and plays it almost immediately.

I know this process may sound confusing or complex, but it's actually very simple. Once you've done it a few times, you'll whip out streaming sound samples in just a few minutes.

Here's a step-by-step overview to creating streaming MP3 files:

1) Record/Save your song to an *.mp3 file.

2) Upload the *.mp3 file to your web site.

3) Create a text file that contains one line: the web address that points to your *.mp3 file on your web host's server.

4) Save your text file with a *.m3u extension to create a metafile.

5) Upload your *.m3u file to the same directory as your *.mp3 file on your web site.

6) Link your web page directly to your *.m3u file.

7) Test the link.

Got it? Simple, isn't it? Just create metafile links for each of your MP3 files, upload them and link to them, and your visitors can stream whichever of your songs they want.

Now, do you want to see something *really* cool? In addition to creating individual metafile links to stream your music, you can create a single metafile that streams *all* your MP3 files in one batch. You can, in essence, create a streaming playlist of your music.

To do this, simply create one single metafile that contains a list of links to all of your MP3 files. So, your metafile might include the following:

http://www.yoursite.com/mp3/artistname_songtitle1.mp3
http://www.yoursite.com/mp3/artistname_songtitle2.mp3
http://www.yoursite.com/mp3/artistname_songtitle3.mp3
http://www.yoursite.com/mp3/artistname_songtitle4.mp3

Then save the file name as artistname_playlist.m3u . When you upload this metafile and open it with your browser, your audio player will stream the first song, then the second, third, and so on in the order that you include them in your metafile. Now you can give your visitor the option to "Play All" so they can listen to your clips consecutively.

One last thing: not every web server supports streaming MP3 files (though most do). So before you go to all this trouble, make sure that your web host actually supports the format.

Troubleshooting Tips: Once in awhile, you may run across a visitor who can't launch your *.m3u file properly. This will happen if the person's computer hasn't been set to associate *.m3u files with their default music player. To properly associate the file in Windows, instruct them to go to their Windows Control Panel, choose the "File Types" tab, then scroll down to M3U. Highlight it, click on "Change…" and choose the audio program they prefer to open it with (Windows Media Player is probably the best option). For Mac users, *.m3u files should open with iTunes by default. If that doesn't happen, refer the visitor to http://www.burroak.on.ca/m3u2itunes.html for information on how to fix this.

What I've mentioned to this point is the quickest and easiest way to make your music available for your web site visitors to sample. If you want to get a more advanced, stylized look, you can embed your music in a flash player. I discuss this below, but first…

Who's "Stealing" Your Music?

One of the most common questions I'm asked on this topic is whether or not the streaming option will prevent people from "stealing" your music, i.e., downloading your music without permission. The answer is no. Anyone who understands how streaming technology works can easily figure out the location of your actual MP3 files and download them to their local computer. However, I wouldn't worry too much about this as *most* people don't have a good understanding of streaming technology. For those that do, if they are determined to download your music samples from your web site they'll figure out a way to do so. The truth is, if you offer your music for streaming or sampling in *any* format, a person with the right tools and know-how can walk away with your music if they really want to. The only way to ensure no one "steals" your music is to not offer samples of it at all, and that's not an option if you want to sell your music to new customers. People who don't know you aren't going to buy your music if they don't have the opportunity to hear it.

If you're really concerned about theft of your sound files from your web site, just offer two-minute clips of your music as I suggested earlier. This gives a potential "thief" less reason to download the file, since it's incomplete, while still giving your visitor a long enough sample to get a good idea what your music sounds like. And there's nothing that says you have to offer sound samples from every single song on your CD. If you feel uncomfortable with offering too much for free, just limit your samples to three or four songs per album. However, keep in mind that the more song samples you offer, the more likely it is a new customer will feel confident buying your music. Put yourself in your visitors' shoes. How much of an album would YOU have to hear to be convinced to buy it?

Embedding Music in Flash

In order to circumvent theft issues, some have suggested the idea of embedding MP3 files in Flash media format. While Flash is a more secure way to protect MP3 files than simple streaming, a Flash stream can still be captured and saved to a computer with the right tools. The other negative to Flash is that, as I mentioned in the previous chapter, not everyone can view Flash. A very small percentage of your visitors won't be able to see your Flash player or listen to your music.

Still, the use of Flash for embedding music does have some big advantages. First of all, your visitor won't need the usual media players (Windows Media, RealPlayer or iTunes) to stream your music. That makes the loading of music clips very fast as they don't have to wait for these other programs to load. Flash audio players can also be very stylish to look at as well. So for *most* Internet users, Flash is an attractive option in terms of offering speed, functionality and convenience.

Here are a few tools to look into for creating Flash music clips if you'd like to research this option:

Wimpy MP3 Player:	http://www.wimpyplayer.com (more details below)
ReverbNation:	http://www.reverbnation.com (more details below)
Secure TSPlayer:	http://www.tsplayer.com/
Web Jukebox:	http://www.coffeecup.com/web-jukebox/
DivShare:	http://www.divshare.com/
e-phonic:	http://www.e-phonic.com/mp3player/
A4Desk Music Player:	http://music.a4desk.com/
Royalty Free Music:	http://www.premiumbeat.com/flash_resources/free_flash_music_player/
XSPF Music Player:	http://musicplayer.sourceforge.net/

Personally, I use the **Wimpy MP3 Player** (http://www.wimpyplayer.com) as the music player on my web site. You can see an example, using my own music, at http://www.davidnevue.com/listen.htm . There are several reasons I prefer the Wimpy MP3 Player over the others; first, the music loads very quickly. I can't tell you how important that is! Secondly, it looks great, and I can customize the design to my liking. Finally, I can encrypt the locations of my MP3 files, making the source files of the music in the player a lot more difficult for people to find and walk away with. I really suggest you look into this one.

The only downside of the Wimpy Player option is that it does take a little technical know-how to get up and running. It's not difficult, but you do need to read and follow instructions to make it work properly, and if you're not familiar at all with HTML, you might find the process of setting it up a bit intimidating.

A simpler option to consider is the **ReverbNation** music player widget. ReverbNation (http://www.reverbnation.com) offers many great promotional tools for musicians, including some of the best Flash player widgets available. Once you create an account with ReverbNation, just upload MP3s of your music into your profile. Once you've done this, visit the "Widget & Apps" section of your "Control Room" to view the available widget apps. There are several music player widgets listed there, and any of them will serve as excellent Flash music players for your web site. My favorite is the "Music Player (Pro)" option (see the example at right), for which you can customize the look, feel and size. Once you're done customizing the widget to your liking, just cut and paste the code provided into your web site and without too much effort at all you have a beautiful music player for your visitors to enjoy! It's really that easy.

A Reality Check About Selling Online…

If you're going to do business on the Internet, you have to come to terms with the fact that if people like your music enough to actually buy it, they are going to turn around and share it with their friends, family, acquaintances. They may even upload your music to some very public places on the Internet. I know this is a distasteful thought to some of you reading this, but if you stop and think about it, is this really a bad thing? Don't you want people to *share* your music? Yes! If a thousand people who love your music share your music with another thousand people, that's a thousand new potential fans who are now aware of your music. And if even ten of those thousand new people go on to become big fans of your music and actually purchase more of it, that's ten more fans than you had before, and ten more than you would have had if your music hadn't been shared or recommended to them by someone they know and trust.

Look, my music is all over the Internet. When I release a new album, it takes no time at all for that entire album to end up all over the file sharing networks, and I certainly didn't put it there. Even so, I sell literally *thousands* of music downloads each and every month. While I cannot definitively prove it, I do believe that fan file sharing does, eventually, lead to more fans as well as actual sales. You should *want* people to share your music. If you have in your possession an amazing treasure, and you protect its secret so much that no one else ever knows about it, then when you die knowledge of that treasure goes to the grave with you. The treasure hasn't benefited anyone. Not even yourself. What's your treasure? It's your music. Let it be found, enjoyed by others, and reap the benefits of that.

Selling Digital Music Downloads

At this point, you are probably wondering how you can *sell* digital downloads of your music, rather than just having people listen to them in your music player. You'll be happy to know there are some nifty ways to combine a Flash music player with a shopping cart system for just this purpose. In other words, your visitors can preview your music in a Flash player, and then purchase your music directly from the player if they desire to.

Before starting down that road, though, you'll want to think about how to best present *all* your products to your customers, not just your digital music downloads. I assume you have other products to sell; CDs, concert tickets, merchandise and so on? If so, start thinking about how you can sell your products together in one manageable system. In order to do this, you may, at some point, need to set up your own shopping cart system and accept credit cards from your web site. How do you go about doing that?

I'll show you in the next chapter!

Recommended Audio Tools

I'm frequently asked to recommend audio file editors. Below are some tools you might want to look into. I've either used these, or had them recommended to me by readers of this book:

MP3Gain: http://mp3gain.sourceforge.net/index.php
This is a great tool for equalizing the volume of all your MP3s.

MPTrim: http://www.mptrim.com/
Great Windows tool for quickly trimming the length of MP3 tracks and adding fades.

MP3 Trimmer: http://www.deepniner.net/mp3trimmer/
Like MPTrim above, but for the Mac.

JetAudio: http://www.cowonamerica.com/products/jetaudio/
Very powerful audio file recorder and converter. Supports every major audio file.

CDex: http://cdexos.sourceforge.net/
Quickly rips CDs to MP3s and converts between audio formats. Free!

dBpoweramp: http://www.dbpoweramp.com/dmc.htm
Reader recommended audio file ripper and converter. Supports virtually all file types.

Audacity: http://audacity.sourceforge.net/
A free audio recorder and editor. This is the one I use for basic MP3 editing. It has a lot of features for being a free tool. Highly recommended.

Fission: http://www.rogueamoeba.com/fission/
A lossless audio editor for Mac users. Fission lets you copy, paste and trim audio, as well as split files, all with no quality loss. Rapidly edit files in MP3, AAC, Apple Lossless and AIFF formats.

Blaze Media Pro: http://www.blazemp.com
Powerful audio editor and converter. Highly recommended by a reader.

SoundForge: http://www.sonymediasoftware.com/products/soundforgefamily.asp
Pretty much the undisputed king of audio editors. Also very costly.

Pro Tools: http://www.avid.com/US/products/family/Pro-Tools
The industry standard for recording studios, but very expensive.

Zamzar: http://www.zamzar.com/
Converts music and other file types online.

Take Credit Card Orders From Your Web Site - In 15 Minutes!

Making the Sale, Taking the Cash!

Accepting Credit Cards - In 15 Minutes or Less

To run a successful business on the Internet, credit card acceptance is an absolute must. There's no way around that fact. Unfortunately, accepting credit cards via your web site typically means setting up a merchant vendor account with a bank, setting up terminal software (and/or hardware), and paying the many monthly fees associated with having an account. This makes accepting credit cards a tough call for most musicians. The situation is very nearly a catch-22: if you accept credit cards, you may not cover your monthly costs; if you don't, however, you'll miss out on a great many sales.

The Redirect Approach

Fortunately, there are options available to musicians that make it possible to accept credit card orders without having to purchase a terminal or pay monthly maintenance fees. In fact, with the first option I'll discuss, you don't need a merchant account at all. You simply redirect your credit card orders from your web site to another company who does the order processing and fulfillment for you. CD Baby (http://www.cdbaby.com) is one such company, and the one I recommend the most.

CD Baby is the largest seller of independent music anywhere, whether online or via retail. It's a *great* place to sell your music. It will cost you $35 per CD title to set up your account (sign up at http://members.cdbaby.com/), but once you do, CD Baby will create a beautiful CD/MP3 sales page for you with everything you need, including audio sampling (two-minute clips) and streaming. All you need to do is direct your visitors from your web site to your CD Baby pages using the "Buy" links CD Baby provides. Here's how:

1) Sign up for CD Baby at http://members.cdbaby.com/ . Send in your music per their instructions.

2) CD Baby will send you an email when your page is set up and ready to go. Once that happens, go to http://www.cdbaby.com/link .

3) Search for your name. When your album title comes up, click on the "Select" button. Here, you'll be presented with several options for linking to your CD Baby pages from your own web site. You can choose from a variety of "Buy" buttons for your CDs and/or MP3 albums.

4) Copy and paste the HTML code CD Baby provides into your web page where you want it to appear.

Now you'll be able to direct visitors to CD Baby to purchase your CDs.

There are several benefits to having CD Baby handle your order processing. First, you never have to pay a monthly fee. CD Baby takes a $4 flat fee from each CD sold via their web site. If you sell your CD for $12.95, your cut of that is $8.95. Second, you never have to ship or fulfill orders. CD Baby ships orders for you as they come in and then provides you with the buyer's info. Third, your visitors can use CD Baby's toll-free number to place orders. So if someone isn't comfortable giving their credit card number over the Internet, they can call CD Baby toll-free to order your CD. Fourth, you get paid, by check, PayPal, or direct deposit as often as once a week for your sales. And finally, your CD is available in one of the largest CD stores on the Internet. If you reach a point where you are selling even just 3 or 4 CDs a day from CD Baby, your CD will be outselling most other artists on the site, meaning it's very likely that YOUR MUSIC will be featured on CD Baby's best-seller lists. This, in turn, results in more exposure for your music to visitors browsing the CD Baby web site meaning, hopefully, even more sales.

I can personally vouch for CD Baby. CD Baby is one of the best, easiest ways to get started taking orders via the Internet without incurring automatic monthly fees. For more information on CD Baby, see the chapter *The Best Places to Promote, Sell and Distribute Your Music Online*.

What about directing visitors to Amazon.com to buy your CDs? Yes, you'll want to get your CDs for sale in the Amazon.com store. However, as Amazon.com takes a 55% cut on the sale of your CDs, sending your web site visitors to Amazon.com to buy your CDs shouldn't be your first choice. A little later in this book I'll talk more about getting your music on Amazon.com and ways to use Amazon.com to your benefit.

When Sales Exceed $100/Month

There are two slight disadvantages to handing your credit card sales over to a third-party web site like CD Baby. The first is that your visitor has to leave your web site to place their order. That's not *necessarily* a bad thing since your customer is presumably leaving your web site to buy your music. Still, that might be a concern. Secondly, at $4 per CD sale, you're paying CD Baby about 30% of your retail price (30% on a $12 CD) to handle your shipping and order processing for you. Now please understand, that's an *exceptional* value if you want someone else to handle all your order processing. But if you don't mind shipping your orders yourself, there are other, less expensive alternatives to consider when the volume of your CD sales begins to increase.

Once you are doing $100 a month total in product sales, take a look at CCNow.com (http://www.ccnow.com). Once you sign up with them and add your products to their database, CCNow gives you HTML code to link your web site *directly into* their shopping cart system. From the customer's perspective, they never actually leave your web site. That is a plus. Another plus is that CCNow takes only 4.99% of your sale (+.50¢/transaction) - a far smaller percentage than the $4/CD that CD Baby takes. The major difference is that with CCNow.com *YOU* are processing and shipping your own orders. CCNow.com doesn't do that for you. If you don't mind doing that, CCNow.com is a great option.

So why wait until you're doing $100 a month in sales to switch to CCNow? Because CCNow has a monthly *minimum* charge of $9.95. If you don't sell anything in a given month, you still pay that $9.95. However, if you are consistently doing at least $100 in sales, you are never charged more than 4.99% + .50¢/transaction. For more details on CCNow's fees, see http://www.ccnow.com/pricing.html .

The only disadvantage to CCNow is that you can only use it to sell physical, shippable product (like CDs, t-shirts, DVDs). If you want to sell a service, subscription, downloadable music or "non-tangible" goods, CCNow won't allow it. In this age of music downloads, that can be a concern. However, keep CCNow in mind as an option, because depending on how you set up your overall store, you can still make use of it. I will tie selling physical products into selling digital products here in a bit.

One great thing about CCNow is that when the transaction is complete, your customer is returned to your web site. In fact, from their perspective, they never really left. Also, in terms of dependability and reliability, CCNow is a well-established business which has been on the Internet for years. As with CD Baby, I can vouch for them from personal experience.

Making use of CD Baby and/or CCNow will help you determine whether it's worth the investment to set up your own merchant vendor account at a later date. Until you do about $500 a month in total credit card sales, you're saving yourself time, money, and a great deal of hassle using one of the above options. Once you are doing $500 a month in sales, it's time to start thinking about getting a merchant vendor account.

When Sales Exceed $500/Month…

It's time to get your own merchant account. The problem is, the process of getting a merchant account is rather convoluted. The first thing most people do when researching this option is contact their bank. If you go this route, you can expect to pay around $35 just to apply. If you are accepted, your bank will provide you with a merchant account and the software you'll need to set yourself up on the Internet. However, when I investigated this option for myself, I found that most of the people at the bank really had no idea how to help me set up my Internet business. They seemed to lack the knowledge to help me get my online store off the ground. What I needed was an Internet-based merchant account provider who understood the needs of an Internet-run business.

Enter Paynet Systems (http://www.paynetsystems.com). Paynet Systems doesn't charge anything to apply for a merchant account and their rates and fees are extremely competitive. Just give them a call at 1-800-809-1989 and they'll walk you through the process of getting your application submitted and approved. The exact fees you'll pay each month will depend upon both the number of your online transactions as well as the value of your sales. For example, let's say your average online sale is $25 and that in a typical month you do 50 transactions from your web site. That means your total online sales would be $1250 per month ($25 x 50). Under this scenario, your monthly costs would be as follows:

> Visa/MC Discount Rate: 2.19% = $27.37 ($1250 x 2.19%)
> Transaction fees: .25¢ each = $12.50 (.25¢ x 50 transactions)
> Monthly service fee: $10.00 (All companies charge a service fee - most charge $10.)
> Monthly gateway fee: $10.00 (Most gateways charge about $20 a month.)
> Gateway transaction fee: .5¢ each = $2.50 (.5¢ x 50 transactions)

Add that all up, and your total monthly fee for $1250 in sales is $62.37. That means you're paying just 4.5% for all your online processing, compared to 4.99% (plus .50¢/transaction) for CCNow and 30% or so for CD Baby. The more sales you make each month, the smaller that percentage becomes. So long as you're doing at least $500/month in sales, your own merchant account is by far the least expensive way to go.

Another Option: In the latter part of 2010, I switched my merchant account and credit card processing to a company called Simplefy (http://simplefy.com) based on the recommendation of a friend. The switch over was a breeze and their customer service has been fantastic! When you're ready to think about setting up a merchant account, you should definitely talk to them.

Important Note: When you sign up for a merchant account, you may want to request that Authorize.net be set up as your payment gateway. Virtually every e-commerce system available supports Authorize.net, and I've found them to be very reliable and easy-to-use. Paynet Systems, mentioned above, uses a payment gateway called Skipjack by default. However, they can set you up for Authorize.net if you request it.

See Also: How to Shop for a Merchant Credit Card Account: http://www.wilsonweb.com/ecommerce/wilson-merchant-account.htm .

Your Shopping Cart - One Easy, Inexpensive Solution

All a merchant account does is give you the bank connections you need to process credit card orders via the Internet. In addition to this, you'll need a separate shopping cart system. Some merchant account vendors will provide you with a free shopping cart solution when you sign up. However, I've found those to be rather generic. So, I researched over 100 different systems on my own, focusing on inexpensive, yet quality solutions. I settled on Mal's E-Commerce (http://www.mals-e.com). The price for Mal's shopping cart is unbeatable, a mere $8 per month for an attractive, customizable shopping cart that hooks directly into your Internet merchant account payment gateway (the system works very well with Authorize.net mentioned above). The cart also includes built-in support for affiliate programs, affiliate reporting, and digital downloads (such as PDFs or MP3s). These features are unheard of in a cart so inexpensive! Not only that, the technical support is, without a doubt, one of the best I've ever received from any software vendor. Whenever I have had a question, I emailed support and have always received a response from Mal himself, the writer of the program, within just a few hours. You won't find a much better or less expensive shopping cart system than the one Mal's E-Commerce provides.

If you find that at some point in the future you need a cart with more features and customizability, take a look at 1ShoppingCart.com (http://www.1shoppingcart.com). I used Mal's cart for years, but in 2004, found that I needed more power than Mal's cart provided, so I switched. I still *highly recommend* Mal's cart for business start-ups. You cannot beat the price or service.

Note: Another shopping cart system was recently recommended to me that looks very promising: E-Junkie at http://www.e-junkie.com/ . It supports the sale of physical products as well as digital products. It's worth investigating.

Your Merchant Account - A Technology Overview

The whole merchant account thing may seem a bit overwhelming. The process is not exactly easy to comprehend, especially when you are just starting out. Here's how the process works:

1) Your customer clicks on a Buy or Order button from your web site.

2) The item is added to their **Shopping Cart**. From here, your customer can opt to either "continue shopping," which takes them back to your store, or they can **Check Out.**

3) Once they **Check Out**, the customer is prompted to enter their name, address, and credit card info.

4) They then **Submit** their info to initiate the order. This information is sent to a payment **Gateway** first, where the credit card number is authenticated and passed on to the issuing bank, then the bank verifies the customer's funds. This is where credit cards are approved or declined.

5) Once **Approved**, the customer returns to your "**Thank You**" page, where they are given instructions about their order.

6) The customer receives an **Order Confirmation** via email.

7) The system sends you a copy of the **Order Confirmation**, with additional details so you can ship the product.

8) Bank funds are automatically transferred from their account, and deposited in your bank account.

You'll find a nice diagram of the process at
http://feefighters.com/blog/wp-content/uploads/2010/10/transaction-flow-infographic.png .

Confusing, isn't it? That's why plug-in solutions like CD Baby or CCNow are so attractive. You don't have to worry about payment gateways, authentication processes, or buying and installing shopping cart systems. You simply plug in a bit of HTML into your web page and you're done. However, once you start doing a lot of business, merchant accounts can save you a lot of money. It's a real headache to set up, but once set up, you can rest easy knowing money is being automatically deposited into your account while you sleep.

What About PayPal?

PayPal is an Internet service that allows registered users to transfer money to and from bank accounts via cyberspace. It's very popular, especially for folks who frequent sites like eBay.com (who, as it happens, owns PayPal). What about making use of PayPal as a shopping cart solution? A couple of readers have asked me this very question, so here's my take on it.

Like CCNow, PayPal offers a plug-in shopping cart solution for your web site. Once you've added the code PayPal provides into your web page, customers can click a single button to purchase your product. At that point, the customer can log in if they have a PayPal account or, if they don't, they can purchase using a credit card. There is no setup or monthly fee for use of this service, and PayPal's transaction fee, which is only 2.9% + .30¢/transaction, makes PayPal a *very affordable* and attractive solution. When a customer makes a purchase, the money is automatically deposited into your bank account. You don't have to wait for a check.

There are two important reasons why PayPal doesn't get my highest endorsement. The first is due to issues of reputation. I have had more than one customer tell me they are actually *afraid* to use PayPal for data security reasons. They fear their personal information may not be secure. Why is that? One reason is that PayPal users have been the frequent target of hackers called 'Phishers' who send emails posing as PayPal requesting personal data such as login information, credit card numbers or bank account numbers (see http://www.antiphishing.org). If the customer is fooled into giving up their personal information, their data is then used and abused by the hacker. Now, this issue isn't PayPal's fault, but because PayPal users are the chief target of these hackers, PayPal has somewhat of an image problem. Thus, if you use PayPal and PayPal alone for your cart system, your customers may hesitate to order because, whether their reason is legitimate or not, they simply don't trust the system.

The second reason I don't recommend using PayPal is because of the way it handles orders. When a customer clicks on your PayPal generated "Buy" button, the first thing they will be presented with is a page to log into PayPal. Now, if the customer doesn't have a PayPal account, and if they don't want to create a PayPal account, this is going to be a big obstacle for them. While technically you don't have to have a PayPal

Midnight Rain Productions

CD - Whisperings: The "Best of" David Nevue | Total with shipping: $15.95 USD

PayPal is the safer, easier way to pay

PayPal Secure Payments

PayPal securely processes payments for **Midnight Rain Productions**. You can finish paying in a few clicks.

Why use PayPal?
- Use your credit card online without exposing your card number to merchants.
- Speed through checkout. No need to enter your card number or address.

Don't have a PayPal account?
Use your credit card or bank account (where available). Continue

VISA MasterCard AMEX DISCOVER BANK PayPal

LOG IN TO PAYPAL

Email:
Password:

Log In

Forgot email or password?

account to place a credit card order through them, the option to order without signing up for PayPal isn't obvious at all.

Take a look at the example above. If I were to create a PayPal "Buy" button for one of my CDs, let's say my CD "Whisperings: The Best of David Nevue," that is what the default order page would look like, and what the customer sees when they click on the "Buy" button.

The very first thing the customer's eye is drawn to, aside from the company name in the upper left, is the "LOG IN TO PAYPAL." screen on the right. Now, if the customer has a PayPal account already, this is very convenient. If they don't, however, and if they *don't want to set up* a PayPal account, then your customer will close the window and abandon the purchase. You'll lose a lot of potential buyers on this screen.

Note that if you look in the lower left hand corner of this page, you see the following text: "Don't have a PayPal account? Use your credit card or bank account (where available)" A customer can click on the "continue" link here to place their order using a credit card without actually creating a PayPal account. The problem is, this text is the last thing your eye sees on the page and if your customer isn't looking for it, they will never find it. People don't study web pages that long. Customers make decisions about whether to proceed with an online purchase in mere seconds, and the first message this page sends to a customer is "LOG IN TO PAYPAL." Upon seeing that, if your customer doesn't have a PayPal account and doesn't want to create one, they'll close the window and move on with their life.

Most shopping cart systems, such as Mal's E-Commerce and 1ShoppingCart.com mentioned above, offer integrated support for PayPal. That means your customer can opt to pay via PayPal from within the shopping cart *if they want to*. This is an excellent way to go, as your customer can choose to pay via credit card or PayPal, whichever they prefer, and they aren't forced into choosing one over the other. About 20% of my customers choose to pay for their merchandise via PayPal.

Selling Digital Music Downloads

OK, now to the good stuff. Selling digital downloads of your music to your visitors.

The music world has changed drastically over the last eight years with much media attention focused on Apple iTunes and other digital music services. While music lovers used to buy just CDs, they are now buying digital music almost as much or more. Without much effort at all, a music fan can go to their preferred digital music store, search for the song and/or album they want, buy it, download it, and transfer it to their portable music device (their iPhone, Droid, MP3 player or whatever). In fact, we're already at a point, technologically, where the music fan doesn't even have to go to his or her computer. They can purchase their favorite tunes "over the air" through their iPhone other portable device.

Experts in this field estimate that in 2010, about 25% of all recorded music (globally) was purchased digitally. If you narrow the market to include just the U.S., about 40% of all recorded music purchases were bought in a download format. Another interesting factor; 80% of all digital music purchases are for song *singles*, not albums. As a result, the music industry is being forced to depend less on album sales and more on the sales of singles. If you're going to stay on top of this trend, you need to start seriously thinking about selling your music as digital downloads (albums and singles) and not just as CDs. So, how do you go about doing this?

There are several ways you can go in terms of selling your music digitally. I'm going to list a few options for you and then I will tell you what *I* would do (and what I am, in fact, doing).

Your digital music sales options:

1) **Sell Digital Music via Your Shopping Cart System:** Mal's E-Commerce, 1ShoppingCart.com and e-junkie.com all support the sale of digital media. If you use any of these cart systems, you can set them up to sell and deliver digital music. If you go with Mal's shopping cart, you'll want to use that in conjunction with a program called Linklok (http://www.vibralogix.com/linklokme/). Linklok is an inexpensive add-on for Mal's cart that provides *secure* download pages for your digital files. While Mal's supports digital downloads by default, the download pages aren't secure. That means someone could bookmark the download page and share the link with their friends or, even worse, post the download link on a public forum somewhere. Not a good thing! Adding the Linklok option to Mal's cart takes care of that problem.

   As for 1ShoppingCart.com's solution, their digital delivery system works very well and is secure, but at $99/month, it's too expensive for most musicians to consider.

   Finally and most importantly, while you can set up these shopping carts to deliver digital downloads, selling digital music is *not their primary function* and so they lack many of the features (such as song previews) offered by some of the other alternatives. The digital downloads option in these carts are really intended for people selling eBooks or PDF files.

2) **Direct Your Digital Music Buyers to Your CD Baby Web Page:** As mentioned earlier, CD Baby (http://www.cdbaby.com) offers its artist's albums in DRM-free MP3 format to buyers. So if you're a CD Baby artist, you can direct your fans to your CD Baby page to purchase your albums and/or singles in MP3 format. Plus, you have your song samples right there for people to preview. The downside: you have to direct your buyers to a third-party site (CD Baby) to purchase your music. Customers have also told me that they found CD Baby's MP3 download process a bit confusing.

3) **Sell Digital Music via Third-Party Software/Player/Widget tools:** There are many companies that have been set up specifically to sell digital music for independent artists. Most of these allow you to sell your music via flash applications and/or portable widgets. Unfortunately, most of them don't do it very well. I can only really recommend a few possible companies to look into at this point…

Audiolife (http://www.audiolife.com) is one of the best when it comes to music sales tools. With Audiolife, you create your own store wherein you can sell not only physical albums, but digital albums, singles, merchandise and even ringtones. Once you have created your Audiolife store, you can insert that "store" as a widget anywhere you like online. Not just your web site, but your blog, Facebook account, MySpace page, email message, and a dozen or so other social networking sites. Your customers can even get their own widget for selling your music on their own web sites and networks! The merchandise option is really cool, as you can create your own t-shirts, hoodies, and accessories right in your store. You can sell physical CDs, or you can upload your artwork and have Audiolife create one-off physical CDs to send to buyers after they purchase. When a customer buys a product, whether it be a CD or merchandise, it's created right there and shipped to them. But the feature I like the most about the Audiolife widget is this: the payment/cart option is included inside the widget. So customers enter their purchase information directly in the widget to buy. The customer doesn't have to go to a third-party site to make their purchase. And yes, the purchase is secure.

The cost to you? There are no up-front costs, which is nice. You pay $5.49 for physical CDs when they are sold (the CDs are created on-demand, one-at-a-time by Audiolife), so if you sell an album for $12.00, you'll profit $6.51, which is more than you'd make if you sold the same CD at Amazon.com. Merchandise pricing varies, but the wholesale prices are reasonable. You set your retail price to whatever you want to determine your own profit margin. For MP3 albums, Audiolife takes $3.00, you keep the rest. For singles, Audiolife takes .30¢ which is near industry standard. You'll make .69¢ on a .99¢ download. For ringtones, you make a flat .50¢ per ringtone sold.

Audiolife gives you a means by which you can go 100% digital and yet still offer one-off, on-demand physical CDs for customers who want them. You can plug your store into almost any web site, anywhere, accept credit cards and be ready to sell. A pretty cool tool.

ReverbNation (http://www.reverbnation.com), which I discussed in the previous chapter, also has a "store" option for selling your music. If you have an account with ReverbNation, click on the "Reverb Store" option in your "Control Room" to create a store where you can sell digital downloads, CDs, merchandise and even ringtones. Once you've uploaded everything you want to sell, click on the "Preview and Place Stores" link. Here, you'll be presented with several different options for your store which allow you to cut and paste code to insert your "store" right into your own web site HTML.

What isn't too obvious, however, is that this "store" portion of ReverbNation is actually a feature provided by Audiolife, and while you can create your entire store right here in ReverbNation, I recommend you work directly with Audiolife to create your store instead.

Nimbit (http://www.nimbit.com) is another slick "shopping cart" add-on option. As with Audiolife.com, not only can you sell physical CDs and merchandise through Nimbit's cart system, you can sell digital downloads too. Nimbit offers three shopping cart style plans, each with its own features. *nimbitFree* allows you to sell downloads only, *nimbitIndie* costs $12.95/month and adds the ability to sell physical CDs and merchandise. Finally, *nimbitPro* is $24.95/month and gives you a custom branded shopping cart, content management tools for your web site and more. You'll find details on each of these options at http://www.nimbit.com/plans-pricing/ .

Like Audiolife, Nimbit's cart is truly portable. It comes with a plug-and-play shopping cart widget called NimbitOMT (Online Merch Table) that you can post literally anywhere, not only your web site but you can plug it in MySpace, Facebook, blog sites and so on. And again, like Audiolife.com, you can provide your fans with code they can plug into their own web sites and social networking accounts giving your fans the ability to directly support you.

The NimbitOMT shopping cart widget includes your digital downloads, streaming samples, your bio with a photo, links to merchandise, eTickets for your concerts, and mailing list manager. So the Nibmit widget does offer a few features that Audiolife doesn't. Here's a snapshot of it:

For a live example of the widget, see
http://www.nimbit.com/gfx/products/omtpage/omtshadowbox.html .

There are four things which, to me, make Audiolife.com a better choice over Nimbit – at least for now:

- No monthly fee with Audiolife.com. You pay only when you sell.
- Audiolife's cart is included in the widget. Nimbit's takes you to the Nimbit web site to purchase.
- Audiolife's widget seems to loads much faster. Nimbit's takes longer to load.
- Audiolife's web site is easy to navigate and understand. Nimbit's is very confusing and hard to understand.

If you want to explore Nimbit, my suggestion is to try out their free service first, see if you like it, and then you can potentially expand into their pay-based tools.

Stop the Presses: Just prior to the release of this edition, Nimbit introduced a new product: *Instant Band Site*, which is available as a free Wordpress plug-in. If you need help installing the site, Wordpress or the plug-in, Nimbit will set it all up for you for $199. For more information on that, see http://www.nimbit.com/instant-band-site/

Bandbox (http://www.bandbox.com/) is the newest addition to this lineup and is very simple to set up. Sign up, create an "album", upload your tracks, and you have a beautiful player from which you can sell digital singles, albums and physical CDs from your web site, Facebook, MySpace, blog and pretty much anywhere else. The cost for the service is $9.95/month (digital only) or $14.95 if you want to sell physical CDs through the player as well. Aside from that, you keep all the profit from sales minus credit card fees. My only caution with Bandbox is that there isn't much buzz about it and as far as I can tell, not a lot of folks are using it at this point. Research this one for sure, but move forward cautiously.

Bandcamp (http://www.bandcamp.com/) . Of all the widget-based tools mentioned here, Bandcamp seems to be the one generating the most positive buzz from musicians. It's really slick. Once you create your Bandcamp store, you can direct your visitors there to purchase both album downloads or physical CDs. One of the great features of Bandcamp is that not only can visitors buy and download your music in the audio format of their choice, you can give them a "name their own price" option if you like. That's something unique to Bandcamp. Bandcamp also offers its members an elegant, simple way to share music directly to Facebook, MySpace, WordPress and many other places online. An account with Bandcamp is free, although they do take 15% of any sales you make. I strongly recommend you check out what Bandcamp has to offer. You may find it very useful, especially if you're seeking a reliable storefront option for selling your music.

Everything I've stated up to this point, I've given you just to let you know your best options. Having shared those, here are my ultimate recommendations for sales of digital music downloads:

4) **Direct Your Visitors to iTunes to Purchase Digital Music.** iTunes is the #1 digital music store out there, bar none. The fact is, if your visitor wants to buy your song as a digital download, chances are they are already very well acquainted with iTunes. Why not let them purchase your music from a source they are already comfortable with? Plus, if your downloads sell well, it puts your music in front of customers already browsing the iTunes store who would not have found your music otherwise. Encouraging visitors to buy and download your songs on iTunes benefits you greatly in the long run.

Here's What I do: I sell my physical CDs direct from my site through my own shopping cart system. For digital downloads, I direct visitors to both iTunes and Amazon.com's MP3 store. They choose. You can take a look at how I put this all together at http://www.davidnevue.com/albums.htm . You'll note that I don't do anything fancy. It's all straight HTML for the most part.

Using one of the widget player/carts above is great for including a widget on Facebook, MySpace or in a blog, but from your official web site, I would recommend sending folks to iTunes directly.

So your next question likely is, *"How do I get my music on iTunes?"* The answer is simple: sign up for CD Baby. Once you have your album (or single) up on CD Baby, you can opt for digital distribution. CD Baby takes just 9% of your portion of the sale, and they distribute your music to more than a dozen digital music stores, including iTunes, Rhapsody, eMusic, Last.FM, Spotify, Amazon MP3, Napster and others. The wait time for getting your music into all these stores varies –a few weeks in some instances – but once your music is in place, you'll likely see sales of your songs just by virtue of them being there.

Digital Distribution Alternative: An alternative to using CD Baby for digital distribution is TuneCore at http://www.tunecore.com . While TuneCore doesn't have the same level of distribution in terms of the number of digital music stores, they have a quicker turnaround (on average) and do cover the most important stores.

For more details about CD Baby and their digital distribution program (as well as iTunes and TuneCore), see the chapter on *The Best Places to Promote, Sell and Distribute Your Music on the Internet*.

To stay on top of emerging technologies in the digital music realm, I highly recommend you subscribe to the Digital Music Newsletter at http://www.digitalmusicnews.com .

Optimizing Your Site for Search Engines - A Step-By-Step Guide

Preparing Your Web Site for the Search Engines

If you've spent any time at all investigating how to promote your web site, you already know the emphasis the world-at-large puts on submitting your web site to search engines like Google. Some folks submit their sites and then become obsessed with their web site "ranking." They continuously strive to reach a point where their web site consistently comes up at a high position when people search for related keywords. Based on the volume of debate on the subject, you would think getting good search engine positioning is the be-all-and-end-all of web site marketing. There's a lot of hype out there! So, what's the real story?

Submitting your web site with the major search engines is indeed an important part of your marketing strategy. However, search engine submission is but *one small part* of your effort. The success of your site does NOT rely entirely upon your rank in the search results. Let's get that myth out of the way! Some people spend hours a week trying to improve their search engine positioning. It's a waste of time. If you spend all your time obsessing over your search engine position, you won't get any other work done! Trust me on this. It's a big time-waster.

The fact is, if you prepare your web page correctly for search engine submission the first time, you can relax about it. You won't have to worry about whether your site is #1 or #20 or even #100 in the search result listings. Your site, if managed correctly, will be a constantly changing, growing web site, so there will be plenty of opportunity for you to populate the search engines with new pages, content and information. As time goes on, more people will find you, and if your web site is a quality site that serves its intended audience well, you'll find that success on the search engines, in terms of search engine placement, eventually does come around. That success does, however, require a great deal of time and patience.

In this chapter, I will explain how search engines work, offer tips for preparing your web site for submission, and show you how to optimize each individual web page to maximize your potential rankings. By "optimize," I simply mean designing your web pages in such a way as to improve your chances of being found when someone searches the Internet for a topic relevant to your web site. The methods I will teach you are the same simple, easy-to-employ strategies I myself use at MusicBizAcademy.com and my other project sites.

Designing Web Pages Around Keywords and Phrases

Before I can go into any depth about how to optimize your web site for the search engines, it's important that you understand the nature of strategic *keywords* and *key phrases*. These keywords and phrases are going to be the axis around which each of your individual web pages revolve. Your keywords, and how you integrate them into your page content, are going to be the heart of your web site as far as the search engines are concerned.

So, what are keywords? Well, what words or phrases do you think people will type in a search engine that *should* result in their finding your web page? Those words, whatever they are, are your strategic keywords. If, for example, you think someone should find your web site when they search the Internet for "Flamenco music," then that's one of your key phrases. Knowing this, take a few moments and think of as many words or complete phrases you can that relate to your web site. Really focus on building *key phrases*, that is, the use of two or more words together. Focusing on entire phrases, rather than just single words, will improve your chances of being found on the Internet. Why? Look at it this way: if you use the Google search engine (http://www.google.com) to search for the word "music," Google returns over 3 *billion* results. If you search more specifically for "piano music," Google returns a list of 104 million sites. Search even more specifically for "smooth jazz piano music" and Google returns just 1 million sites. As you can see, the more *specific* you get with your keyword phrases, the more likely you are to be found by someone searching the Internet using that particular phrase. The more specific your phrase, the more you narrow down your competition.

If you have difficulty thinking up key phrases, try making use of the Google Adwords Keyword Tool at https://adwords.google.com/select/KeywordToolExternal . Using this tool, you can input any keyword or phrase, submit, and it will return a list of related keywords and phrases you may not have thought of.

My favorite keyword tool is Trellian's Free Search Term Suggestion Tool at http://www.keyworddiscovery.com/search.html . Using this tool, you can input any keyword or phrase, submit, and then see how many instances of that keyword or phrase were searched for during a given month via a wide variety of search engines. For example, type in the word "guitar" and you'll see a list that looks something like this:

Results 1 - 100 of 148997   Page: 1 2 3 4 5 6 7 8 9 10

Search Term	Total ?
guitar	67950
guitar tabs	16484
guitar hero	14974
electric guitar	13944
acoustic guitar	9897
ultimate guitar	8900
guitar pro	8317
guitar flash	7569
download guitar pro 5.2	7440
the complete idiot's guide to playing bass guitar	7436
k.i.s.s guitar book	7436
guitar flah	7436
the complete idiot's guide to playing bass guitar download	7436
forum guitar learning	7436
filetype pdf guitar guide	7436
how to self learn play guitar	7436
learn on your own guitar	7436
guitar center	7131
bass guitar	6996
guitar hero world tour	4906
guitar chords	4852
guitar amp	3345
guitar tab	2258
classical guitar	2137

and so on....

Not only can this tool provide you with more ideas for individual words or phrases, it also shows what phrases people are actually using to search the Internet. What this tool allows you to do is compare your potential keywords to determine which keywords are *really* the most likely to bring targeted traffic to your web site. If the audience you want to target is guitar players, and you had to choose just one key phrase to target them, would you use "guitar tabs" or "guitar chords" as a keyword phrase? With this tool, the choice is obvious. There's no guesswork involved. As you can see, many more people search for "guitar tabs" than "guitar chords."

If you want more tools like this, check out the list of 14 Keyword Suggestion Tools at http://www.seocompany.ca/tool/8-keyword-suggestion-tools.html . The Wordtracker Free Keyword Suggestion tool at http://freekeywords.wordtracker.com/ is also very useful.

Information like this can really come in handy when you are researching who your audience is and how to best target them. Once you have completed your list of keywords and phrases, organize them, listing the most powerful and most relevant keywords and phrases first.

Now that you have a basic understanding of keywords and phrases, let's talk about how search engines work...

Creepy-Crawlies: Bait for the Spider

When you register your web page with a search engine (I will show you how to do this in the next chapter), the engine sends what is commonly referred to as a spider, a crawler, or a robot to index your web site. This spider examines the text and links it finds within your pages and uses that *content* to determine what your web site is really all about. Everything the spider finds as it travels through your site gets added to the search engine *index*, which is essentially a huge database that contains every page it finds. Sometimes there is a lag time between the crawling and the actual indexing, which is why, in some cases, it can take several weeks before your site is included in search engine listings.

The key to optimizing your web site for crawling search engines is to create web pages that are spider-friendly. You, in essence, want to help the spider *learn* what your web site is about. To do this, you design your site in such a way as to *impress upon* the spider the *content* you want it to notice. This all sounds very science-fiction doesn't it? While I'm giving you the impression the spider is more intelligent than it really is, I'm doing so to make a point. Web page content matters, and to some degree your task is to arrange your web site in such a way that the spider gets the food it's looking for while, at the same time, you feed it content that will most benefit your search engine positioning. So, how do you do that? That's where your keywords and phrases begin to come into play.

There are three things that really matter to crawling search engines in deciding how they rank your web site in their listings: your page title, your page relevancy, and your page popularity. I'll begin by discussing your page title.

Your Page Title Says it All...

The single most powerful tool you have to draw traffic to your web site via the search engines is your web page title. Your title, which appears in the top bar of your web browser, is also the text that displays in the search engine results. It's the text the searcher will see and click on to go directly from the search results page to your web site home page.

Your web page title has more influence over your search engine listing (and whether someone actually clicks on it) than any other single aspect of your web site. Therefore, placing your strategic keywords in your title is of utmost importance. Not only because you need to create a page title that says to someone, "click on me," but because when someone searches the Internet for a particular phrase, pages that contain that *exact* phrase in the page title will, in most cases, be displayed above other pages which do not have the same exact phrase in the title.

Let me give you an example. Using Google (http://www.google.com), if you search the Internet for "lemon meringue pie," the top returning results will, in most cases, contain that *exact* phrase. Thereafter, sites containing "lemon pie" or just "lemon meringue" in the title are listed, and after that sites containing just "lemon" or "meringue" or "pie" or variations on those words are listed.

The point is, choose your page title very carefully. Word the title of your main index page (your home page) in such a way that you make use of your most powerful keywords and/or phrases so that search engines find your exact match. At the same time, keep in mind people are reading your page title and using that to determine whether or not your link is worth the effort of clicking on. So you can't just squeeze every possible keyword combination into that one, single page title. If you do, the title won't make a whole lot of sense to the searcher! You may find it helpful to think of your page title as a one-line ad. Your task is to make that ad stand out when listed on a page with nine other ads.

Finally, as you ponder all of this, remember that as you build and grow your web site, you're going to be adding more and more pages to your web site. Each of those individual pages represents another opportunity to be included in the search engine index. So, as you move forward designing and organizing your web site, build your pages around variations on your keywords and phrases. This creates diversity within your web site, and creates a variety of pages that can each target your potential customers in slightly different ways. I'll be talking a bit more about this in the chapter, *Targeting Your Customers to the Max*.

Creating a Page Title: If you don't know how to give your web page a title, simply follow these steps: First, open your HTML document in a text editor. In the <HEAD> portion of the document (between the two HEAD indicators), use this tag:

<TITLE>My Web Page Title</TITLE>

Put it on a line by itself, then save your text file as an *.html document. When you view this page in a browser, the title will appear at the top in the browser title bar.

NOTE: I need to emphasize that your page title will be of absolutely no benefit to you if it doesn't reflect your actual web page content. Remember, the spider is looking at more than just your page title – it's examining the whole of your page content. So whatever keywords or phrases you use in your page title, those same topics, whatever they are, should be addressed within that page. In short, for best results your page title should be a one line, short description of what that page actually contains.

Your Web Site Relevancy

Having covered your web page title, I'll now talk about a second important factor a search engine uses to determine how to position your web site in its listings: relevancy. Once the page title has been established, search engines tend to sort pages based on the density of keywords or key phrases within a document. In other words, a calculation is made to determine the *frequency* of your particular key phrase within a page when compared to all the other text around it. The resulting calculation is translated into a relevancy rating, which determines how relevant your web site is to a particular phrase searched for.

There are a number of factors that enter into calculating your *relevancy*. When your web page is indexed, search engines tend to give more importance to text that appears high in that page, usually in the first paragraph or so. So, to improve your relevancy for a set of keywords or phrases, include as many of them as is reasonable to do so in the opening paragraph describing your web site. In other words, put together a good, basic description of your web site, include as many keywords and phrases as you can, and place that description near the top of your web page. As with the page title, remember to make sure your description reads naturally. Don't stuff the top of your page with keywords and phrases just for the sake of impressing the search engines! The resulting concoction may be altogether unnatural sounding! Use your keywords and phrases, but work them into a natural-sounding reading. One reason for this, aside from the obvious (it reads well to a human being), is that some search engines (like Google) use random text from your web site to display a site description on their results page. So, as with the page title, you want a description that's going to appeal to human readers.

NOTE: If you are making use of tables in your page design, include your description text and strategic keywords within the top, left-hand cell of your table. Search engine spiders read table text before the remainder of the page.

Another way to improve your relevancy is to keep your web pages relatively short. The longer your page goes on and on with endless text, the less each of your keywords or phrases will stand out. Why? Because the more text you have, the less relevant each key phrase becomes for that page. Have you ever noticed how many web sites give you just a bit of information on one page, and then make you click "next" to go to page 2, page 3 and so on? Ever wonder why they don't just put it all on one page? There are three primary reasons for this: First, the more your visitor has to scroll down to read your page, the more likely they are to become impatient and leave. People easily get overwhelmed seeing too much information all at once. Secondly, the more pages used, the more page impressions are generated for advertising revenue (I'll discuss this more later). Finally, and in this context, a shorter page generally means a higher relevancy.

By the way, this relevancy issue also means you need to have actual HTML text on your page. I often run into web pages made up entirely of graphic images or Flash content. The problem with this design is that if your page is made up entirely of graphic images or Macromedia Flash, you'll get zip for a relevancy rating. You need text for the spiders to feed on. They can't read your images, and their ability to make heads or tails of your Flash content is limited. So, whenever possible, use text. Your human visitors will appreciate that as well. As I mentioned in the chapter on web design, Flash is cool looking, but it doesn't sell product. For more on Macromedia Flash and how it affects your search engine optimization, see http://searchenginewatch.com/2200921 .

ANOTHER NOTE: Again, don't stack your page content with *extra* keywords and phrases for the explicit purpose of getting a higher relevancy ranking with the search engine! Use common sense. The above suggestions are made to help you strategically place your content on your web pages, not to imply you should fill your pages with useless clutter!

Just a Popularity Contest?

Finally, a *big* factor that determines search engine ranking is web site popularity. Web sites that are frequently linked to from other web sites are considered to be *higher quality* web sites than web sites no one is linking to. Why? Because, a search engine reasons, if "Bill's Web Site" has more people linking to it than "Ted's Web Site" does, then the probability is that Bill's web site contains more useful content that visitors want. So, when someone searches for your keyword phrase, the top sites returned will not only contain the exact phrase in the page title and have relevant content, they will also have many other web sites linking to them.

This logic, while it makes sense, does make it very difficult for brand new web sites, no matter how good they are, to compete with web sites that already have a well-established web presence. This doesn't seem very fair, does it? So how do you overcome this popularity contest to improve your web site ranking in the search engines? There are several ways, most of which I will discuss in detail later in the book. However, so as not to leave you hanging, these ways include, but are not limited to:

Building Reciprocal Links with *Quality* Web Sites: Find the web sites that already rank high in the search engines when searching on your keywords and phrases, then contact the webmaster and inquire if they will exchange links with you. The higher quality the web site is that links to you, the more this link will help you in your quest for a higher position in the search engine results. Why? Because search engines count not only *how many* other sites link to you, but *how popular* the sites are that link to you. In other words, if 10 *quality* web sites link to you, it will do you more good than if 50 *poor quality* web sites link to you.

Increasing Your Press Release Distribution: Write a press release or human-interest story that talks about, and links to, your web site. Include your most powerful keywords and phrases in the press release title. Now take that release and use a service like PRWeb (http://www.prweb.com) to announce your press release to the world. If the story is compelling, many news-oriented web sites will pick it up and post it on their own web site. In a very brief period of time you'll have a large number of web sites linking to you using content that you, yourself created. The end result is more web sites linking to you, increasing your link popularity.

Creating Exposure via Social Media, Blogging and Networking: Social networking became mainstream in 2007 bringing us services like Twitter, Facebook, StumbleUpon, Digg and others. Plus, there are hundreds of professional bloggers out there who are writing stories on every conceivable topic. You can write articles, blogs and commentary for these social-based web sites to quickly draw attention to your own web site, your blog and/or the services you offer. I'll talk more about how to do this a bit later in the book.

Investing in Paid Search Engine Exposure: You have the option of paying for exposure on the search engines using pay-per-click advertising. It can be expensive, but it's a good way to gain some visibility. I cover pay-per-click engines in more detail in the next chapter.

Getting Creative With Your Key Phrases: Some keywords and phrases are unique enough that searches on those phrases return significantly fewer results, meaning it's much easier for you to rank well when you use those phrases. This would be one case where going for the most commonly searched for key phrase may not do you as much good as targeting a lesser searched for, but more unique, key phrase. This really comes down to knowing and understanding your target audience to determine what it is they are *specifically* searching for on the Internet. Again, I will be addressing the topic of targeting your audience in more detail later in this book.

Creating Quality Content: This seems obvious, but if you create a quality web site with information people want, they will link to you from their own web sites. That will, over time, improve your popularity ranking.

Most search engines lean heavily on link popularity to determine their search results. While your page title is the most important thing to use to ensure you get listed for a particular phrase, ultimately, the highest ranked sites are going to be the most popular sites. Please do not get discouraged about this! As I mentioned at the very beginning of this chapter (read it again if you need to), the search engines are *just one way* to bring visitors to your web site. You must keep this in mind! There are *many* other ways to bring targeted traffic to your web site, so don't fret too much about your search engine positioning. Using the marketing methods I will address in this book, you will be able to both improve your web site popularity (by creating a buzz about it) and as a result, your search engine ranking. Don't sweat the search engines. There's more to the Internet than getting listed on Google!

Article of Note: Reciprocal Linking vs. Mutual Linking
http://www.rightclickwebs.com/seo/reciprocal-linking.php

Helping Spiders!

I want to summarize some general things you can do to help search engine spiders crawl your web site. Here's how to feed a spider well:

1) Create a page that links to all of the major pages within your web site. That page will serve as your "site map." Now, link to this site map page from your home page. That makes it easy for the spider to find the pages you feel are most important – plus your web site visitors will make good use of it!

2) Use text links throughout your web site and link often between important pages.

3) Keep your descriptive text high in the page and easily accessible.

Killing Spiders!

Here are a few things that kill spiders, stop them cold dead, or severely handicap their ability to crawl your web site. You'll want to avoid...

1) The use of Flash content only (especially on the all-important home page), providing no text links to follow.

2) The use of graphical content only, resulting in no text links to follow.

3) The use of frames.

4) The use of dynamic pages that use CGI for page delivery. Most spiders can't read this information. The use of SSI, however, is fine.

5) The use of symbols in your URLs, such as the '?,' which is often used as a command parameter. Once a spider sees the '?' symbol in a web address, they'll go no further.

The above information will help you organize your web pages in such a way that you can maximize your potential for most any crawling search engine. However, I have a few other tips that might (and I repeat, *might*), in certain circumstances, help improve your positioning. I'll start with everyone's favorite "magic bullet": meta tags.

Meta Tags: Much Ado About Pretty Much Nothing

At one time, the proper use of meta tags in your web page was considered to be the "secret" of search engine optimization. Many people still use them today to try to influence rankings. While it's true that meta tags once had great influence on search engine positioning, today meta tags aren't that important at all. In fact, none of the major search engines even look at meta tags. Still, a few minor search engines do look to them, particularly your "description" tag, to find key information about your site. Therefore, it's useful to have a good understanding of how to best make use of them.

What are meta tags, you ask? If you view the HTML of your web page in a text editor, you should see your meta tags at the very top, in the <HEAD> section of your document (commonly called the page header). Your web page header will look something like this:

<HEAD>

<TITLE>My Web Page Title</TITLE>

<META Name="description" Content="Write a web site description here">
<META Name="keywords" Content="Insert your keywords and key phrases here">

</HEAD>

While you may see other tags listed there, the *description* and *keyword* tags are the only two you really care about. It is possible that by default, you have no meta tags listed. If this is the case, simply add them like you see in the example above. Make sure you place them between the two <HEAD> tags. Once this is done, save your text file as an *.html or *.htm document (either extension will work).

NOTE: In case you are wondering, the items in your page header do not display in the web browser. Only items within the <BODY> section of your HTML document (below your page header) are displayed in a browser.

Write a good description of your web page using 150 characters or less (including spaces) and insert this into your *description* meta tag. This description might be the same exact description you place high in your web page to help create relevancy, as discussed earlier. As you did with that description, include as many of your keywords and key phrases as possible. Again, don't just stuff your description with keywords for the sake of stuffing it with keywords (I'm really beating this horse dead!). Some search engines make reference to this description tag when listing your web site in their search results. So use your keywords and phrases in a logical way, resulting in a description that makes sense and appeals to the reader.

Now take your top 8 or 10 keywords or phrases and include them in your *keyword* meta tag. Here's an example a Flamenco guitarist might use:

<META Name="keywords" Content="flamenco, spanish music, flamenco guitar, latin music, flamenco dance, ottmar liebert, spanish guitar, dance music, jesse cook">

Use all lower case and don't repeat your keywords or phrases. There is some debate as to whether using commas to separate your key phrases makes any difference to search engine crawlers. Some prefer to simply string all the text together, leaving out the commas. I have no opinion on this issue. Personally, I use commas. It just seems more organized.

NOTE: It's very important that the keywords or phrases you use in your meta tags actually exist within the content of your page. For example: if you use "guitar tablature" as a keyword phrase to attract guitarists, but that phrase does not exist anywhere else in your page (or there isn't any guitar tablature, period), then the search engine spider will consider your page irrelevant to that keyword phrase. You must keep your keywords relevant to the actual content within your page!

A Keyword to the Wise

Avoid using keywords in your meta tags that are vague or open-ended. Earlier, I illustrated how ineffective using the keyword "music" alone would be. The term is so generic that it would be extremely unlikely that anyone would find your web site when performing a search for that single word. Why even bother using that as a keyword? Instead, focus on unique keywords or phrases that are more *specifically* representative of who you are. Also, don't get cute by using keywords that have nothing to do with your web site just because they are commonly searched for. What good would it do you to use "Paris Hilton" as a keyword phrase for your music site? Sure, her name is one of the most searched for on the Net, but do you really want to target an audience that's in search of Paris? Probably not! (Unless Paris Hilton is the name of your band – there's a thought!) Even if such a keyword increased your traffic by a few hits a month, that's not the way to target customers who are likely to buy your products! It's not the quantity of traffic that's important, it's the *quality*. Again, I'll discuss the topic of targeting your audience in more detail in the upcoming chapter *Targeting Your Customers to the Max!*

Related Tip: If you're curious what the most popular searches actually are on the Internet, check out Google Trends at http://www.google.com/trends . Yahoo's Buzz Index (http://buzz.yahoo.com) is also an interesting read.

The "Spam"-ish Inquisition

Speaking of getting cute with keywords, not only should you avoid using unrelated words or phrases in your tags, you should avoid the *overuse* of the same keywords. Repeating the same words over and over in your meta tags is considered to be "spam." Anything you do that is designed to artificially pump up your keyword relevancy is spam. Sites deliberately stuffing their meta tags (or their page content) with the same keywords repeated over and over usually end up getting penalized in their ranking, and may even be dropped entirely from the search engine index. If you think you have found some unique way to trick the search engines into giving you a better listing, think again. By trying to outsmart the search engines, you may end up being your own worst enemy! Play it safe, use sensible keywords and phrases, and place them logically and strategically in your page without overdoing it. There's a careful balance to maintain. If your goal is to increase your search engine ranking, do so by growing and improving your page content, building reciprocal links, and creating a web site of value for your target audience.

See "7.5 Ways to get Banned or Penalized by Search Engines":
http://www.searchenginejournal.com/9-ways-to-get-banned-by-search-engines/4152/

More Meta Tag Tips

Here are a few more tips for creating keyword meta tags:

1) Add the letter "s" to the end of every word where appropriate (or add the plural of the word to the list in the case of words like cactus/cacti). For example, if you use the phrase "guitar tab" change that to "guitar tabs." A search for "tab" will also find your keyword "tabs," whereas the opposite is not true.

2) Some search engines consider capitalized and lower case words to be two different words. For example, MP3 and mp3. If you think a particular keyword or phrase is likely to be typed both ways during a search, you might include both variants in your meta tags. Keep in mind, however, that when most people use search engines they type using all lower case.

3) Don't forget misspellings. If one of your keywords has a common misspelling as a variant, use it. Do people commonly misspell your name? How might they try and spell it? For example, is it "Sarah McLachlan" or "Sarah MacLachlan?" Do you see the variant? Chances are, both are searched for.

4) Geographical location is important. If you're a band in Athens, Georgia, indicate that in your meta tag, description and content. If a particular venue is looking for a local band or artist, they may include the city name in their search. For example, "lounge singers in boston."

Other Somewhat Useful Tips

Here are a few other ideas for improving your web site's relevancy with search engines. These tips *might* help with a few crawling search engines, and they might not. I put them here for your consideration as you go about building your web site.

Location, Location, Location

If you can use a strategic keyword or phrase in your web site address, you can, to some degree, use this to increase your relevancy within your actual HTML. For example, if you have a site designed around the topic of Flamenco music, including the word "flamenco" in the web site address would be a logical thing to do. For example: http://www.flamencomusic.com.

Now, let me show you how you can build on that. Let's say John's home page is located at http://www.flamencomusic.com. He has several articles he's written on Flamenco guitar technique and has created web pages for each of these articles. Where should John put those articles on his site to create maximum impact with the search engines? If I were consulting John on this, I would advise him to create a sub-directory within his site called "guitar," then one further called "technique." Now, if he has several articles on technique, these should be placed in the http://www.flamencomusic.com/guitar/technique/ directory.

Now, from his home page, he lists several of these articles and links directly to them. He now has links pointing to:

http://www.flamencomusic.com/guitar/technique/tromolo.htm
http://www.flamencomusic.com/guitar/technique/legatos.htm
http://www.flamencomusic.com/guitar/technique/tempestad.htm
and so on...

Now, if John views the HTML of his home page, he will see these URL links complete with some powerful keywords. When the search engine spider comes along to index John's Flamenco page, this URL text is indexed as well, and as a result, may boost the relevancy of John's Flamenco music site when someone searches for information on specific Flamenco guitar styles.

The point? If you're going to have links to other pages within your site, you might as well design your directory structure in such a way as to include your strategic keywords.

Tagging Your Images

If you make use of graphic images on your web site, you can use those, to some extent, to create more text for the search engine spider to feed on. How? By taking advantage of the ALT command for your images. The purpose of this command is to put text in place of images in the event your images don't load. The command was used frequently in the early days of the Internet for text-only web browsers.

Here's an example of a standard HTML graphic image reference:

<IMG SRC="flamenco_sampler.gif" HEIGHT=142 WIDTH=171>

Now, here's an example that employs the ALT command:

<IMG SRC="flamenco_sampler.gif" ALT="Free Flamenco Music Sampler!" HEIGHT=142 WIDTH=171>

The addition of the ALT command creates a text description for your logo or graphic. To see this effect on any web page, move your mouse pointer over the logo and if you see a text area float over the logo or graphic, you know the ALT command is in use. A few search engines will read that ALT information as it gathers information about the site.

Heading Tags

A heading tag is different than a page title tag. The heading tag tells the search engine which text on your web page consist of the "main points" – the headlines. These are referred to as H1 and H2 in your document HTML and will look something like this:

<H1>Flamenco Music to Make the World Dance Uncontrollably</H1>

and a sub-heading tag would look like this:

<H2>Spanish Guitar Duo Rocks the House</H2>

These tags tell the search engines what lines are most important in your page. If you include your strategic keywords in your headings, it may add some additional relevancy to the particular words and phrases you're trying to target for the search engines.

Link Text: Get Specific

It has been theorized that when determining relevance, some search engines lend additional weight to text that is hyperlinked on your web site. In other words, text you link may be seen as more relevant than text you do not. For example, let's say you have links to your articles on Flamenco guitar styles from your home page. Instead of using text like this...

"For some great articles on different Flamenco guitar styles, click here"

and then linking the "click here" text, do this...

"Check out these articles on Flamenco guitar styles."

and link the words "Flamenco guitar styles"

Some in the search engine industry speculate that this will create more relevancy for the phrase "Flamenco guitar styles" within that page. If this is true, you could see why you'd want more weight placed on the words "Flamenco guitar styles" than on "click here."

The Exclusion Clause

There may be an occasion when you do NOT want a web page indexed by a search engine. If you want to exclude a page from a search engine, just include the following meta tag:

<META Name="robots" Content="noindex">

Put that line between the <HEAD> tags of any page you do NOT want indexed and the spider will leave the page alone.

Optimization Summary

The point of this chapter is to help you design your web page with search engines in mind. Now that you know what kind of content search engines are looking for, you can build your site around that.

To summarize:

1) Search engine optimization is just one small part of your music promotion strategy. Your success as a musician on the Internet does not rely on the search engines.

2) Design your web pages around the keywords and phrases that target the customer most likely to be interested in your product. Each page is another opportunity to catch the attention of a different customer using a slightly different phrase to search the Internet.

3) Design your site to *impress upon* the search engine spider the *content* you want it to notice. From your home page, use *text links* to link to important pages deeper in your web site. You want to make it easy for the search engine spider to locate your most important content.

4) The three things that matter most to crawling search engines are your page title, page relevancy, and page popularity.

5) Think of your web page title as a one-line ad for your web site. Use a page title that says "click me" to any potential customer viewing it on a search engine results page.

6) Create content around your key phrases to establish relevance. Write a web page description, containing the appropriate keywords and phrases, and place it high in the page.

7) Search the Internet for sites that rank high using your keywords and phrases, contact the webmaster for these sites, and offer to swap links. This will increase your popularity ranking.

8) Meta tags do not, in most cases, have any effect on rankings since the major search engines ignore them.

9) Do not stuff keywords and phrases unnaturally in a web page for the sole purpose of trying to artificially inflate your relevancy rate. Use keywords and phrases logically, skillfully and appropriately using common sense.

10) When all is said and done, what matters is *content*. Design a web site that offers something of value to your target audience, and not only will they return, but eventually others will begin to take notice.

Here are more articles you might want to read through on this topic:

44 Internet Marketing Articles Everyone Should Read:
http://courtneytuttle.com/2007/10/15/43-internet-marketing-articles-that-everyone-should-read/

Web Sites Every SEO Should Know:
http://www.seounique.com/blog/25-websites-every-seo-should-know

Beginners Guide to Search Engine Optimization:

http://www.seomoz.org/article/beginners-guide-to-search-engine-optimization

Key Site Ranking Factors:

http://www.seomoz.org/article/search-ranking-factors

There you have it. Now I'll show you how and where to submit your web site to the search engines...

Search Engine Submission - How to Put Yourself on the Internet Map!

Search Engines: The Changing Landscape

If you haven't noticed, the search engine world has undergone drastic change in the last few years. It wasn't all that long ago that twenty or more Internet search companies were duking it out for market position. Today, most of those companies have all but disappeared. As often happens in the corporate world, the little guys can only fight so long before they are overtaken, bought out, acquired or otherwise disassembled by bigger guys with more money, resources and power. As of this writing, there are only three search engines that are seriously competing for the Internet search market, and very soon that number will dwindle down to two.

This is a good thing in one sense. It's made our job, as Internet music marketers, much easier. A few years ago you had to put a lot of effort into getting your web site listed on *dozens* of search engines. Today, you can submit your web site to all the search engines that matter in less than ten minutes.

Should You Hire a Search Engine Professional?

You may wonder if you are really up to this task. What if you make a mistake when submitting your web site to a search engine? Should you hire a professional to do that job for you? Let me assure you, submitting your site to the search engines is not difficult to do. In fact, you'll be surprised at how simple it is. While there are search engine optimization specialists who will gladly take your money to optimize and submit your web site for you, there's no need to go that route. Save your money for something else.

Yes, Virginia, it Really is That Easy...

Here's all you have to do:

First, make sure your web site is optimized and ready to go per the previous chapter. Second, go to the submit links I refer you to below for each of the recommended search engines. Third and finally, enter the web address for your home page (i.e., http://www.yourwebsiteaddress.com) in the appropriate field on the search engine submit form and then hit the "Submit" (or "Add") button.

That's all there is to it.

Once you submit your web site, the search engine will take that as a notification that your site needs to be crawled. In due time (usually not too terribly long), the spider will come and add your web site into the search engine's database. Now remember, as I stated in the last chapter in the "Helping Spiders" section, in order for the spider to crawl your *entire* web site, you need to have *text links* to your important pages from your home page, and links from those secondary pages to deeper pages and so on. That way, when the spider comes along, it will follow the links from your home page to the other important pages on your web site.

Once you've submitted your web site, check back with the search engines periodically to see if they've listed you yet. If you perform a search on the *exact phrase* for your web page title – and if that page title is unique enough – you should see it come up near the top of the search results once your site has been indexed. Another way to check the status of your web site is to simply search on your web site address. For example, I can search Google for "musicbizacademy.com" and see that indeed, the web site is in Google's index. If I want more specific detail, I can type "site:http://www.musicbizacademy.com" (no quotes) and see every page under that domain that Google has included in their database.

The Search Engines That Really Matter

In previous editions of this book, I spent a great deal of time delving into the long and tangled history of search engines; where they came from, what their marketing strategy was, who bought out who, and what search companies came and went and why. I've left all that behind. Frankly, I doubt most of you really care about the history of search engines. What you need to know is that while there are literally *thousands* of search engines on the Internet, only a few of them matter in today's world. Virtually any search performed anywhere on the Internet today goes through one of the three companies listed below. Even if someone performs a search on a less-popular search engine, such as AOL.com, in most cases the search results actually come from somewhere else (for example, AOL's primary search results are provided by Google).

Without further ado, here are the most important search engines to submit your web site to….

Search Engine	**Submission Guidelines: How, Where and How Much…**
Google (http://www.google.com)	**Submit** your web site via http://www.google.com/addurl.html
	Notes: Google is the **first place** you should submit your site as it is the most used search tool on the Internet. According to recent figures by Net Applications, 66% of all search results on the net are provided by Google.
	Cost: It's free to submit, but Google also offers a paid advertising option called AdWords. I will discuss that shortly.

Yahoo (http://www.yahoo.com)

Submit via http://search.yahoo.com/info/submit.html
Yahoo's service descriptions are quite convoluted, but for most people, the "Submit Your Site for Free" option will suffice.

Notes: At one time Yahoo was the dominant search engine player. Now it's #2 after Google, sitting at a mere 16% of all Internet searches. In fact, Yahoo has abandoned search. By the second half of 2010, Yahoo's results will be provided by Bing (below).

Cost: Yahoo offers both free and paid submission options. Take the free option. Neither Yahoo's "Search Submit"(at $49 + .15 cents per click) or the $299/year Directory option are a good value in my view. The "Sponsored Search" option you see listed is the "Yahoo Search Marketing" advertising program. I will discuss that shortly.

Bing (http://www.bing.com)

Submit via http://www.bing.com/webmaster/SubmitSitePage.aspx

Notes: Bing (formerly MSN Search) is the third most used search tool, sitting at 3% of all Internet searches. By the second half of 2010, Bing will provide search results for Yahoo as well, which should bring them up to about 12% of the search market.

Cost: Free. Paid "sponsorship" options are available via Microsoft's sponsored ad program called adCenter. More on this shortly.

Believe it or not, that's the extent of it. Those are the *only* search engines you need to worry about. Once your web site is listed in Google, Yahoo and Bing, you'll be in a position to get exposure to 94% of the total Internet audience either directly or indirectly. Now, as I previously stated, there are *many* more search engines out there. Just try counting the ones listed at http://www.searchenginecolossus.com for starters. However, even if you *combined* the thousands of search tools you see listed there, they still account for less than 6% of all Internet searches. So spending much effort on those is, relatively speaking, a waste of time.

Testing and Resubmitting Your Keywords

As I previously mentioned, once you've submitted your main page to a search engine, it will send a spider to crawl your entire web site. This means you don't have to submit each of your pages separately to the search engines. Despite this, I do still recommend submitting your most important pages individually. By doing so, you will ensure you populate the search indexes with your content. Once your web site grows to 60, 80, or 100 pages, you'll find your stuff popping up all over when you do a search on your strategic keywords and phrases. More pages mean more opportunities for visibility!

Once you are listed, you'll want to check back with the search engines periodically to ensure your pages stay listed. To keep your listings fresh, a good rule of thumb is to reevaluate your content and resubmit a page any time you make major modifications to it.

Don't get frustrated if you find getting a high ranking (in the top 20) on one or more of the search engines a difficult task. It's not easy. In fact, your web site may not be given a decent ranking for close to a year after you submit it. There is speculation that Google has put an "aging delay" into place for new web sites. If you have a brand new domain or website, Google puts your submission into a "waiting queue" for ranking that's six months to a year long. While your web site *will* be indexed and included in the database, it won't rank highly on your keywords no matter how well you optimize your pages until this period has passed. Why is Google doing this? No one knows for sure, but many believe it's an effort to combat fraud and identity theft. Web sites designed to trick people into giving away their credit card information (such as fake web sites soliciting aid for various charities and benefits) come and go very quickly. This waiting period reduces the chance that a web site of questionable origin will appear anywhere near the top of the listings for a particular keyword or phrase.

If you hang in there, eventually your web site will start turning up where it should in the listings. Until it does, keep developing your content and make a serious effort to get other web sites to link to you. Above all, don't stress out about it. As I said at the beginning of the last chapter, search engine success takes time and patience. Sometimes you just need to focus on building a quality site, all the while keeping the optimization rules I mentioned in mind. Eventually, as you gain in popularity via the marketing strategies I'll get into shortly, your search engine ranking and visibility will increase.

Helpful Article: Ten Tips to the Top of the Search Engines: http://www.highrankings.com/tentips

Now, let me address another key question....

Should You Pay for Position?

On the submission guidelines page, I mentioned the Google AdWords program as well as Microsoft's adCenter program (via Bing). These are pay-for-position advertising tools that allow you to bid for advertising spots (i.e. "sponsor ads") that appear on a search engine result page (see example below). The more money you agree to pay each time someone clicks on your listing, the more visible your "ad" link will be when someone searches for your particular keyword or phrase. So, if you want lots of clicks through your ad to your web site, you have to be willing to pay more than your competitor to get the higher, more visible position. In this competition for position, the person with the biggest pile of money wins.

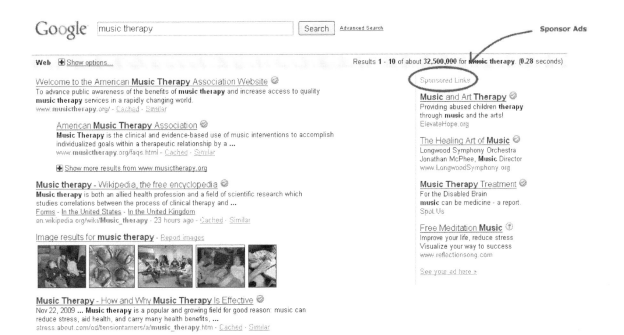

Now the big question: is investing in a "sponsor" ad campaign with Google or Bing a worthwhile option for selling music? The answer, in most cases, is no. The minimum adCenter lets you bid for a keyword is 5¢ per click. That means that you'll pay $5.00, at the very *least*, for 100 click-throughs. The problem is, because sales conversion rates are so low and because you don't have a very high profit margin on CDs (or digital downloads), it's a losing wager. I haven't seen *anyone* sell independent music successfully (and come out ahead) when using a pay-for-position marketing strategy.

Now, if you're selling a product that targets a very precise audience, these advertising options can be beneficial. I use Google AdWords to promote this book and I come out ahead on that deal. But the reason I make money on it is that I'm targeting people searching the Internet with terms like "how to promote music" or "selling music online." So my target audience for this book is very well defined. I have a higher sell-through rate and a higher profit margin to help pay for those ads.

When you're selling CDs or downloads, however, it's very difficult to generate enough sales to make a profit using pay-per-click advertising. The only time when that might *not* be the case is if your band is one people are specifically searching for. For example, I sold a copy of this book recently to *The Wiggles*. *The Wiggles* is a very popular children's program from Australia (see http://www.thewiggles.com.au if you're curious.) I'm sure a lot of folks are searching the Internet for Wiggles-related merchandise for their kids, and in *that* case, *The Wiggles* could probably make very good use of this advertising model. But without that kind of established name brand, an independent musician will find it much more difficult to make a profit.

If you'd like to research your sponsor ad options, you'll find the information at…

Google AdWords	http://adwords.google.com/
Microsoft adCenter (Bing)	http://advertising.microsoft.com/search-advertising
7Search.com (another alternative)	http://www.7search.com/

Recommended Reading:

Here are some great places to do more research on search engines...

Search Engine Watch:	http://www.searchenginewatch.com/
HighRankings.com:	http://www.highrankings.com/
SearchEngineGuide:	http://www.SearchEngineGuide.com
Pandia Search Central:	http://www.pandia.com/
Virtual Promote:	http://www.virtualpromote.com/
37 Ways to Promote Your Web Site:	http://www.wilsonweb.com/articles/checklist.htm
10 Tips to the Top of the Search Engines:	http://www.highrankings.com/tentips
Bruce Clay Tactics:	http://www.bruceclay.com/web_pt.htm

For search engine mastery, I *strongly* recommend you subscribe to HighRanking.com's free newsletter. It really is a must for anyone trying to keep up with the search engine world. I also highly recommend the SearchDay newsletter from SearchEngineWatch.com. Both of them are high on quality content, and low on advertising.

Targeting Your Customers to the Max!

Pick Your Target and Aim Carefully!

While it's important to properly design, prepare, and optimize your web site for the search engines, search engine placement is only the very beginning of your music marketing plan. If selling music on the Internet was as simple as submitting your site to the search engines, then you really wouldn't need this book! So, let's dive into the all important topic of targeting your audience.

The first audience you need to target is your existing fan base. As I will demonstrate shortly, your fans are going to play a big part in how you lay the groundwork for future marketing strategies. It may be, however, that you are just starting out in the music business and feel like "I don't have a fan base." If this sums up your situation, think again. You have family, friends, co-workers, classmates, former classmates, church members and neighbors all around you. If you sit down and start writing down the names of every person you've ever known in your life, you'll be very surprised how quickly that list grows without much effort. Doing *this very thing* is exactly how I started promoting my music way back in 1991. Don't underestimate the power of your friends, family, coworkers and circle of acquaintances. You've heard of the fabled "six degrees of separation." Well, you really only need two of those six degrees to begin building a pretty large mailing list.

Voices from the Past...

So where do you start? To build a foundation for your mailing list, one of the first things I recommend you do is pull out your old high school and college yearbooks. Remember Joe? Brenda? Jimmy? I'll bet you forgot all about some of those old chums of yours! Go through the class pictures and write down the names of anyone you think would be interested in your music career. Now you just need to find them!

The easiest way to find old friends on the Internet is to make use of Facebook (http://www.facebook.com), the Internet's largest online community. Facebook is extremely popular and is, as of this writing, still in a rapid growth phase. You can bet a lot of your pals from the past are on it. If you haven't already, set up a Facebook account. As you do so, you will be prompted for your current location, the high school and/or college you graduated from (and the years attended), and where you worked at different times in your life. Once you've entered that information in your Facebook profile, you can use that information as a base point to search for others on Facebook who have "lived life" in the same places you have. You will quickly find yourself hooking up with people you haven't seen or heard from in a very long time.

As you approach these friends from the past, be mindful of how you make your initial contact. You don't want to come across as if you're contacting them after all these years just to sell them something – even if that's true to some extent. Just drop them a note and say "hi." Let them know you found them on Facebook and wanted to catch up. If they care about you and are interested, at some point during the "let's catch up" conversation, they will probably ask you what you've been up to. It's at that point you can bring up your music career. Invite them to visit your web site to listen to some of your music. If they respond positively, ask them if they would like you to let them know when you are playing a concert near them. If they say yes, get their email info and plug them into your mailing list database. It's a simple as that.

Aside from Facebook, there are other resources you can use to research old school chums online. Most everyone knows about Reunion.com (now MyLife.com), but there are other similar sites. Here are a few places to begin your search:

MyLife.com (formerly Reunion.com)	http://www.mylife.com/
Classmates.com:	http://www.classmates.com
USAReunited:	http://www.usareunited.com
MySchoolReunited:	http://www.myschoolreunited.com/
GradFinder:	http://www.gradfinder.com/
Alumni.net:	http://www.alumni.net
SchoolNews:	http://www.schoolnews.com/
CuriousCat Alumni:	http://www.curiouscat.net/alumni/

While you're on these sites looking for old acquaintances, don't forget to register your own name, class, and contact information. You never know when old friends may come to one of these sites looking for *you*. In most cases, it doesn't cost anything to add your own profile. MyLife.com, for example, only charges a fee if you find someone you know and want access to their contact or personal information.

Listed below are other web sites you can visit online to search for people. These are more hit-and-miss, and you have to wade through a lot of advertising, but if you're desperate to find one particular individual (say an old girlfriend or boyfriend?), then you may find these tools valuable:

Spokeo:	http://www.spokeo.com
ZabaSearch:	http://www.zabasearch.com/
Pandia People Search:	http://www.pandia.com/people/index.html
PublicRecordsNow:	http://web.public-records-now.com/
Intelius:	http://www.intelius.com/
Lycos People Search:	http://peoplesearch.lycos.com/whitepage/
AnyWho:	http://www.anywho.com/
Knowx:	http://www.knowx.com/
PhoneNumber:	http://www.phonenumber.com/
U.S. Search:	http://www.ussearch.com/consumer/index.jsp

Developing Relationships in Cyberspace

Resources like those mentioned above make it fairly easy to find old friends. However, don't get so busy delving into your past that you forget to explore your *current* relationships as well. Many of those in your circle of friends, family and coworkers are probably active to some degree on Facebook, so you'll want to make that connection with them. As those folks become more aware of what you're doing with your music, they may, over time, become more interested and supportive, not only because they (hopefully) like your music but because they know you and want to help you. You may find that some of your biggest networking assets turn out to be people you already know but haven't developed an online relationship with yet.

Relationship-building is a very important part of marketing your music, and social sites like Facebook make developing those relationships a little easier to do. This is your hope; that friends from the past and present, your family and co-workers, will fall so in love with your music that they feel compelled to share it with their own friends, family and co-workers. And then, in the best of worlds, those friends will share it even further with their own friends and acquaintances. And on it goes.

This is how you grow a fan base and a mailing list, by developing relationships and cultivating interest in your music. This leads to more sales, as well as performance opportunities which in turn, again, leads to more sales, more mailing list signups, more people hooking up with you on Facebook, MySpace and Twitter. It's a continuous process. The more your music spreads, the more contacts you are able to make, and the more people you have around you to help you further spread your music and grow your career.

This is also why you need a web site – so that there's one central place people can visit to find out more about you and your music. Your overall objective with just about everything you do online is to drive people to your web site, encourage them to sign up for your mailing list and to, of course, sell your music. So from this point forward, I'll assume your web site is completed and ready for visitors to discover. That being the case, let's talk about....

Making Use of the Microphone

If you are a performing musician, you have one advantage over musicians that don't regularly perform. You have a captive audience to promote your music and web site to every time you play. Once you have center stage, take advantage of the limelight. Pick up that microphone and use it. Here are a few suggestions for promoting your web site at your gigs:

1) Are you ever at a loss for words when doing a sound check? Do you feel silly walking up to the mic and saying "test, test, test" to the annoyed, impatient look of the crowd? Isn't that embarrassing? Make good use of that moment and integrate your web site address into your sound check. Say the address over and over again in creative ways while you're doing your sound check. You can also use the opportunity to invite folks to hook up with you on Facebook, Twitter and MySpace, search for you on YouTube and so on. If you're going to talk, make it count.

2) Hang a large banner over the stage with your web address in large, easy-to-read letters. If you can use black light to light up bright, neon colors on your banner, all the better. It looks very cool, and everyone will take notice. Imagine that "first impression" moment on stage before you play your opening chord – the lights in the room go out, the black light comes on and your banner blazes in the darkness – then you hit them with your first riff: the crowd goes wild (or so you hope)! You can get banners made fairly inexpensively at http://www.vistaprint.com . I've used Vistaprint for my own marketing materials and highly recommend them.

3) Pass out business cards that contain your contact information and web site address. Business cards are dirt cheap advertising, so give them out like candy. On your business cards include a one-line catch-phrase about your act that sums it all up, and point it out to people when you hand them your card. Want to get some inspiration for some very cool business card designs? See http://www.toxel.com/inspiration/2008/12/09/40-creative-business-card-designs/ You can order business cards online at http://www.vistaprint.com . Upload your own design or start by using one of their templates.

4) Rubber stamp the hands of all concert attendees with your web site address as they enter the venue. When they get home after the show, your web site information is still on their person. Yea, they'll wash it off eventually, but they'll remember it the next morning when they hit the shower. You can purchase a customized rubber stamp fairly inexpensively at http://www.vistaprint.com or http://www.rubberstamps.net/ .

5) Create flyers that double as coupons and pass them out at your show. On the flyer, include offers for CD discounts, merchandise discounts and other incentives that are *only* redeemable via a special order page on your web site. Once you design your flyer, you can have them printed at any local print shop. I use Fed Ex Office (http://www.fedex.com/us/office/) for most of my printing needs of this nature.

6) Use the stage to promote a contest where attendees can win free merchandise, dinner dates with the band, or cool band-name-branded gadgets. Make the prize something unconventional to get the attention of your crowd. The contest entry form is, of course, available at your web site.

7) Got an iPhone? Hold it up from the stage. Remind the crowd that they can purchase your music on iTunes *right now* using their iPhone.

8) Announce the availability of sheet music, guitar tabs, or lyrics for your songs available for purchase and/or free download from your web site. Fans who are musicians themselves *love* that kind of stuff.

9) Offer free MP3 downloads of new, unreleased material from your web site and announce from the stage that you are seeking fan feedback on those new songs.

10) Include an up-to-date performance schedule on your web site and at the end of the show let fans know they can go there for event times, dates, or to order tickets early. You might even offer discounts for tickets purchased via your web site by a certain date.

11) Invite the crowd to connect with you on FaceBook, Twitter, MySpace and anywhere else you spend a good deal of time online. Make your appeal to your audience *personal*. "If you like the music you hear from the band tonight, hook up with us online on our MySpace, FaceBook and Twitter pages. Wherever you hang out online, we're there too! So drop by, friend us and we'll friend you back." You get the idea.

Be *aggressive* about marketing your music and web site at concert events. Most artists are much too timid with promotion at gigs. They do their show, then afterward sit at a table and wait for people to come to them. This is the WRONG approach! If you've got CDs and merchandise to sell, you should have someone working the audience, actively taking your products into the crowd while you're on stage. It's the same approach food vendors take at pro or semi-pro ball games. Food vendors don't wait for you to come to them; they go into the stands and bring their goodies to you! Take this same approach with your audience and you'll find you have much better CD and merchandise sales at events. I recommend you hire two or three "agents," people you pay a buck or two for every CD they sell, and then send them out to work the crowd. It's quick money for them and quick sales for you.

Obvious (or maybe not so obvious) Tip: The more you pay your "agents" per sale, the more motivated they will be to spend their time pitching your product at your shows rather than just hanging out in the crowd. You want *enthusiastic* sales people who like to smile. The more enthusiastic your sales people are, the more product you will sell through them, as people *enjoy* buying products from people they perceive as likeable, friendly and happy.

Get the Folks on Your Mailing List: When you're playing a show, you want as many people as possible to sign up for your mailing list so you can keep in touch with them about new releases, concert dates, web site updates and so on. At every show, have your sales people hand out mailing list sign up cards to fill out. Don't forget to hand out pens as well (order personalized pens at http://www.inkhead.com or, of course, http://www.vistaprint.com). Then, during your show, let people know you will be collecting the completed cards at the end of the concert and drawing names to give away free merchandise, tickets, drink vouchers, CDs, MP3s, DVDs, sheet music – whatever. If you give people an incentive to fill out the card and sign up for your mailing list, they will be more likely to do so. I use this approach at every one of my shows and it makes it very easy to gather names and email addresses to expand my mailing list.

Additional Reading: Success at the Merch Table, The First 10 Ideas…
http://indieuniverse.wordpress.com/2009/06/09/success-at-the-merch-table-the-first-10-ideas/

Put Your Fans to Work!

Read this article: 1000 True Fans: http://www.kk.org/thetechnium/archives/2008/03/1000_true_fans.php

Your fans are a *very* powerful asset for you. I can't stress this fact enough. For every hundred fans you have, there's going to be at least one out there that lives and breathes your music. These are the people you want to enlist to help you. Just a few "true" fans can go a long way in getting the word out about you and your web site.

Will fans really help? Yes, your true fans will. People want to feel important to the people they love, and though it sounds a bit strange to say, your true fans do fall in love with you in a way. If you've been playing long enough, you've seen that starry-eyed look in people. It's very recognizable, and though it can, at times, be a bit disconcerting, you can put these fan emotions to work for you in a positive way. When you see that look in a fan's eyes, ask them if they'd like to help you promote your music. If they say "yes," then you are on your way to creating your first "street team," as it's commonly referred to in the music industry.

One of your primary tasks at performances should actually be to seek out and find true fans for your street team. Think of it as recruiting. True fans will usually jump at the chance to work for you, even on a volunteer basis. They'll pass out flyers and posters for you, design web sites for you, create videos for you and post them on YouTube, sell CDs for you, help you set up and tear down equipment, and even spend the time and energy necessary to help you promote your music online.

Once you have created your own personal team of fans, arrange a special get together, a private "by invitation only" dinner party for them. Host the party at your home, or if that's a bit too personal just invite them out for a Coke and pizza. Once you have everyone together, grab a pencil and notepad and start in with the questions:

"Who here spends much time on the Internet?"
"How much time a day, do you think?"
"What do you like to do online?"
"What kinds of things do you search for on the Internet?"

"Who are your favorite artists and bands?"

"What hobbies do you have, and do you use your hobby on the Internet?"

"What type of research, if any, do you do online?"

"Where do you go online to chat about the music you like?"

"Are you actively involved in any chat rooms or discussion groups, and if so, which ones and where?"

"Are you actively involved in social networks like MySpace, Facebook, Twitter , YouTube or _____?"

"How much time to do you spend on Facebook compared to doing anything else online?"

"Where do you listen online to music most often?"

"Where do you go online when you want to find new music?"

"What is your absolute, #1 favorite thing to do online?"

"What is your preferred way to receive updates and news about my music? Email? Facebook? _____?"

The answers you receive to these questions will usually lead to even more questions. Listen carefully, keep the conversation going and **take detailed notes** on what your fans tell you. You might even record (or video) the meeting! If there are a few in the group who seem reserved and shy, use your charming personality to bring them into the conversation. Let them know their feedback is important to you. You need input from every single person on your team. Knowing and understanding these people who love your music will help you know and understand the audience you want to target on the Internet. By getting to know the fans you *do* know, you'll better get to know the potential fans you *don't* know. That's the whole point of this exercise. Marketing firms pay tens of thousands of dollars to gather this kind of information for their clients. You can get it for the price of a dinner and a few drinks!

Once your private party is over, find a quiet place by yourself and analyze your notes on the comments your fans made. Find the commonality between your team members. What do all these people have in common? What hobbies, likes and dislikes? Where do they spend their time online? If you can find *common interests* between these true fans that you know enjoy your music, chances are others who share similar interests will dig your music as well.

In addition to meeting face-to-face with your local fans, you can have online gatherings with your Internet-based fans. Why not send out an email to the fans already on your list and invite them to a group phone conference? You can have a sit down meeting with your fans from around the world, but do it online. At FreeConferenceCall.com (http://www.freeconferencecall.com) you can host a free teleconference for up to 96 people. Just create an account, set up a time, and let your fans know you will be there for a live teleconference and that you'd like them to join you to answer some questions that will help you better promote your music. The only cost to your fans is the cost of the phone call. If you prefer, you can spend .06¢ per minute and make the call toll-free for your fans. The service even lets you record the call for free so you can go back and review it later to take notes. On your first call you may only get four or five fans to join you, but you can be assured that those fans are serious about your music, and representative of the very people you want to target online.

For something a little less interactive, you can use a service like Survey Monkey (http://www.surveymonkey.com/) to create a survey with your questions and send it out to fans. You'll gather important information and you can graph the survey answers into valuable data reports that you can hang onto for a long time. Bravenet.com also has a great survey tool called Vote Caster that's free to use. Check that out at http://www.bravenet.com/webtools/vote/ .

This information you gather, whether it be face-to-face, via a teleconference or an online survey, will help you better target new customers on the Internet, which brings me straight to the next point....

Targeting New Customers - When You Do it Right, the Future Looks Bright!

OK, so you've done your research and you now have a much better idea who your target audience is. That's all fine and dandy, but how can you use the information you've gathered to bring new customers to your web site? After all, the number of musicians already established on the Internet is overwhelming. How can you possibly compete with them all? How can you ever hope to be heard when so many other web sites are out there demanding your potential customer's attention?

First of all, don't worry about creating a buzz about your music on the *entire* Internet. That would be an unrealistic goal, rather like playing a gig and expecting the whole world to hear. What you want to do is create a buzz at very specific locations online where people will be most responsive and open to hearing your music. Where are these places? To find out, use the information you gathered from your street team. Where do members of your team hang out on the Internet? Where are they going online to chat about the music they love? Where do they go online to *share information*? These are the places you want to focus on, and the best way to make an impact *quickly* at these locations is to ask your street team to actively participate in generating interest in your music among their peers.

Taking Aim at Social Media Circles, Groups, Chat Rooms and Forums

When you're ready to begin targeting new customers, one of your first tasks should be to send your street team into their favorite social networks, forums, newsgroups, chat rooms, and discussion groups to talk up your music. Since they visit these places often, it's not like they are doing any extra work. They're just talking about the music they love and sharing it with their online friends. The places they talk you up do not necessarily need to be music-related venues, either. Remember, you are targeting people who have common interests, and it's through this common connection that your street team can introduce your music to others.

This kind of thing is done all the time in the professional music biz. If you're in a chat room for the band "The Killers," for example, and you see two people chatting back and forth about this other amazing up-and-coming band, do you think that's an accident? Well, it might be, but it might also be a couple of street team members for that "amazing" band (who might have a sound similar to The Killers) trying to drum up some interest in a chat room where they have an audience receptive to their style of music.

Of course, you don't have to rely solely on your fans. You can do your own self-promotion. Having spent time interviewing your true fans, you know what they are interested in, who their favorite bands are and some of the commonalities between them. Find forums, chat rooms and discussion groups where your target audience is likely to hang out. When people post questions or comments on a topic that is in your area of expertise, respond and get involved in the discussion. Become a forum expert, and every time you post a message or respond to someone, use a very specific email signature. For example, here is mine:

David Nevue
Solo Piano Artist & Creator of Whisperings: Solo Piano Radio
http://www.davidnevue.com
http://www.davidnevue.com/listen.htm
http://www.solopianoradio.com
http://www.twitter.com/davidnevue

CD REVIEWS from Buyers...
http://www.davidnevue.com/testimonials.htm

WIN a FREE CD!
Subscribe to David's 'Notes from the Piano' newsletter.
Details at http://www.davidnevue.com/subscribe.htm

You don't even have to blatantly promote your music when posting your messages. If fact, you *shouldn't* do that as people will dismiss you as an opportunist. Let your email signature do the work, giving you "billboard-style" promotion whenever you post a message in response to others. Answer questions, join in discussions, offer advice on the topic at hand and get involved. If you post messages frequently and if you are a pleasant person to talk to in the discussion group, people reading the messages will be curious about you and your music and will eventually check out your web site. People might ask you questions about your music in the discussion group, and *then* you can talk about it all you want in the appropriate context. You'll make many new e-friends and web acquaintances, and if you are targeting your audience well, new fans.

Where do you find these forums, discussion groups and chat rooms to post in? Start your research with the big three: Google, Facebook and MySpace, where so many people spend their time.

As it relates to **Google** (http://www.google.com), there are lots of web sites that cater to your particular target audience and many of those have active visitor forums. To research this, go to Google, and do a search on your "target topic" and add the word "forum" to it. For example, if you know fans of your music also tend to be fans of guitarist Jack Johnson, go perform a search for "Jack Johnson Forum." Now just look how many forums there are… all folks you can drop in on, develop relationships with, and casually introduce your own music to. You'll find the most active discussions on specialized web site forums like these.

For **Facebook** (http://www.facebook.com) perform a search for a targeted term and related pages and groups will come up. For example, search for "U2" and you'll find the band under "Musician" pages. On the left menu, you'll see a link where you can break the search results down into "Groups." Click on that and you'll find dozens of places to join in on discussions. You'll want to explore the groups/pages with the most fans. You can also search Facebook for topical discussions, for example, "guitar playing," for other places to get involved.

On **MySpace** (http://www.myspace.com) just click on the "More" drop down menu near the top of the web site and you'll see the forums and groups options. Choose one of those and you can browse and/or search for discussions in the forums that you may want to look into.

Other places online you can apply this marketing approach include…

Zhift (forum search tool):	http://www.zhift.com
Hi5:	http://www.hi5.com
Yahoo Groups:	http://groups.yahoo.com
Google Groups	http://groups.google.com
Google Chat & Forums:	http://directory.google.com/Top/Arts/Music/Chats_and_Forums/

Access to all of these places is free and they are all fairly easy to navigate. Just perform a search in any of the above for your strategic keywords and phrases and see what discussion lists come up as a result.

Once you dive into the world of chat and discussion, you'll find plenty of opportunities to promote yourself (or to send your street team) while taking an active part in conversations. You'll also find that hanging out in chat rooms, newsgroups and discussion groups is a great way to get to know your target audience. If you get involved, and get your street teams involved, you can build up a following very quickly. Best of all, it's FREE advertising.

Targeting by Site

I would now like to introduce you to a marketing strategy I call "targeting by site." This strategy is one I would consider an advanced marketing technique, especially in terms of the time required to execute it. However, for the purpose of targeting new customers, targeting by site can be very effective.

To target by site, you really need to have a clear picture of who your target audience is and what it is they are searching for on the Internet. You must be able to put yourself in the shoes of that potential fan out there and know how to get their attention. They've never heard of you or your music, but what *have* they heard of? What are they looking for? What do they want and what do they *need*?

The idea behind targeting by site is that you figure out what topic or subject your potential fan is looking for on the Internet and actually build a web site around that theme. This web site is *in addition* to your own personal band or artist home page. Let me make that clear. While aspects of this strategy can most certainly be used with your personal artist web site, you will have much more flexibility if you create an entirely new web site expressly for this purpose. You'll see why in a moment.

To illustrate this strategy, let me once again use the example of John, the Flamenco guitar player. John has a brand new Flamenco guitar album that he wants to advertise to Flamenco music fans. The problem is, he needs to get their attention. After a few meetings with his street team, John has a good idea what kinds of things Flamenco music fans are interested in. These include Flamenco guitar strumming techniques, gypsy music, Spanish guitar, and the history of Spanish guitar music styles. Some of his fans are also big fans of Jesse Cook and Ottmar Liebert, two well-known Flamenco-style artists. With all this in mind, John designs a web site with pages centered on the discussion of these topics. The site features not only a forum for interactive discussion, but Flamenco videos embedded from YouTube, on-topic articles, blogs, interviews, guitar playing tips, Flamenco music album reviews written by fans, chord charts and more. He calls this web site, dedicated entirely to Flamenco-related topics, www.FlamencoWorld.com. One by one, John finely tunes each individual page of his site with keywords and key phrases so they each target one particular topic. Once completed, John submits this custom-made web site to the search engines. Now John has a *general topic* web site specifically designed to appeal to the people who are *most likely* to be interested in his style of music. The more topic-related content he has on his web site, the more pages he can populate the search engines with. And the better job he does creating a quality web site around his topic, the more people that will find it, bookmark it, and link to FlamencoWorld.com. Traffic will generate more traffic as word gets out to similar web sites, blogs, chat rooms, forums and discussion groups.

So what happens when a potential new customer visits FlamencoWorld.com? How does doing this help John promote his music? He does it by including a highly visible promotional ad for his music on each individual page, one that links directly to a secondary page from which he pitches his Flamenco music CD and/or digital music downloads. This ad might be as simple as one, highly-visible link, saying something to the effect of, "Flamenco Guitar Rocks! Listen to This Month's Featured CD," or, for more impact, John's "ad" might be a short capsule review of the album designed to stir up interest in the reader. That review includes a photo, audio clips (perhaps a flash music player) and a link to a page with more details and of course a "buy" button.

Are you following the logic of this approach? Notice that, in this case, John didn't design a web site for the sole purpose of selling his music or promoting his name. He created a web site that promoted Flamenco music as a whole to attract his target audience. Only then, when a visitor with an affinity to his particular style of music arrives, does he draw their attention to the music he's selling. By using this technique, the artist gains more exposure and gains the additional benefit of having a much better chance of being found by the search engines. You see, John knows that his potential fan has never heard of him, but he also knows the kinds of things Flamenco music fans search for on the Internet. So, he uses that knowledge to his advantage.

Want another example? Who do fans say your act sounds like? Maybe your band has a real moody alternative grunge sound and everyone says you remind them of Alice in Chains, Nirvana or Pink Floyd. Rather than trying to sell your own name, which no one knows at this point, create a web site that targets fans of Alice in Chains, Nirvana or Pink Floyd and promote it. You can use their popularity to your benefit. Create fan pages for these bands (on Facebook too!), review their CDs, start a bulletin board or chat room service based on those bands. Talk about them in your blog. Now, on each of these pages, advertise your "featured artist," which is, of course, you. Are Nirvana fans looking for a new musical buzz? Tell them how much they will love the new album by this "great new band" you are featuring and provide sound files to listen to. Do you see how this works? The fan comes to your targeted site, checks out the featured artist he's never heard of, then, if you are successful with your sales pitch, takes a chance and buys your music.

You can take this idea in all kinds of directions. Is your music soft like a lullaby? Perhaps you should create a site that targets moms looking for advice on how to get their babies to sleep through the night. Is your music groovy piano jazz? Maybe an "online jazz bar" will bring in some curious customers. Brainstorm with your street team and see what kind of creative ideas you can come up with. Think of your targeted web site as a *product*. What kind of *product* does your target audience need? What are they *already* searching the Internet for? Find that, use that, and design your targeted web site around that concept. Then you have something that will attract potential buyers who have a predisposition to your style of music.

One of your goals with your own targeted web site, aside from using it to put your music in front of visitors more likely to enjoy your music, is to encourage those visitors to subscribe to your monthly newsletter, your *Targeted Site Mailing List*. Visitors who appreciate the information you provide on your targeted web site might also be interested in subscribing to that site's newsletter, giving you the opportunity to email them web site news, updates and announcements on a regular basis.

Once you have your visitor's email information, send updates on a periodic basis that encourage subscribers to return to your targeted web site. You can use the newsletter to announce new articles you've written, linking to those articles on your web site. You can create a poll of some sort and direct your mailing list subscribers to your web site to participate. You can sponsor a contest, and send your readers back to the web site to enter. The point is, use your targeted site's monthly newsletter to keep subscribers returning to the site. Why? Because your targeted site includes advertisements for your music. Your hope is that eventually they'll try your music and take you up on one of your special CD/MP3 Package offers. Once that happens, you begin the process of converting that targeted customer into a fan.

Now you can see why I consider this target by site marketing strategy to be "advanced." It takes a lot of work. If you put this strategy to use, not only are you managing, maintaining and promoting your own personal artist home page (plus any social networks you're involved in), but now you're managing, maintaining and promoting a topic-related site (or sites) as well. From my own experience, however, I can tell you that this idea works. If you find the right *something* to promote online that your would-be-fan really wants, you have, by creating this targeted web site, built a bridge to a person who would have never heard of your music otherwise. Yes, it's time consuming, and yes, it's a lot of work, but it does sell product. You can expand on this idea as well, by taking your "targeted web site" and creating a blog for it, a Facebook page for it, a Twitter account and even a YouTube channel featuring related information. These are all tools you can use to drive traffic to your targeted web site all for the purpose of pointing them to your music.

I recently ran across a perfect, real-life example of a company using a "targeting by site" philosophy to promote their services. Check out http://www.press-release-writing.com/ . These guys have some great articles on how to write a press release, including "10 essential tips" to ensure your press release makes the news, sample press releases, a press release template and more. Guess what service they sell? Press release writing and distribution. Do you see what they've done? In creating these articles and getting them indexed in the search engines, they've targeted the very customer they want to sell their services to. In fact, the way I found them was searching for easy-to-read articles on how to write a press release to add to my reference list in the next chapter. So, as you can see, by offering these free articles, these folks attract the attention of potential new clients and draw them into their web site where they can pitch their writing services.

Divide and Conquer!

When you make use of the target by site strategy, you will eventually end up with a web site that contains an abundance of pages each addressing very specific sub-topics beneath your more general topic. For example, I categorize the online directory at the Music Biz Academy (http://www.musicbizacademy.com) into sub-topics about CD manufacturers, musician communities, talent agencies, radio promoters, music law and so on. Each page has its own strategic keywords and phrases which I submitted individually to the search engines. The end result is that each of these individual pages attracts new visitors who are searching the Internet for very specific services. I get more traffic to my general topic web site by focusing on very specific, narrow topics for each page. This brings in more newsletter subscribers, more contacts, and more customers. More exposure means more business.

Dividing up one's web site into many sub-topical pages also allows you to test the effectiveness of new pages, marketing ideas and keyword strategies. You may find that one particular page (or sub-topic) of your site becomes very popular on its own merit. When this happens, consider taking that page concept and spinning it off into its own domain name and web site. What is the advantage of doing this? The search engines give listing priority to the "top pages" of any web site. So if one of your secondary pages does well on the search engines, imagine how well it would do if it had its own domain name. That's exactly how the *Music Biz Academy* came to be. Originally, the Academy concept was a sub-topic of a larger, more generic music site. When it became obvious the Music Biz Academy section of the site was a hit on its own merit, I spun that off into its own domain name and launched it as a new web site. Just search for "music biz" on Google and you'll see the kind of effect it has had. As of this writing, The Music Biz Academy is the #1 web site result returned.

If you have a hit web page and decide to spin it off to its own domain, that doesn't mean you stop cross-selling the services, products, CDs, or information you offer from your original site. In fact, you'll want to cross-sell your products and services even more. Use your most popular web site to promote your other, less popular ones. Doing this not only keeps traffic flowing back and forth between domains, but it increases your overall exposure and it may boost your link popularity rating with the search engines.

Creating spin-offs like this is how you grow and diversify your online music business. You test new ideas, find what works, and then put your energy behind building and expanding those web sites that generate income for you. Over time, as you find more success and branch off into other areas, you'll find yourself creating your own little Internet Empire!

Isn't it Nice to Share?

Your visitors, whom you've already targeted, can help you further increase traffic to your web site. One way to do this is to allow them to share your web pages with others, either via email or via the social networks they are involved in. Check out AddThis.com (http://www.addthis.com/). A few simple clicks, a cut and paste, and you have a sharing tool added to your web page that will allow others to share your content with others. It's pretty slick.

Targeted Link Partnerships

Go to Google.com and search for some of your most powerful keywords and phrases for your web site. Take note of two things: first, which web sites are in the top twenty or so for each keyword? Secondly, which "sponsor" sites pop up when searching on your keywords?

It will be to your advantage, both in terms of targeting your audience and for link popularity reasons, to try and create link partnerships with these top ranked and sponsor web sites. If you are able to make your site accessible via a link from sites already getting a high volume of traffic, you will benefit from their promotion also. You benefit both because these sites already enjoy high search engine positions for your particular key phrases and because they target the very same audience you are trying to reach. If your prospective customer is visiting one of these popular web sites, it would be nice if there was some way for that customer to click from that web site and go directly to yours!

So, how do you approach these web sites to ask for a link to your web site? Think of something you can offer the webmasters of these other, more popular web sites. What does your web site have that would benefit their visitors? Perhaps you can offer a service, information, or a product. Even just offering to exchange links for the sake of cross-promotion is perfectly acceptable.

Sometimes it can feel awkward coming right out and asking other web sites to link to you. There is an easy way around this. Consider managing a directory of web sites you feel you can recommend to your own, targeted visitors. These might be your personal favorites or those that position well in the search engines on your own strategic keywords. Each week, feature a new site and contact the webmaster to inform them that you are featuring them. After handing them the compliment, graciously ask if they will consider linking back to you.

For example, at *The Music Biz Academy,* I find and review web sites I feel are beneficial and valuable to the independent music community as a whole. These web sites are sorted by topic in my Musician's Internet Resource Directory (see http://www.musicbizacademy.com/directory). Whenever I find a music-related site I really like or would like exposure on, I review their web site, providing a link from my directory to their site. I also feature their site on the Academy home page and in our newsletter, *The Music Biz Academy Digest.* Once the review is up, I contact the webmaster of the site with an email similar to the following:

Subject: Your Web Site Featured at The Music Biz Academy!

Message: Dear Mr. Smith, (If at all possible, use the name of the web site owner. It will make your email more personal.)

I wanted to let you know we are featuring your web site this week at the Music Biz Academy! You can see your review at http://www.musicbizacademy.com . Your listing will be permanently included in our directory, as well as featured in the next issue of our *Music Biz Academy Digest,* which is emailed to thousands of opt-in readers. Please take a look!

If you feel our web site may be of interest to your visitors, please consider linking back to us. We would very much appreciate that! Once again, congratulations on a great site, and thank you for your consideration.

Best regards,

David Nevue
The Music Biz Academy
http://www.musicbizacademy.com
http://www.twitter.com/musicbizacademy

Not only do webmasters visit the Academy to check out the review I gave them, they are often impressed enough by what they see to link to my web site from theirs. Using reciprocal links, you can generate a lot of goodwill, and you will find, over time, that by doing this you will begin to develop strategic relationships with other musicians just like yourself. You will be able to help each other. I have met some of my best contacts this way! Goodwill generates good word-of-mouth, and word-of-mouth makes for great publicity!

Spy vs. Spy: See Who's Talking About You...

One of the best ways to target new fans is to track who is talking about you and/or linking to you, and then follow up with them personally. Here's how...

Who's Linking to You?: You can easily use Google to find out who is linking to your web site. To do this, just type the following in Google: "link:www.mywebsite.com". That will result in a list of web sites that are linking to you that Google has indexed. Yahoo has a similar tool. To make use of that, go to https://siteexplorer.search.yahoo.com/mysites . Once there, insert your web site URL, click the "Explore" button, then once the results come back, click the "Inlinks" button. That will show you sites linking to you that Yahoo has indexed. You can use this to either follow up with those web sites or to create possible partnerships with down the road.

Who's Talking About You? Google offers a fantastic tool for monitoring who is talking about you. It's called Google Alert. Visit http://www.google.com/alerts , enter the search term you want to monitor along with your email address, and Google Alert will send you an email each day with a listing of web sites making reference to your selected search terms. It's a great way to monitor when people mention you, your web site, or any other search term, keyword or keyword phrase you want to track. For example, I monitor my own name, "David Nevue." Whenever someone mentions my name and that page gets indexed by Google, I get notified. So when fans post blogs about my music, or they post a video of them playing my music on YouTube, I get an alert about it. I can then follow up with that fan directly if I want to – posting my own comment in response.

I get a real kick out of this tool. It's not uncommon for pianists to post videos of themselves playing my music on YouTube. When they do, I get a notice from Google Alert, I can watch the video and if the pianist (usually a young piano student) does a great job, I can write them a personal note to pat them on the back for their work and encourage them. It's a GREAT way to build relationships with your fans.

You can also use Google Alert to monitor bloggers who talk about you, link to you, or when folks talk about a particular keyword of importance to you that you're following. Once you receive the alert, you have an opportunity to jump into the conversation and post your own comments on the topic (along with your signature and web site link of course!)

Google Alert is a free service, although they have paid options as well for deeper, more thorough results if you want them. I love it and use it every day.

Another great tool is Zhift forum search at http://www.zhift.com . Just enter your name to see if anyone is discussing you. This is a great tool to use to find forums where your targeted keywords are discussed as well.

Maintaining the Sales Machine

The bigger you get, the more web sites you expand into, the more maintenance you'll have to do. Any web site you create should be updated on a regular basis to keep up with new and innovative technologies, as well as to keep your site appearance and site information current. Doing so gives your site life, and it encourages your visitors to return. The more they return, the more opportunity you have to promote your music or other products.

I recommend you check any links you have to other web sites on at least a monthly basis. This is fairly easy to do using online tools like LinkAlarm (http://www.linkalarm.com). I also recommend you check all your pages to ensure they are loading quickly and properly. If you find another site layout you like better than yours, use the inspiration to redesign your site. If you continually update and change your site(s), you will find that visitors will return again and again to see what's new.

"But," you say, "I don't have time to do all this. This is way too much for me." If that's how you feel, I can totally understand. The targeting by site concept in particular can be very overwhelming, especially if you find it difficult enough just to complete and market your own personal web site. If this is the case for you, then don't worry about trying to develop this strategy right now. Tuck this information into the back of your mind for later, when you have more web experience. This style of targeting is fairly advanced, and there are other ways to bring new customers to your web site, as I shall demonstrate shortly. All I'm trying to do right now, since we're on the topic of targeting customers, is pass the knowledge I have to you so you can decide what works best for you.

Get the Hits That Really Count!

Here's something to remember: if you receive 1,000 hits a day on your web page, it won't mean a thing if only one of those visitors is interested in your product. Use your time and energy to generate publicity that brings you a meaningful, targeted audience! Don't worry about getting *thousands* of random hits on your site. It's the targeted visitors who will buy your product that you really want!

Recommended Supplementary Reading:
How to Target an Online Niche: http://www.searchengineguide.com/kalena/2005/0606_kj1.html

The Power of Words -
What You Know Can Sell Your Music

Do You Have the "Write" Stuff?

As you saw in the previous chapter, creating an entire web site just to target your audience is a lot of work. It's well worth doing, but takes considerable time and effort to set up, get going, and then maintain. If you're not quite ready to take on such a large project, there is an alternative you can do *right now* that is simpler, faster, and doesn't require a lot of maintenance; something you can do almost immediately that will suffice until you have the time to get your targeted web site up and running: write.

Writing is an action you can take that doesn't require too much effort. No, I'm not talking about writing a book; I'm talking about writing a paragraph or two to express your thoughts, feelings and opinions. Did you know that you can promote your music online just by expressing your thoughts and opinions in written form every day? You can. And that action is what this chapter is dedicated to: how to write to your target audience and how to use your words to interest people in your music.

Targeting by Topic: A Blog Well Done

I've mentioned "blogging" in passing many times up to this point and even covered it in some detail in the chapter on *Planning a Web Site* (see *Blogging Your Web Site* section). Now let's dive into the topic more fully.

To review, a "blog" (short for "web log") is basically an ongoing commentary of life, career, events, and everything the blog writer cares about. The concept of "blogging" hit the Internet about three years ago and has reached a point now where blogs have become one of the biggest sources of content online. Surprisingly, people have made careers out of professional blogging. They have become "opinion leaders" just by writing about what they know and love, including politics, religion, music and marketing. Many people actually look to individual bloggers as a voice of authority on some subjects. Why? Any time something is written down, it gains a certain aura of authority and authenticity. Write intelligently on a subject frequently enough and people come to trust and believe you. Words are a very powerful thing.

So all a blog is, really, is a commentary on subjects that matter to the writer and the writer's audience. YOU can be that writer. YOU can be that blogger. And if you market your words intelligently, the blogs you write will be sucked up by the search engines, meaning the topics you write about will become searchable and found online as people search on your keywords and key phrases. Get into the practice of writing a blog, and people interested in what you're writing about are likely to find you sooner or later.

Let me give you an example from my own personal life. One of my very good friends was pianist Dax Johnson. Dax was a special performer who had an incredible charisma about him. People were drawn to him wherever he played. Dax's "thing" was playing piano at malls all over the country. Every weekend, thousands of people would see and hear him playing the piano and purchase his CDs. He'd just start playing and before you knew it, there was a huge gathering of people around him transfixed by his music and his performance. Between songs, Dax would chat with his "guests." He was very approachable, and had a way of talking to people that made them feel special and important. In doing so he touched hundreds of thousands of lives.

In 2005, Dax passed away. As his friend, and as someone who had shared the stage with him on a few occasions, it hit me pretty hard. One of things I did in response was to write a blog about him and his music. I felt the need to offer some kind of tribute, to express my feelings, my experiences, and to somehow immortalize him. While my purpose in doing this was personal and had nothing to do with marketing, the blog did have an unintended result in marketing my music.

Go to Google and perform a search for "Dax Johnson." The #3 listing that comes up (as of this writing) is my blog tribute to him. Many people who knew Dax have found my blog while searching for updated information on him. The unintended effect of all this is that quite a few of Dax's fans have gone on to become fans of my own music. So you can see how the blog has become a tool to "target" an audience with a predisposition to my own style of piano music.

Every time you write a blog, it's like writing a new article on your topic of choice and putting it out there for the world to discover. What topics could you write about that potential fans of your music would be interested in? You can write commentaries about popular artists who have inspired you, comment on news events, charitable organizations or politics and then – and this is key – *find a creative way to tie those commentaries into your music*. Every blog you write is one more opportunity for potential fans to find you. You can use the blog to direct people to your web site to sample your music or embed a flash player containing your music right in the blog.

Need some ideas on what to write about? Your brain is an excellent source for content. You'll find all kinds of good stuff in there (I presume). Here are some ideas to get your brain churning…

1) **Write Reviews:** Review movies, books, products, television programs, music, web sites, YouTube videos and even other blogs (yes, write a blog to review other blogs!) There are plenty of things to review out there. What is your target audience searching the Internet for *right now*? What is the hype? Write about it, review it, and when you do, use a captivating title that will rouse curiosity and grab the attention of someone who sees it.

2) **Write About Stuff You Know:** What do you know about that other people find confusing, hard to do or understand? Write about it. Write your own "how to" guides. Conduct an experiment and talk about the results, take a poll and talk about the results, do a case study, discuss technical matters and take something people perceive as "hard" and show how easy it really is.

3) **Write About Personal Experiences:** Who inspires you? Write about them. How did you get to where you are now? Write about it. Where did you play your last concert and what were some crazy things that happened backstage the night of the show? Write about it. Do you take lots of photos? Share them… and then write about them! How about that last concert tour? Write about it. What are some of the biggest mistakes you ever made? Write about them. What makes you laugh? Write about it.

4) **Interview People:** Find someone out there who has a big audience and interview them – perhaps a celebrity or semi-celebrity, perhaps an "expert" in your field, perhaps another blogger with an already

well-established readership. Make your interviewee look good and not only will you have a new blog entry to promote, but your interviewee will likely promote the interview to his/her own readers too, bringing your blog new readers.

5) **Create Lists:** People love lists. 101 Ways to Cope with Stress, 10 Ways to Live Longer, 330 Ways to Enjoy Toast, 18 Ways to Stay Focused at Work, 5 Ways the Music Industry Can Save Itself. All real blog titles. You get the idea.

6) **Take a Stand on Something:** What do you feel VERY strongly about that draws others to you who share your views? Write about these things.

7) **Sex, Religion, New Technologies and Politics:** The most popular blogs on the Internet dwell on these topics. Find a way to combine any or all of them with your music and you might have a winner.

Now, regarding the last two items especially, you do need to be careful. Posting your thoughts and opinions can have unintended negative consequences. If you get too preachy, negative, depressing, insulting or even political, it can turn people off and even turn them against you. So whatever you write, consider carefully the possible reactions people might have to what you express. Think about who your targeted audience is. Will your words inspire them? Or will your speaking your mind offend the very audience you want to draw? Being controversial can be good, and it may be that you *want* to be controversial because that very thing may make you unique and stand out. But doing so can also flip the other way. Tread carefully. Think twice before you publish that commentary. Once you put your blog out there, you can't take it back. Every word you write is archived somewhere forever.

As you see by the list above, there are plenty of things you can write about. If you can find a way to take these topics and relate them to your own music, you are creating dozens more avenues for people to discover who you are and what you do. If you are a prolific writer and properly promote your writings (I'll talk about this shortly), you'll soon find that your blog becomes a big source of mailing list signups (and eventually sales) for you.

Your #1 goal is to have your blog, video, or music go "viral." What does that mean? It means that what you've created is so interesting that people feel compelled to share it with other people. One person shares your post with six of their friends, who each share it with six more, who each share with six others and so on. Within a week, you're a semi-celebrity and thousands of people know who you are. That's the aim. It's not easy to do, but it *does* happen. It may be that the blog you write today will bring hundreds or thousands of people to you tomorrow. Expressing a few thoughts and opinions might get you a gig, an interview or a licensing deal. Every word counts.

So the next obvious question you may have is… "How do I go about creating a blog?"

Blogging Basics: How to Get Started

There are several ways to go about creating a blog, and I'm going to cover some of them here. However, and I want to warn you about this up front, some of what I'm about to discuss *sounds* complicated. There are new technical terms to learn, and as you know, anytime you start talking in techno-speak it adds confusion. I can see how you might read the next several pages and find your eyes beginning to gloss over. I will do my best to explain things in a simple way. Let me just say this: if you do your research and take the time to *read, explore and experiment*, you will find that blogging (and promoting your blog) is fairly easy to do. However, if you just read what follows, and do nothing to explore the option further, it will seem more difficult than it really is. If you're like me, you don't learn so much by reading, but by *doing*. Learning to blog and promote your blog, when you haven't done it before, is definitely one of those kinds of skills. You must read and then *follow up and do*.

First, you need the tools to create a blog. Two very popular (and free) tools for writing and posting blogs are Wordpress (http://www.Wordpress.com) and Blogger (http://www.blogger.com) . In either case, your blog is hosted online at Blogger.com or Wordpress.com so you don't have to worry about installing software or maintaining a web site. Both tools are fairly intuitive to use and come with pre-made blog templates. The templates make it easy because you can choose one to represent the look and style of your blog and just start writing. Of course, you can customize the look and feel of your blog to your heart's content, if you desire to, with few limitations. But with the default settings, you can just create an account, pick a template and start writing, which makes it a snap to do.

Now go do it. Visit Wordpress.com and/or Blogger.com, create an account, and play around with it. If you want my opinion (and I presume you do as you bought this book for my opinion, right?) I prefer Blogger.com. I just like it better. I like the templates better, I like the interface better, and to me, the directions you find in the tool itself read more like a human wrote them. Most serious bloggers I know seem to prefer Wordpress, however. Choose whichever you like best. Either will work.

When you create an account on Blogger or Wordpress, you'll receive a site-based URL (web address) by default. For example, your blog might be located at mymusicblog.blogspot.com (that's a Blogger URL) or mymusicblog.Wordpress.com (a Wordpress URL). A URL like that can make your blog location hard to remember for some folks. Wouldn't it be nicer to have your blog web site address read something simple like mymusicblog.com? That is something you can customize without too much trouble. Both Blogger and Wordpress give you an option to "map" a domain address you already own to your blog URL. So you can map your Blogger mymusicblog.blogspot.com domain to mymusicblog.com, for example, which makes it an easier address to remember for your regular readers. Of course, for this to work, you must own the domain address you want to map to. If you don't own it already, go to DirectNIC (http://www.directnic.com), find a domain address you like that's available, and then purchase it. Then, in your blog tool options you can map your URL to that domain name. (If you have a Blogger account, just look under your Settings/Publishing tab for mapping information).

Are your eyes glazing over yet? I know, it sounds complicated. So many techie words in there; domain, address, URL, mapping, ARGH! It's really not too bad. **Go do it and see!** It's the only way to learn.

If you do happen to be technically inclined, you can install the blog software on your own domain server rather than doing a mapping redirect. Take a look at http://www.Wordpress.org (note that's dot.**org**, not dot.com). At Wordpress.org, you'll find instructions on how you can download and install Wordpress to your own server. In fact, many web hosts offer one-click Wordpress installs now, making it a lot easier. For more information on this, visit http://Wordpress.org/download/ . Wordpress offers a list of suggested web hosts. I use http://www.powweb.com, and a hosting account there includes the one-click Wordpress install option.

Why Blog? How One Artist Made $3,000/Month in Music Sales by Blogging

So why do the "blog" thing at all? Do you need more encouragement to see the value in it?

Here's a snippet from an article called *Sex, Drugs and Updating Your Blog* posted in *The New York Times*. This might get you excited about the possibilities of marketing your music online using a blog…

> *Jonathan Coulton sat in Gorilla Coffee in Brooklyn, his Apple PowerBook open before him, and began slogging through the day's email. Coulton is 36 and shaggily handsome. In September 2005, he quit his job as a computer programmer and, with his wife's guarded blessing, became a full-time singer and songwriter. He set a quixotic goal for himself: for the next year, he would write and record a song each week, posting each one to his blog. By the middle of last year, his project had attracted a sizable audience. More than 3,000 people, on average, were visiting his site every day, and his most popular songs were being downloaded as many as 500,000 times; he was making what he described as "a reasonable middle-class living" — between $3,000 and $5,000 a month — by selling CDs and digital downloads of his work on iTunes and on his own site.*

You can read the rest of the article at http://tinyurl.com/2gytwc

That's pretty inspiring, isn't it? Look at the kind of income Jonathan was able to generate simply by doing one thing, doing it well and doing it often. It shows how tenacity and dedication can really pay off. The key to marketing anything online is *consistency*. You can't just write a blog for two weeks, get bored of it (or too busy to do it) and then stop. To develop a regular readership, you have to deliver something on a regular basis, something that your targeted audience will keep coming back for. The longer you do it, the better your content, the more people will return, link to you, and spread the word about what you are doing online.

At this point, I want to include an article by Lance Trebesch of TicketPrinting.com (http://www.TicketPrinting.com). The article fits so well here, it's almost as if Lance wrote it exclusively for my book! He didn't, but I am using his article with permission. I have also included some of my own comments (which are noted) interspersed within his article. With that introduction, here are…

20 Steps to Creating a Successful Blog for Your Band
By Lance Trebesch, lance@ticketprinting.com, http://www.TicketPrinting.com

Blogs prove to be a tricky field to conquer, especially when it comes to gaining an initial reader base. However, once you get that reader base, great potential for increasing your online reputation is created. Successful blogs keep their status by following these 20 rules from the start and throughout their blog's lifetime.

1) **Focus the topic**. Thousands of different blogs exist on the web. Only the well-established ones can post general news and see success. Instead, focus your blog around a niche. The more narrow the subject, the more likely you will get a steady reader base.

   David's comments: To use your blog to promote your music most effectively, cover topics that will draw interest from your *targeted audience*. As each blog populates the search engines, it creates one more doorway to your music, not only from the search engines, but from others who are linking to your writings. When you're writing your blog, always think about your potential keywords. While you do want to "stay within your niche" to some degree, if you hit the same keywords over and over again, you're not really expanding your reach. The key here is balance. Write to a niche, yes, but allow for the occasional topical diversion to keep it interesting and to attract new readers who might find you and then get turned on to your music.

2) **Search similar blogs and subscribe**. Because there are so many blogs on the Internet, chances are somebody somewhere will also be talking about your subject (for example, see "Electric AND Guitar at http://www.technorati.com/search/electric+AND+guitar). Find these sites and subscribe to them so you get instant updates. The best action to take is to read up on these blogs and know what they talk about regularly.

   David's comments: Lance here makes reference to Technorati (http://www.technorati.com), arguably the largest blog tracker on the Internet. Know it, love it, and use it to search for other bloggers talking about the same things you are. It's a great place to find other blogs to review, people to Interview, and even subject matter ideas. He also makes reference to "subscribing" to a blog, by which he is referring to RSS feeds which I discuss in detail below.

3) **Create business relationships**. By helping out someone else and their blog in some way, they will, in return, help you and your blog. One good example is devising a list of online radio stations you can submit your music to and give them (*i.e.: the other blog writers*) the list so they can use it for their benefit as well. By becoming business friends, you can promote each other by talking about one another's webpage, music, blog, etc.

   David's comments: In other words, create relationships with other blog writers in your focused topic and cross-promote each others' blogs. Your blog entry one particular day might simply be a short introduction to another writer's blog and vice versa. You make reference to their blogs, they make reference to yours. This sort of cross-promotion is very common in the blog world.

4) **Make quality content**. Just writing a blog is not enough. You have to make sure what you are writing is good content. No one will comment or read your blog if the content seems worthless and poorly written. Also, write grammatically. Misspellings are one of the most painful things to witness in blogs.

5) **Work on the title**. The title is a necessity. The first thing people look at and what makes them read your blog is the title. Titles that hint of content with lists and bullets also draw people in due to the pleasing layout and more white space of lists. If the title perks their interest, they will click on your blog to continue reading. Take the time to think about an interesting title and log which titles draw more readers.

   David's comments: Not only is the blog title important in terms of whether someone decides to click on the link, it's also a key factor in terms of search engine optimization and placement. Search engines treat blog page titles just like web page titles. Keep this in mind.

6) **Submit to directories**. After creating a good content-and-keyword-rich blog, submit it to different directories. Top Blog Area (http://www.topblogarea.com/) and BlogFlux (http://dir.blogflux.com) are two good sites to submit blogs to according to the category of blog. Another option is to write just one blog for an established blogging site (for example, http://www.rockandrollreport.com) in the rock music industry and tell them why they should feature your blog on their site. If they choose to put the blog on their site, you will see greatly increased traffic.

David's comments: See also…
20 Essential Blog Directories to Submit Your Blog To
http://www.searchenginejournal.com/20-essential-blog-directories-to-submit-your-blog-to/5998/
Since you may be just getting started, I would wait to submit your blog until you have a good month or two of regular blog entries. That way, the directory will be able to get a feel for the particular niche your blog covers and your blog won't appear "unattended."

7) **Get a friend to submit your blog to Digg, StumbleUpon, Technorati, Netscape, and Reddit**. These search sites generate a ton of traffic to your site if viewed frequently (or "digged," "thumbs up" "favored," etc). However, people view down on you if you constantly submit your own content to these sites, so instead, make a buddy submit your blogs, videos, or podcasts to these sites one or two times a week. Eventually, your good content will make it to the homepage of these content-search sites, generating an unimaginable amount of traffic to your blog.

David's comments: You can add a little "chicklet" to the bottom of your blogs (see http://www.addthis.com) that makes it easy for readers to share your blog with others and/or bookmark it on the sites Lance mentioned. Asking your regular readers to share their favorite posts is a great way to go.

8) **Ping every site**. Some submission sites allow you to 'ping' them, which means they get an automatic update when you post a new blog (see http://bit.ly/9b9dN5 for an example). This is good so they always have your latest posts in their records. These sites also allow you to put in key tag terms. By inputting a tag term, your blog will pop up if someone searches for the term you used. For instance, if you are writing about *electric guitar comparisons* (tag terms) and the searcher inserts "compare guitars," your blog will show as a result. You must utilize pings and tags to increase your blog popularity.

David's comments: To clarify, a "ping" is another term for "automatically submitting my blog to the blog search engines" so don't let the new term confuse you. Some blog tools, like Wordpress and Blogger, can be set to do this automatically.

9) **Write regularly and stand out**. The only way to gain a steady reader base is if you write a blog regularly. The best blogs update their content daily or sometimes several times a day. As an upcoming artist, though, weekly will suffice if you write on a consistent day around the same time every week. In addition, you need to stand out from other bloggers. Write properly, but *use your personality*. Personality keeps the blog interesting and keeps readers coming back. In addition, readers like to be treated as humans, so drop the business lingo. Blogs are for entertainment, so engage your audience. Write for them.

10) **Host your blog on your website domain**. Using a different host (such as Blogger) for your blog not only confuses your readers, but also reduces the amount of quality traffic to your site. The only smart way to host a blog is through your own website. If readers like what they read, or you mention something about your music in the blog, they can easily navigate to your website to find out more information. Creating a blog serves the purpose of promoting your music online, which you can only do if your reader can easily access your website from your blog.

David's comments: I agree with this in concept, though you don't need to install Wordpress at your domain if you don't want to or if you feel like it's too technical for you. Just do the domain mapping redirects I described above. Both Blogger and Wordpress allow this. Plus, you can always link back to your official web site from your blog, regardless of whether it's being hosted at Blogger.com, Wordpress.com, or somewhere else.

11) **Ask people to subscribe**. RSS feeds (http://feed.informer.com/) allow users to subscribe to your blog and receive an update when you add new blogs. This makes it convenient for readers so they do not need to check for blog updates. An alternative is to send the updated blog through email, so having both an email subscription and a RSS feed is necessary. Also, make the sign-up process simple and prominent. Display the RSS button everywhere and occasionally mention it in your posts to sign-up. The simpler the process to sign-up, the more chance the reader will go through with the process.

   David's comments: "RSS feed" is another new, technical-sounding term I haven't introduced in this book up to this point. RSS Feeds are simply a way that web sites can easily distribute their content to people who subscribe to them. It's kind of like an automated content delivery system for subscribers. They don't have to wait for you to send an email notice, they get your latest blog entries automatically in their feed reader whenever you post something new if they are subscribed. It's something akin to a customized newspaper. Wordpress and Blogger both create RSS feeds automatically. For more information on this topic, if it interests you, see Feed 101 at http://www.google.com/support/feedburner/bin/answer.py?answer=79408 . I will also be addressing this in more detail in just a moment.

12) **Offer a bribe to sign-up**. Take an example from Marketing Pilgrim (http://www.marketingpilgrim.com/), by offering a $600 cash giveaway by signing-up for a RSS feed (see http://tinyurl.com/287w64). The code to register for the money is in an RSS-only message. Receiving $600 free is pretty convincing to sign-up. Other options to get people to sign up are free e-books related to your topic ("How to Get a Record Deal"), or send a personalized autographed picture of you or the band to those who sign-up.

   David's comments: Personally, I don't care to give up $600, but I do like the latter ideas. Lance's point is to come up with creative ideas that will strongly motivate readers to subscribe to your feeds and/or sign up for your newsletter.

13) **Comment on forums**. Comment on blogs. Comment on chats. And comment by providing a link back your blog. By injecting your opinion and showing your personality through these comments, people will notice you and want to find out more. Make sure the comments are meaningful and not just some form of spam to create a link back to you. People appreciate when an expert adds their knowledge, so write truthful comments that will help the audience. Comments are the biggest promotion of your blog in the beginning months of the blog.

   David's comments: We more or less covered this last chapter. Just add your blog link to your signature when you post on other sites' forums, chat rooms and blogs.

14) **Leave blogs open for discussion**. If compiling a list, ask for comments to add their suggestions for the list. The 5 Rules of Social Media Optimization (SMO) blog by Influential Marketing Blog (see http://rohitbhargava.typepad.com/weblog/2006/08/5_rules_of_soci.html) became instantly popular by people linking to it, posting comments and recommending the blog. After writing a general blog that

does not include a list, ask a question at the end to encourage comments and blog discussion. The more interesting the discussion, the more people will link to your blog, promoting it.

David's comments: A great way to make your blogs more interactive, as is….

15) **Respond to comments**. Read your comments daily and respond when someone asks a question to you through the comments. Once you start getting a steady reader base that begins posting comments, do not discourage them by never responding back. Respond rapidly to make your reader happy.

David's comments: It's always good to develop those relationships. If folks go to the trouble of commenting, it's good practice to respond in kind.

16) **Start a podcast**. A podcast (http://www.how-to-podcast-tutorial.com/) is a great way to promote both your blog and your music. Podcasts are an audio blog, but you should not update it as often as your blogs (unless you just want to run an audio blog exclusively). On the podcast, talk about interesting subjects related to your blog and mention your music often. Play a fraction of your music just prior to and just after your podcast, promoting both your music and your blog.

David's comments: I'll be covering Podcasting later.

17) **Invite guest bloggers**. **Be a guest blogger**. Your blog gains interest if you occasionally – monthly, quarterly – invite guest bloggers to write. Your business pals become a good place to start when thinking about whom to invite to be a guest blogger. The guests then feel flattered by your interest in them and in return promote your blog or music. On the other hand, ask your business friends to guest blog for them, which immensely promotes your music or blog through their site. Whenever you get an opportunity to guest blog, take it.

18) **Add videos, pictures, MP3s, etc**. Just having words on every blog gets boring. Perk readers' interest by putting a funny YouTube video in your blog, adding a unique MP3 or taking a snapshot of the website you mention in the blog. Any item out of the norm to create a change will boost your blog's appeal. Every once in awhile, make your blog a video-blog through YouTube where you narrate the blog (and act as well). You can also create a music video (http://www.youtube.com/watch?v=dTAAsCNK7RA) for you or the band and advertise it through your blog.

David's comments: Definitely check out the YouTube video link provided. The video is quite famous now as it went viral and resulted in a huge career boost for the band. Also, photos do work. Some of my most popular blogs with fans have been the travelogues I've written featuring photos of my kids. In general, the use of images (tastefully) is a good thing. It gives your blog some personality and makes it more enjoyable.

19) **Use tracking software and analyze**. Find out how many people are visiting your blogs and which ones generate the most traffic. You should re-create titles and content that receives many views. The tracking software can also tell you how people are hearing about your blog through Digg, Google, etc. It can give you a great insight on your viewers and many other marketing hints if you are creative.

David's comments: If you're using Blogger or Wordpress for your blog and posting your content to their web site, you'll need to use a third party service to insert a stats counter on each blog page. Just

Google "tracking blog stats" and you'll find many options. If you're hosting the blog on your own domain, your web host should be able to provide you with page stats.

20) **Build a brand**. You want people to recognize your blog as an object, not just another blog. Make your blog worthwhile to the reader. Promote the blog with any sources you have. Tell your friends, family and strangers about it. On your website, promote your blog and on your blog promote your website. Do the same with social networking sites, YouTube videos, podcasts, live performances, etc. By marketing in a bunch of different places, you spread your name and have more sources to promote your blog and music.

David's comments: In other words, promote your blog via social networking, which I have discussed and will be discussing more.

Your blog will only see success if you follow all these steps and promote it as often as possible. Blogging takes a lot of dedication but pays off in the end with increased music sales. Never stop blogging and remember, you are writing for your audience.

By Lance Trebesch
lance@ticketprinting.com
http://www.TicketPrinting.com

So there you have it. Two articles in one. Lance's article, and my comments on his article.

In this day and age of Internet marketing, blogging has, in many ways, become the new "search engine strategy." It's a great way to get your content out there to your target audience, and then use that content to promote your music and your own web site.

Blogging on MySpace? One of things you can do very easily on MySpace is blog. If you have a MySpace account, log in, click the Profile/My Blog menu. Then on the left click on "Post New Blog." Now start writing and when you're done, "Preview and Post." That's all there is do it. Ta-da! You're done. MySpace is possibly the easiest way to blog. But there's a serious downside. If anything should ever happen to your MySpace account, you lose your blog. Everything you've written is gone in a flash. *Puff*, it's gone, or at the very least, inaccessible to you. I can't tell you how many people have had this happen to them. One day they have a MySpace account, the next they don't. MySpace has banned their page for some reason. It happens. So while blogging via MySpace is a great way to start out, if you want to get serious about blogging and make sure your blogs aren't vaporized someday, you'll want to make use of Blogger or Wordpress. Sure, you can post your blog on MySpace, but I would suggest you make Blogger or Wordpress your blog home.

Here are a few more articles to check out on blogging if you want to research this further:

Blogging 101
Blog? Yep, and Here's How: http://bit.ly/92LtUh
Blogging for Beginners: http://www.problogger.net/archives/2006/02/14/blogging-for-beginners-2/
Blogs 101:   http://www.searchengineguide.com/ross-dunn/stepforth-tutor.php
Learn How to Blog: http://www.blogbasics.com/beginner-tutorials.php

Optimization and Inspiration
25 Blog Optimization Tips Even Dad Can Do: http://tinyurl.com/5e4qe5
7 Ways to Keep Content Flowing on Your Blog: http://ow.ly/uI6

Want more? Just search Google for "how to blog" or "blog tutorial."

How and Where to Promote Your Blog

Once you starting writing blogs, you'll want to *immediately* start promoting them. The whole point of a blog is to increase your readership and to do that you need to get your words out there. One of the keys to doing this is to first make sure your blog generates an RSS (Rich Site Summary) feed. Most blog software (like Wordpress and Blogger) will generate RSS feeds by default.

So what's an RSS feed? Well, think of it this way. You, as an avid reader and traveler of a thousand web sites, could go and visit those thousand web sites every day to see what's new. But what if those web sites could come to you? What if they could send an update to a single web page you've set up where you could view all these web site updates at once? That's exactly what an RSS feed reader does. It brings blog and web site updates right to you.

So you can see why you would want to offer RSS feeds to your visitors. If they like your blog enough, they'll subscribe, and that means you can reach those same people every time you update your blog and/or web site. They don't have to come to you, you automatically post to them.

If you're in need of an RSS feed reader, Google offers a free one that is very simple to use. You'll find the Google Feed Reader at http://reader.google.com .

For an easy to understand explanation of RSS Feeds, watch this video:
RSS in Plain English: http://www.commoncraft.com/rss_plain_english

The only thing your visitors need to subscribe to your RSS feed is your feed URL. If they don't have it (or can't find it), people can use their feed reader to search your web site to find your feed URL. If one is present, the feed reader will, in most cases, find it.

It's easy to create an RSS feed if you don't already have one. A popular RSS feed generator is FeedBurner (http://www.feedburner.com) which was recently acquired by Google. If you spend any time at all reading the FeedBurner web site, you'll figure out how to use it pretty quickly. In fact, if you use Wordpress, Blogger, or even MySpace to write your blog, FeedBurner offers easy to understand quick-start guides for each one of those (See http://www.google.com/support/feedburner/bin/topic.py?topic=13055). A quick read through that will walk you through the process of creating a feed for your blog that your visitors can subscribe to in no time flat. Best of all, the FeedBurner service is free.

Once you get the hang of publishing your feeds, FeedBurner offers all sorts of other promotion options for you, including "PingShot" which automatically sends your feed to feed aggregators, search engines and (if applicable) podcast directories.

Beyond setting up an RSS feed for your blog, here are other things to do to promote your blog. Lance covered some of these in his article. I've added several more options of my own:

1) **Include your blog address in your signature** so that when you post in forums, chat rooms, or comment on other blog posts, your blog address is listed there.

2) **Search for other blog posts** at Technorati (http://www.technorati.com) or via Google Blogs Search (http://blogsearch.google.com) that cover the topics you and your target audience are interested in. When you find a great blog, post a comment on it, build a relationship with the blogger, or even write your own blog about the other blog.

3) **Submit your blog** to the appropriate blog directories listed at http://www.searchenginejournal.com/20-essential-blog-directories-to-submit-your-blog-to/5998/

4) **Submit your blog as an "article"** to these article distribution sites (be sure to include a byline with a link to your music/blog/web site!):

Articles Factory:	http://www.articlesfactory.com/
Go Articles:	http://www.goarticles.com/
FreeSticky:	http://www.freesticky.com/stickyweb/
EzineArticles.com:	http://www.ezinearticles.com/
IdeaMarkers.com:	http://www.ideamarketers.com/

   Top 25 Article/Content Submission sites:
   http://www.wilsonweb.com/linking/wilson-article-marketing-1.htm

5) **Submit your RSS Feed** URL to the RSS Network (http://www.rss-network.com/submitrss.php)

6) **Develop a regular posting pattern**, so that your readers know when to expect a new post. If you post every Friday, for example, people will know to check back on Friday for an update.

7) **Link to other blogs often** when you comment on them, and post a comment on the actual blog posts you make reference to.

8) **Invite feedback from readers.** Ask their opinions, thoughts, and commentary. Not only does it develop relationships, a reader's comment might give you more to blog about. You might also ask readers for feedback on what they want you to write about.

9) **Be the first to blog about breaking news** of interest to your target audience.

10) **Make it easy for your readers to share** your blog with others by using a bookmarking tool like http://www.addthis.com or http://www.addtobookmarks.com/

11) **Ask readers to submit your blogs to Digg** (http://digg.com) and **StumbleUpon** (http://www.stumbleupon.com), two of the most popular bookmarking and content sharing services on the Internet. More on these shortly.

Want more information on blogging? Check out some of these…

Everything About RSS:	http://www.rss-specifications.com
How to Promote Your Blog:	http://www.search-this.com/2007/04/23/how-to-promote-your-blog/
25 Paths to an Insanely Popular Blog:	http://tinyurl.com/26buvf
Is Your Mom Your Only Reader?	http://bit.ly/1xW3sb
Free Essential Tools for Bloggers:	http://tinyurl.com/2wwj34

Can't commit time to blogging regularly? Then try *microblogging* via Twitter (http://www.twitter.com). You never have to type more than 140 characters to get your point across. More details on Twitter in the next chapter.

Social Media: Marketing Your Life

Taking Aim at Social Media Circles

Blogging is hugely popular on the Internet, but what is more interesting, I think, is what came about as the direct result of the blog society: social media. Social media has become a massive part of our culture, especially here in the United States. Social media has *changed* our culture. It is to our culture today what television was to our culture fifty years ago.

Prior to the blogging craze (I'd say pre-2006), the Internet was comprised mostly of content that communicated one-way via web sites. You searched for what you wanted via Google or Yahoo and found a web page that gave you the information you were looking for. There was no real "relationship" formed with the web site itself, or even the web site owner. The information was one-way, for the most part.

When the blog-craze happened (it peaked in 2007), people starting posting more than just information. They were posting *conversation*; opinions, thoughts and observations which people could respond to and comment on themselves. Millions of people jumped in and starting taking part in what became a continuous dialogue. Over the course of just a few months, the Internet was transformed. Rather than being static and one-dimensional, it was *personal*. People took ownership over their little corner of the Internet and became emotionally attached. What happened online was now a part of *real life*.

This great change is part of what some have called "Web 2.0." It all started with blogging, MySpace and YouTube, and now includes Facebook, Twitter, Flickr and bookmark sharing sites like Digg and StumbleUpon.

The reason I get into all this is that marketing your music in a "Web 2.0" society has become a necessity. Your fans *expect* you to be a part of their world now. It's not enough to just have a web site where people can try out your music. Your fans want to *know* you and they want to *follow* you. They want to *comment* on you and what you're doing. They want you to be part of their daily routine. They want *you* to be a part of *them*. Yes, it's a bit creepy. I'm going to give you some tips on coping with that here shortly.

But first, I want to give you a brief list of the most important social media hotspots to familiarize yourself with. There are *thousands* of networking web sites you could frequent, but as with search engines, there are really only a few that seriously matter at the moment. Here are the ones I think you should be most aware of:

Facebook (http://www.facebook.com) **:** I've talked about Facebook at great length already. I won't add anything here other than to say… if you're not on Facebook yet, get on there now. It's the largest and most active social network of the current age. In fact, as of March, 2010, it regularly gets more page views than even Google does.

Twitter (http://www.twitter.com) **:** What's Twitter? It's a microblog. You have just 140 characters to write something meaningful. People use Twitter to tell the rest of the world what they are doing, feeling and experiencing *right now* in short bursts of text. It sounds silly, and it is, but your true fans will follow you because they care about you and want to know what you're up to. It's a great way to communicate with dedicated fans (who are also on Twitter) on an almost instantaneous basis. Set up an account if you haven't already. It's going to be a very useful tool for you.

YouTube (http://www.youtube.com) **:** Any video that matters on the web is on YouTube. You can post your own videos or video commentaries and share them with the world. Think blogging for video. You can be your own talking head and spout off audibly, or create music videos and/or slide shows that incorporate your music and share them with fans. Fans can subscribe to your video ramblings. You can invite fans to add videos to comment on your videos, or invite fans to record and share videos of them playing your music. I'll add more on the topic of YouTube shortly.

Flickr (http://www.flickr.com/) **:** While YouTube is a social network based on video-sharing, Flickr is dedicated to photo-sharing. Like MySpace or FaceBook, you create a profile, add friends, join groups, jump in on discussions and, of course, upload your photos. Naturally, uploading photos of your band, "behind the scenes" shots, fans, studio time, album art and concert performances is a must. But you can also upload photos of other things you are interested in that might also be of interest your fans. Think about what photos you can upload that might draw people to you and your music. How can you tie your photos to your music, making them one seamless presentation? Use your photos to tell a story, celebrate your fans, promote a benefit or charity, or involve people in an event or social experiment they might take part in.

Another nice thing about posting photos to Flickr is that you can use your Flickr account in conjunction with other sites to promote your music. For example, check out Moo.com (http://www.moo.com/flickr/) . You can merge Moo.com with your Flickr photos to create business cards, greeting cards, postcards, gift certificates and more. Also check out http://www.delivr.net/ for using Flickr to deliver eCards to your fans that feature your Flickr photos.

Digg (http://digg.com) and **StumbleUpon** (http://www.stumbleupon.com) are social bookmarking web sites. In other words, when you find a web site, page, or article you like, you "bookmark" it in one or both of these tools. By doing so you share your favorite places on the web with anyone else who might care. These are *great* promotion tools for your blogs! If one of your blogs catches fire with Digg or StumbleUpon readers, you might find these sites bring you a lot of web traffic. However, and **this is important**, users of these sites heavily frown upon people posting their own content! They consider it SPAM. So you want your blog readers to recommend your content to Digg and StumbleUpon for you. Don't post your own pages!

There are many social bookmarking sites out there. Digg is by far the most popular, so if you have to choose one to focus on, Digg it. Here's some suggested reading for you:

> *The Beginner's Guide to Digg:*
> http://www.pronetadvertising.com/articles/beginners-guide-to-digg.html
> Check out the additional resources section for more info.
>
> *The Beginner's Guide to Getting Massive Traffic from StumbleUpon*:
> http://www.subhub.com/articles/get-massive-traffic-from-stumbleupon
>
> *The Top 15 Most Popular Bookmarking Websites:*
> http://www.ebizmba.com/articles/social-bookmarking

The best way to get familiar with "social bookmarking" is to just sign up and start using them. When you write blogs, articles or other content, be sure you include bookmarking links for Digg and StumbleUpon in your blog pages so that readers can easily share them with readers of those services. You can do this using http://www.addthis.com or http://www.addtobookmarks.com, or you can add the Digg and StumbleUpon buttons directly on to your pages. See http://about.digg.com/downloads and http://www.stumbleupon.com/buttons/ for information on those.

Putting Spin on the Social Circle of Life

As you get familiar with all these social networking tools, you'll find it becomes second nature to start tying them together. That's when it gets rather fun. You can write a blog, for example, then let your fans know about your new blog post via Twitter, Facebook and MySpace on one hand, while on the other hand you submit your new blog post to the search engines and invite readers to bookmark it on their Digg and StumbleUpon accounts. You can notify fans of new Flickr and YouTube posts, and use those same photos and videos to promote your music and web site, all the while integrating Flickr photos and YouTube videos into your blog and web site to help make them come alive and feel more interactive. Then, when readers comment on your posts, you can respond to them, develop those relationships, and invite them to sign up for your newsletter, follow you on Twitter/Facebook/MySpace and so on. It all ties together. Every aspect of social marketing ties into every other aspect. It's the social networking circle of life.

Here's some great reading material for putting it all together:

Tools for Engaging in Social Media:	http://tinyurl.com/d6kp6e
A Blogger's Guide to Branding with Social Media:	http://tinyurl.com/59zhp8
The Role of Social Media in a New Blog Launch:	http://traffikd.com/blogging/smm-blog-launc/
How to Influence Powerful Social Media Users:	http://tinyurl.com/yp6ztz
How to Target the Right Social Media Sites:	http://tinyurl.com/6c585s
35 Must-Read Articles for Social Media Marketers:	http://tinyurl.com/6arhjn
The Ultimate Social Media Etiquette Handbook:	http://tinyurl.com/5tuf4s

And some lists:

Categorized List of Social Media Sites:	http://traffikd.com/social-media-websites/
List of Social Media Networking Sites:	http://en.wikipedia.org/wiki/List_of_social_networking_websites
A Collection of Social Networking Stats:	http://bit.ly/4r8Mqr

Social Media: A Lesson in Self Defense

As I mentioned just a few paragraphs ago, with the advent of Web 2.0 and Social Media, your fans now *expect* you to be a part of their world. Your fans want to *know* you, they want to *follow* you and they want to *interact* with you via Twitter, Facebook, MySpace and other social networks. On one hand, this is a good thing. When it comes to Internet marketing, developing relationships with your fans is a key element. It always has been. But now, as you get involved with Facebook or Twitter and start posting your "status" several times a day for the world to see, things begin to get personal, perhaps a little bit *too* personal. How do you cope with this?

Having been active in the social media world for a while now, I've discovered the importance of setting boundaries for what I do and do not post for the world at large to read. I have learned that if you cross these boundaries, there can be social consequences. Have you ever really thought about how the words you post come across to your fan base? What you post can drastically change your reader's opinion of you in both good and bad ways. While a fan might be thrilled to find you on Twitter or Facebook at first, after following your posts for a while they may actually become bored with you, disappointed in you, turned off by you or even angry at you.

Social interaction with your fans is a good thing... to a point. But it would be wise to give yourself a few rules to go by; rules to help protect you not only from yourself (you may be your own worst enemy), but also those who follow you who may or may not have your best interests in mind.

Consider this a lesson in social media self defense. Here we go:

1) **Measure Your Words Carefully. Then Measure Again:** Think twice about every word you're about to post before you actually post. When you first get involved in social networking, the most natural thing do to is to just "be yourself" and post your true feelings, thoughts and opinions about everything under the sun. This can be a two-edged sword when it comes to how your fans perceive you. Your fans like your music because they relate to it somehow and as a result on some level they think they know and understand you. But the truth is, they don't know you at all. That means that with every word, thought or opinion you post there is the potential to taint someone's image of who you are. Always measure how your words match up with your public image. If you write beautiful love songs, but your posts are filled with cynical ramblings, crass language and sexual innuendo, how does that affect your fans' image of you? Destroy your fans' image of you, and you will cost yourself future sales. So, before you post your opinions on this or that, always make sure what you post is truly how you want to represent yourself to your fans. This means you should…

2) **Be Wary of Discussing Politics, Religion and Controversial Subjects.** That is, unless those very things *define who you are* as an artist. If your music is political by nature, you can be political in your commentary. If your music is not political, and you spout off in a negative, cynical way about politics or the leadership of your country, you'll likely put off some of your fans who may respond as if you are attacking them personally. The same is true about religion. If your faith in God defines you and your music, then by all means be that person of faith. Don't hold back. But if your music isn't defined by your faith, just know that if you start praising the Lord in your posts you might put off some of your fans. Politics and religion are potentially divisive topics, as are abortion, gay-rights, immigration and even extreme environmentalism. Just *saying* those words, in any context, can rile some people up. Being controversial can be good for publicity, but when you're trying to develop relationships with your fans, going on and on about your political, social, or religious views can be the very thing that turns them against you. Be very careful not to use your status update as your own personal soapbox to preach from, *unless* you feel so strongly about those things that you don't care if you lose fans and sales over it. It may be that you don't care if you lose fans over expressing your opinions. If you don't, then go for it. Be who you want to be. Your strong opinions will likely appeal to a few like-minded thinkers. Just be aware of what you post, how it might come across, and whether you're OK with how it affects others' perceptions of you. The question I always ask myself before posting something potentially controversial is; "does what I'm about to write define me as an artist and a person? or am I just venting?" My politics, for example, have nothing to do with my music. So I keep my thoughts on politics to myself, generally speaking. I am not defined by my politics. *I am defined* by my faith in God, however, so I personally have no problem praising the Lord in my status updates. I just do it tastefully.

Not every post I write says "Hallelujah," but I'm also not afraid to thank God publicly for my wonderful family or a beautiful day. It's all about balance, and being watchful of your public persona.

SUGGESTION: When it comes to politics, especially, I understand how hard it can be to restrain yourself from venting political frustrations in your status update. If you find you simply can't resist doing that, let me suggest you create a separate outlet specifically for your political rants. Perhaps a Twitter account specifically set up to let you express your political views, one that doesn't have your name on it. Then you can have the satisfaction of expressing your opinions to the world at large without destroying your relationships with fans of your music that have an opposing viewpoint.

3) **Stay Positive. Don't Worry. Be Happy.** Listen, no one likes a complainer. Don't use your status update to tell the world how lousy you feel, how stressed out you are, how hard life is, how unfair you've been treated, how misunderstood you are, or how much you hate your job. People tire of whiners quickly. Do you enjoy listening to people complain? Neither does anyone else. Complaining is the fastest way to lose friends and followers (in real life too). Whatever you do, when you post a status update, be positive and encouraging to others. Present your life as good, blessed and happy, even if it isn't at every single moment. If you are a joyful person, people will be drawn to you. When you post, do so with a smile, and you'll make your reader smile. Smiling is good.

4) **Be Interesting. Be Inspiring.** If you're going to update your status to tell the world what you're up to, find ways to make your posts exciting to read, even if it's just the way you phrase something. Don't post an update that says… "checking email" or "watching tv" or "just chillin'" Blah. Who cares? Be creative. Be imaginative. Be specific. Make every post count and mean something. If the post you're about to write isn't something you'd care about if someone else wrote it, then why bother writing it yourself? Make sure that, from your readers' perspective, you lead a very interesting life. If you don't feel like your life is very interesting, then do something about it. Don't just sit there staring at the TV. Make your life interesting. It's in your power to do so. Then talk about it in happy, positive ways. Make your life sound like the "dream life." Your fans don't expect you to be dull. Life is too short to be dull. Don't be dull!

5) **Watch Your Back.** Guess what? Not everyone who follows you is a "fan." Did you know that people might follow you who don't care about you or your music? <GASP> It's true! It's easy to forget this sometimes. You just happily post away assuming everyone loves you and thinks you're terrific. But you never know who's following you, and not everyone who follows you is friendly toward you. People who are curious about how you do business might follow you. Your ex-girlfriend with a grudge, a stalker boyfriend, or an overzealous fan might follow you. People looking for ways to tear you down might follow you. People who want to test your integrity might follow you. People who are looking for good ideas might follow you. People who want to copy what you're doing might follow you. Always be aware that people might be following you who don't have your best interests in mind. So don't be giving away all those family/trade/business secrets and don't be too revealing about yourself. Don't give your enemies ammunition to use against you.

6) **Keep Your Private Moments Private.** Doing something cool and fun with your family? Use social media to tell people about it, *after* the fact, not before. Don't post a status update saying… "Taking my kids bowling at Lois Lanes in a few minutes. Should be fun!" That will just invite curious fans to come down and join you. Might be OK. Might be weird. Instead, wait until you've finished your fun family outing, and then post a message about the great fun you had earlier in the evening. There are, of course,

times when you want your fans and followers to meet up with you somewhere; when you're playing a show, or just a special meet and greet with fans, for example. But keep your private moments private.

7) **Don't Ignore Your Fans. Respond With Enthusiasm.** When you start posting frequently, fans and others will respond to your comments with comments of their own. Respond back, acknowledge them and be positive, enthusiastic and encouraging. If folks respond to your comments and you repeatedly ignore them, some are bound to take it personally. Always engage your fans. If they comment on a song or an album of yours, thank them and let them know how much you appreciate it. Just think; every day you can chat with dozens of total strangers, encouraging them to share your music with their friends and family. Do you realize the power of this? If a hundred people are following you, that's a hundred people you can ask, via your status update, to spread the word about your music. With social networking, you always have a crowd at your fingertips. Work the crowd.

Social media is a great thing, and a fantastic way to stay in touch with your fans on a day-to-day basis. However, words are powerful, lasting, and shape people's perceptions of who you are. Always be watchful of how you present yourself in writing. Think twice before you post, stay positive, be enthusiastic, and avoid being negative or boring.

Audio and Video Blogging

Some of you might be more comfortable talking than you are physically writing. For those of you in this category, you might want to look into creating audio blogs rather than written blogs. However, if you take this course, know you might be at a slight disadvantage – at least in one sense – when it comes to online marketing. Why? Because online marketing is about content and as far as most search engines are concerned, *written* content is where it's at. After all, *words* are what we search for on Google, not *sounds*.

The biggest problem with audio-only blogging is that it's one-dimensional. Imagine a visitor coming to your web site, hitting the *play* button, and hearing a faceless voice. What is there to engage them visually? Within two minutes, your listeners will become distracted, browsing the Internet in another browser tab while you're yakking it up. Before long, they'll tune you out completely, and then turn you off. The only hope you have of keeping your listeners' attention is to give your audio some real zing through the force of your personality, the strength of your topic, and the use of music and sound effects to make your audio more exciting to listen to. Even with all those elements, you'd better get to the point quickly, because people aren't going to stay attentive to an audio-only stream very long, especially since they're sitting in front of their computer. It's one thing to listen to audio-only talk-radio (or an audio book) while you're in your car driving. But when you're at the computer, it's much harder to stay focused on what is being said. The Internet is far too distracting.

If you're going to go to the technical trouble of creating audio, why not just go all the way and create a *video*? It's easy to do these days. Most laptops come with a web cam built in and you can purchase a decent video camera for a couple hundred bucks at Best Buy. With video people can see *and* hear you, which allows you to be much more personal with your viewers. If you include the video blog (or *vlog* as video blogs are commonly referred to) on your web site, it gives your visitor something engaging to watch. People will be less likely to tune you out since your video gives the impression you are speaking to your audience directly, almost as if you were with them in person. Plus, with video blogging, you have all kinds of promotional opportunities, which I'll get into momentarily.

How to Make Your Video

I'm not going to take time in this book to teach you, step by step, how to make your own video. The ins and outs of video production are a book unto itself! However, I can point you to some resources that I think you'll find very useful.

First of all, let me direct you to the video, *How to Make A Video*. You'll find that on YouTube at http://www.youtube.com/watch?v=3zFePU1uvtc . This simple, ten minute, "how to" video was produced by Tim Carter of AsktheBuilder.com and while it doesn't address music videos specifically, it addresses a lot of the basic "gotchas" of creating a video that is both interesting and entertaining. Good, common sense stuff, but a great place to start.

In the beginning, you probably won't be making "music videos" so much as you will be recording video blogs (vlogs). I'd advise purchasing a simple web cam for this purpose. If you have a laptop manufactured in the last year or two, your laptop likely came with a web cam built in. If not, drive down to your local Best Buy store (or its equivalent) and check out your web cam options. Write down the product names and prices, then return home to research those cams and brands online. Read reviews to help you determine what the best "plug and play" cams are. You want to find something easy to use that will still give you a decent picture and sound.

> See Also…
> Getting a Web Cam: http://www.youtube.com/watch?v=XLjpZUsFEXo
> How to Edit a Video: http://www.youtube.com/watch?v=gmvjvlOnBYw

Once you have a cam, spend some time at YouTube.com watching vlogs to see what others are doing. To do this, just go to http://www.youtube.com and search for "vlog." You'll find plenty to view, some good, some not so good, but certainly lots to watch. Pay close attention to those vlogs that you find interesting to watch.

As a viewer, what is it that makes this or that video blog interesting to you? Take notes on those things, so that you can take the "best" ideas of the vlogs you find to integrate into your own vlog. During this process, you'll probably find a number of vlogs that are "how to" videos about the process of vlogging. There's no shortage of them, so watch and learn from those who have gone before you.

Some general tips about making your video:

1) **Be Entertaining:** Don't just sit there. Be animated. Be Funny. Be interesting to watch. Don't be a bump on a log. Move it, move it.

2) **Eye Contact:** Talking to an audience on YouTube is like talking to a live person, and when you're talking to people, eye contact is key. If you look people in the eye, you radiate confidence and people will like you more and respond to you better.

3) **Keep Your Videos Short:** People have very short attention spans. Make videos that range anywhere from 15 seconds to a maximum of two to three minutes. The longer you go, the less likely it is people

will take the time to watch as most people won't commit to spending several minutes watching a video on YouTube.

4) **Use Lots of Cuts and Shots:** Keep your video zippy. Again, people have very short attention spans. Use lots of quick cuts to give your video a sense of action. How? Just edit out all your "ums" and "ahs." Your video doesn't have to be one long ramble with one camera shot. In fact, you don't want that. Edit out your natural pauses for a quick, snappy video.

5) **Plan What You're Going to Say Ahead of Time:** Don't wing it. Some improvisation might be fine if you're gifted at it, but even so, write a script. Know what you're going to say before you say it. Have a point to make and know how to get there, step by step. Have a sense of direction. Don't wander. Don't ramble.

6) **Watch the Lighting:** Without artificial lighting, videos shot inside tend to appear dark. You don't have to spend a lot on special lighting equipment. Just use a lamp or two, and experiment with your lighting levels until what you see on your video looks natural, warm and pleasing.

As you watch vlogs and other videos on YouTube, you'll likely find videos that you wish to respond to. I recommend you do so. In fact, recording video responses to a vlog made by someone else is the best way to get started. Doing so gives you an opportunity to fine tune your video persona and technique before creating a regular vlog of your own.

As always, when in doubt about "how to" do something, search Google or YouTube. There's so much free information available to you online it's amazing. You might be interested in reading "How to Create a Video Blog" at http://desktopvideo.about.com/od/videoblogging/ht/howtovlog.htm . The article contains some basic information, but contains many links to more details you can follow up on.

As to making an actual music video, or at least something interesting for your fans to watch, one tool I recommend you try is Animoto.com (http://www.animoto.com). Create an account, upload your favorite digital still photos, add one of your tunes and just watch Animoto turn it into a stunning video. It's amazing. Want an example? Here's a video I created combining Animoto and my original piano music. http://www.youtube.com/watch?v=BjZT0rO-WtQ . The video includes favorite photos from my many travels. As you can see, I take my family with me on many of my concert tours. Pretty cool, huh? Obviously, this isn't a true music video so much as it is a clever slide show with some very cool transitional effects. But Animoto adds so much movement that it *feels* like a video. And it just shows you what you can do without knowing anything at all about video production.

If you want to dig deeper into creating videos and editing them, I suggest you start mining YouTube.com for information. There's so much great material there to help you get started, everything from video editing software recommendations to tutorials that walk you through the video editing process for specific software programs. To start you off, check out "How to Choose a Video Editing Program" at http://www.youtube.com/watch?v=yiQ6OtLHgX4 . After that, just let your natural curiosity guide you. There's no end to the amount of helpful, easy to understand information you can find on YouTube.

Promoting, Marketing and Distributing Your Video

So you have a video or a video blog. How do you go about promoting and distributing it? Let's start with the video itself.

What makes your video interesting and potentially "viral" isn't *you* so much as it is the topic you're covering in your video. Yes, your video (or vlog) must be entertaining, funny and engaging – and that is up to you – but folks who don't know anything about you will never find your video unless…

   a) someone else recommends it to them
   b) you manage to get your video featured on YouTube or
   c) someone stumbles upon your video while searching for a related topic they are interested in.

Let's be honest; option "b" isn't too likely, and option "a" requires that someone discovers your video in the first place. So you need to start at "c" and to do that, you need to make your video findable when someone is searching for a particular topic or phrase.

Obviously, the place you want to focus your video promotion is YouTube.com. Anyone who spends any time online is familiar with YouTube and let's face it, most of the videos that are shared with other people are streaming from YouTube (YouTube's actual market share of the video/multimedia web site world, as of November 2010, is 75%. See the complete data at http://www.marketingcharts.com/interactive/top-10-video-multimedia-websites-november-2010-15333/).

When you upload your video to YouTube, you give it a *title*, a *description*, and keyword *"tags."* Sound familiar? It should, as that's exactly the same process you go through to optimize a web page for the search engines. You want to use the title, description and tags to target your video to your potential audience. Put as much relevant text as you can into your description and tag fields to make your video easier to find. The YouTube "tags" are the equivalent of the keywords and key phrases you use in web site optimization.

The search facilities on YouTube work somewhat like Google in that video search results are going to come back based, in large part, on the video title, description and keyword tags. Search results come up by "Relevance" by default. So you want your video title, description and tags to not only accurately describe your video, but to also contain keywords and phrases related to your video topic. Your title and description should also generate *curiosity*, so that when someone reads the title, they are compelled to click and check out the video. So obviously, you don't want to title your video blog "John Smith's Vlog." Who's going to click on that? Instead, use a title and description that will grab the attention of someone who doesn't know who you are. Focus the title on the subject matter or topic and create a title that says "click on me, I'm interesting."

One aspect of successfully promoting yourself and your music online is to be relevant to what's going on *right now* in the world around you. In other words, find out what people are talking about and insert yourself and your music into that conversation. So what are people talking about *right now*? To find out, visit the YouTube home page and view the most popular videos at any given moment (you'll see them all listed by category). That will tell you what people are watching, searching for and thinking about at any given time. Another great tool is Twitter's search tool. Go to http://search.twitter.com/ and at the bottom of the page you can view Twitter's "Trending Topics" to see what a large number of people are talking about *right now*. You might also enjoy this blog post; *15 Fascinating Ways to Track Twitter Trends*:

http://mashable.com/2009/04/04/twitter-trends/ . And finally, you can view what people are searching on and reading about via the web at http://google.com/trends or http://buzz.yahoo.com/ .

Once you know what's hot on people's minds, you have something you can talk about or comment on that's guaranteed to be of interest to people. So there are two ways to approach this; one is to find videos that are already popular on a particular topic and then create a video response to that video. A second option is to create your own video or vlog based on that topic. This is a marketing strategy that I like to call *Newscasting.* You find out what people are talking about, and then target your video, your written blog, your music and even your web site to these topics. If you align the content you create with subjects that are popular right now, you might be able to insert yourself - and your music - right in the middle of that conversation. The trick is to find a clever way to make your video not only relevant to the topic at hand but also a vehicle for promoting your music.

Here are a few other promotion tips for your video:

1) **Widespread Video Distribution:** YouTube isn't the only place you can post your video. There are dozens of other video-based web sites where you can place and promote your video. Here's a *small* list:

Google Video:	http://video.google.com
Yahoo Video:	http://video.yahoo.com
Dailymotion:	http://www.dailymotion.com
Blinkx:	http://www.blinkx.com/
Flurl:	http://www.flurl.com/
Veoh:	http://www.veoh.com
Metacafe:	http://www.metacafe.com
Vimeo:	http://vimeo.com/

To make the process of video distribution easier, take a look at **Tubemogul** at http://www.tubemogul.com/ . This fantastic and FREE service allows you to upload your video to one place (Tubemogul) and have it automatically distributed to not only YouTube.com, but also to more than two dozen other popular video services. Another similar alternative is Vidmetrix (http://www.vidmetrix.com/)

2) **Target Your Audience:** Search YouTube (and other sites as you have time) for the same keywords and tags you're using in your own video. What are the most popular videos that come back in the search results? Take note of what tags are used in the top videos you find and edit your video to add the same tags that are appropriate for your own video. Then when people watch those videos that are most popular, chances are better that your video will be recommended to that viewer as a "Related Video." Create a video reply for those same popular videos and people who discover those videos may stumble across yours as well.

3) **Encourage Interaction:** Most of these video services, including YouTube, are based on social network principles similar to Facebook. Those who view your videos can comment on them and rate them. In your video description (and even in the video itself), invite comments, ratings and responses from those who watch your video. That will get some dialog going, giving you a chance to respond and make connections with other active users.

4) **Put Your Video Everywhere:** Embed your video on your web site, as well as Facebook and any other social networks you're involved in. Post links to your video in message boards and forums you're involved in. Search for blogs related to your topic post there. Invite friends, family and co-workers to watch your video, rate it, share it, and comment on it. I mentioned earlier how YouTube video results are ranked by relevance. Other factors that determine how your video is ranked on YouTube include the video ratings, how many times it's been viewed, shared, number of comments, playlist additions and how many web sites are linking to it. You definitely want to get others involved in helping you spread the word about your video. You want your video shared on as many web sites as you can.

5) **Spread the News:** If you've got a GREAT video that is getting a *lot* of viral traffic, write a press release about its success to create even more of a stir (a chapter on writing and submitting press releases is coming up next!)

Don't Forget! The whole point of all of this is to promote your music! So when you create video blogs and commentary, find a way to tie it to your music. Include your web site address in not only the video description, but also in the video itself to drive traffic to your web site.

See Also…

ReelSEO: Online Video Marketing News, Tips, Trends & Observations
http://www.reelseo.com/

YouTube Sharing and Optimization Tips:
http://www.reelseo.com/seo-for-video/#youtube

How to Go Viral on YouTube – Video Marketing Tips for Musicians
http://arielpublicity.com/2009/04/29/how-to-go-viral-on-youtube/

Now, let's talk about your press release....

Your Internet Press Release -
How to Write It and Where to Send It!

Making Noise About Your Web Site!

If you're doing anything worthwhile with your music or at your web site, you ought to be sending out press releases on a periodic basis. These press releases can be sent to your music fans, subscribers to your email list (covered in detail later), or the music industry at large. However, be careful who you target your press release to. The last thing you want to do is start sending your press releases to people who don't want them. The line between sending out appropriate press releases and "spam" can be a very thin one. For example, a press release for your band's new album would not likely be considered real news to the music industry at large (sorry, but unless you're a mega-star, it wouldn't), so you should avoid sending emails to announce your new album to music industry people. That would likely irritate the very people you wish to attract! I myself receive unsolicited press releases from artists that, after the umpteenth time, I really don't want. Their email address has permanently been placed in my "nuisance" spam filter. That's exactly the kind of thing you don't want to do!

If you want to send out a press release about your brand new just-released album, ask yourself the question, "Who cares about my new album?" Your fans do, so a news release sent to them would be appropriate. Any time you prepare a press release or news announcement, ask yourself "Who cares?" The answer to that question is a good test to determine whether your news item is worthy of widespread distribution. Here are some real life examples:

When I release my brand new CD or get an album up and ready for purchase on iTunes, *who cares?* My fans do, so the news release would be sent to them, as well as those who have subscribed to my personal email list. When my Midnight Rain record label releases a CD sampler of solo piano music, *who cares?* Piano music fans in general might. So the press release would be sent to any Internet newsgroup or discussion group where piano music is a topic of interest, as well as any piano-related music sites that host advertising or solicit news releases. When I release a new edition of this book, *who cares?* Pretty much any working musician may potentially be interested, as well as some in the independent music industry, so the press release would be sent to the appropriate discussion groups, independent music sites, announced to online music e-zines and so on.

So, are you working on a project worthy of widespread recognition? Do you have an event or news you want to get the word out about? Here are a few places online to consider sending your press release and/or marketing materials:

Mi2N: The Music Industry News Network (http://www.mi2n.com/input.php3) is the first place to go to find out what's going on *right now* in the music industry. Every day, you'll find dozens of new stories, and you can submit your news release for free. Some items also get published in MusicDish (http://www.musicdish.com), owned by the same people. Don't miss this one.

CD Baby News (http://cdbaby.org/contrib.php) is a terrific place to send your release if your news is something that would be of interest to other musicians. It's free.

Beat Wire (http://www.beatwire.com/submit) is a press release service designed specifically for musicians that I've consistently heard good things about. Your news is delivered directly to the desktops of over 10,000 music editors at daily newspapers, magazines, news agencies, top web sites, radio stations, and other outlets. You can submit your press release to music critics, journalists, editors, and radio programmers. The cost is $149.95.

RapidPressRelease.com (http://www.rapidpressrelease.com/music+band+press+release/) sends your music news release to "DJ's, producers, labels, radio hosts, reporters, journalists, editors, online news outlets and music groups." They personally review each and every release and match it to a tailored audience to have optimal impact, so this is a highly targeted service. Cost is $269 for one release, $497 for three.

PRLog (http://www.prlog.org) is a general purpose press release service. It's not targeted to the music industry, but it is free to use. Releases are distributed to Google News, numerous search engines and RSS feeds. It's probably one of the best of the "free" PR services.

PRLeap (http://www.prleap.com) is another general purpose press release service, but it goes a bit further than PRLog. For $99, your release gets sent to not only Google News, but also the Associated Press and the United Press International, as well as Social Media sites (like Twitter) and bookmarking sites like Delicious, Digg and StumbleUpon. It's also very easy to use.

PR Web (http://www.prweb.com) is arguably the Internet's top news release service and it's the one I use the most. Their releases get over 50 million page views per month. All press releases are posted on the site indefinitely and, depending upon how much you "contribute," get widespread distribution through their syndicated newsfeed service as well as on Google, Yahoo News and more. PRWeb also maintains a list of over 30,000 opt-in bloggers and journalists who receive a daily email that includes press releases matching their selected criteria. I like this one a lot, but depending on how much exposure you want, it can start getting expensive. PR distribution packages start at $80 per release.

If you want to go for broke, try eReleases (http://www.ereleases.com). For $399 they will submit your press release to 100,000 opt-in journalists. They also have a *targeted* music distribution list which you can add on for no additional charge. The latter list covers most of the mainstream music magazines such as Rolling Stone, Hit Parade, Circus, Keyboard Magazine and so on.

Finally, EWorldWire.com (http://www.eworldwire.com) is interesting as you can target very specific groups, which include major newswires, trade/industry specific, local distribution, top 100 newspapers, European markets, college & university press, and pretty much any ethnic group. Their fees start at only $99.

And you'll want to check out these *20 Free Best Press Release Distribution Sites*: http://www.pagetrafficblog.com/20-press-release-distribution-sites/6839/ .

There are many press release distribution services out there, many of which overlap in terms of who actually sees your release. Check out the above services and if you want to compare these with others, simply search Google.com for "press release distribution."

Pay-for-Promotion Services

Here are a few services that do more than just distribute your press release. If you're looking to hand off your promotion work to someone else, these may be options for you:

Ariel Publicity (http://arielpublicity.com) is the best of the best when it comes to organizing and running a full publicity campaign for you. Campaigns are entirely Internet-based, focused on social media makers, bloggers, podcasts, Internet radio stations and digital music stores, with the goal of increasing your exposure and sales. For those of you out there who just want to hire someone to do the grunt work for you, Ariel Publicity is a great option. "Cyber PR" publicity packages run from three to four months, with rates starting at $1,995.

Evolution Promotion (http://www.evolutionpromotion.com) is a service founded by Karen Lee, former promoter for Elektra and IRS Records (The Cars, Motley Crew, Metallica and others). Services include radio promotion, tour promotion, direct customer marketing, Internet radio and marketing, web design and consulting. The Evolution Promotion team has a very impressive clientele list, and they create custom campaigns for each one.

The MusicDish Network (http://www.musicdish.net) Another branch of MusicDish, MDN marketing campaigns are custom designed for your music and include syndicated marketing, online street teams, MySpace marketing and distribution.

Music SUBMIT (http://www.musicsubmit.com) isn't so much a press release service as it is a widespread music release service. Once you sign up, they'll take your music and information and submit it to hundreds of Internet music resources all at once. These include Internet radio stations, online music magazines, blogs, music directories and podcasts. It's a nice way to kick off a new music release, but there's a downside: the press releases aren't targeted at all, so your information may go out to a lot of folks that aren't interested in your particular sound. This one is hit and miss, making the value of the service difficult to assess. Fortunately, it's fairly inexpensive. Promotion packages start at $34.95.

SonicBids.com (http://www.sonicbids.com) is one of my favorites. Sign up, create an electronic press kit, and they'll email you just about every day with new opportunities for gigs, contests, promotion and so on. When you see something you want to submit to, you just sign in and submit your electronic press kit with a single click. The price to subscribe is between $6-$11/month, depending on the options you choose.

How to Write a Press Release

Looking for help writing a press release? Writing is definitely an acquired skill.

First, *Pick a Good Title* - Everything I've written before about using strategic keywords and key phrases for your web pages, blogs and videos is true here, too. Remember, you're writing for the web, so it's very possible that the press release you send out will be posted on dozens of web sites, many of them much more popular than yours. That's cool, because you can benefit from the link popularity of these other, more well-known web sites. Use a title that will result in people discovering your press release when they search the Internet on your keywords.

Next, *Write a Story* - Whatever it is you're marketing, whether it be your band, your CD, blog, digital release, web site or a product, write your release in such a way that it tells a story. However, rather than writing a story ABOUT your product, write a story about the NEED that it fulfills. What need does your web site/music/gig fulfill? Write a story that demonstrates that need and then shows how your product (or music) fulfills it. You want your press release to create *desire* in the reader; the desire to fulfill that need, whatever it is.

Here are some additional bullet points provided by Christopher Knab, one of my business partners at the MusicBizAcademy.com web site (http://www.musicbizacademy.com/knab/)

1) When to Write a Press Release:
- Concert/Show and or Tour information
- Record, Publishing, Merchandising Contract/Deal Announcements
- Important Band Personnel Changes/Additions
- CD, DVD, Single, Video Release Information
- Promotional Events/Marketing Plans/Benefit Concerts/Misc. Announcements

2) What The Print and Broadcast Media Need:
- News or announcements related to *their* target audience
- Submission deadlines met for calendars and event listings (often that's 30 days)
- Event or information in proximity to their coverage area

3) Layout and Essential Information:
- The phrase "For Immediate Release" centered near the top 1/3 of page
- Date press release is sent out
- Contact information: Specifically, the person the media can call for more information. Include phone number, web site and email address.
- Printed on company or artist/band stationery with full address info
- One page long (unless for major event or project)
- End with the marks ### centered at end of the body

4) The Press Release Structure:

The Slug Line (Headline)
- Short, but attention-getting headline phrase
- A hint of the purpose or topic to be presented

The Lead Paragraph
- Should include the 5 W's and the H (if needed): Who, What, Where, When, Why, and How
- Summation of the basic topic/information
- Begin with the most important part of the information
- Who is in the beginning sentence, followed by Where and When
- Why, What, and How follow in the next few sentences
- No unnecessary details should be included in the lead paragraph

The Body
- Elaboration on the theme or purpose of the press release
- One thought, one paragraph. Cohesive, single ideas in each paragraph
- Write information in descending order of importance
- Keep information *factual*. Opinions only in quotes with proper credit
- Use simple sentences (Subject - Object -Verb) and *avoid too much hype*
- Ending option: Recap essential information from first paragraph
- *Proofread several times* for spelling, and/or grammatical errors

Here are some other valuable resources to look to for help writing your press release:

Sample Press Release:
http://www.press-release-writing.com/press-release-writing-tips-sample-press-release/

How to Write a Press Release:
http://www.publicityinsider.com/release.asp

How to Write a Successful Press Release:
http://webdeveloper.internet.com/management/manage_write_press_release.html

Writing a Press Release – What to do, What not to do:
http://www.rapidpressrelease.com/tips/writing.asp

The Anatomy of a Press Release:
http://www.pressflash.com/resources_anatomy.php

Press Releases 101:
http://musicians.about.com/od/musicindustrybasics/tp/pressreleases101.htm

The Ten Commandments of a Press Release:
http://www.musicdish.com/mag/?id=12018

Proven Strategies for Selling Your Music

How to Turn Your Visitors Into Dollars

I've talked about how to prepare your web site for the search engines. I've taken you step-by-step through how to target your customers using keywords, meta-tags, news, targeted sites, reviews and articles. But how do you effectively sell your music once you have attracted a visitor to your web site? That's the topic I will address in this chapter; specifically, how to convert visitors into sales.

Limit Your Visitors' Options

First of all, there is a golden rule to marketing any product on the Internet: limit your visitors' options. Too many link options on one page will totally overwhelm your potential buyer. When someone visits your web site for the first time, they have no idea what to expect, nor do they know what YOU expect them to do. From their perspective, your web site is a maze of new information to process and navigate. There is one question on their mind: "Where do I go now?" So, your job, as the web site designer, is to make the answer to that question obvious.

When designing the navigational layout of your web site, set it up in such a way as to draw your visitor gradually, but inevitably, to your order page. How do you do this? You keep the links to your *power pages* front and center at all times. What are your power pages? They are the pages that make up the absolute core of your web site, and the pages that represent a "call to action." They include your "sample music" page, your "order" page, your "booking" page, your "license music" page, your "mailing list signup" page and any other page whose job it is to *sell your music* and/or *services*. These are the pages that result in the customer *doing something* other than just reading information. They are either *listening, buying, subscribing, licensing* or *booking*. As you design your web site, include links to your power pages at the top of every page you build and make them stand out. Make them obvious.

In terms of laying out your home page (your main index.htm page), make the links to your power pages central to that. Then *below* them, include links to your *secondary* pages. Secondary pages are for those folks who desire *information* and who want to *explore* and *dig deeper* into who you are. These pages include your bio, your news page, your blog, your photo gallery, articles you may have written and other similar pages. These pages are secondary because while they provide *information* about you to your visitors, they don't necessarily sell your music on their own. So they get second billing under your power pages.

Whenever a visitor clicks from your home page to a secondary page, such as your bio, the only link options you should give them are to either return to your home page or to move on to one of your power pages. So they either move forward to a power page, or back to the home page. By doing this, you ensure that your visitor never gets lost and that no matter where they go, they are always just one click away from taking some kind of *action*, whether that be sampling your music, signing up for your mailing list or, best of all, purchasing your music.

If you'd like, you can take a look at my own artist web site at http://www.davidnevue.com . You will notice the priority my power pages are given. Your eye is drawn to the links to my most important pages first (My CDs, iTunes downloads, sheet music, concert info, music player, booking and licensing info) and then to the secondary pages below. Finally, no matter where you go on my web site, you'll see the same link options at the top of every page that either return you to the home page or move you on to one of my power pages.

For another example, check out the web site of the band Rondellus (http://www.sabbatum.com). I'm very proud of these guys. Their producer was one of my early clients and put the advice of this book into practice. He recently emailed me to let me know that Rondellus sold over 3000 CDs from their web site in nine months. Good going!

Back to my point. A mistake I often see artists make is that they attempt to link every page on their web site to every other page on their web site. It becomes a tangled mess for your visitor to navigate. Keep it simple! The fewer links you have on your web site, the more likely your visitor is going to click on the link you really want them to - the "BUY NOW" link.

NOTE: I might suggest you put a link to a site map at the bottom of each of your pages, also. This is more for the benefit of search engine spiders than your visitors, but your visitors may check out your site map to get an overview of everything you have to offer, as well.

Article of Note:

Choice Kills Conversion:
http://www.optimizeandprophesize.com/jonathan_mendezs_blog/2006/10/choice_kills_co.html

Customers Given Too Many Choices are 10x Less Likely to Buy
http://sivers.org/jam

Below are a few more suggestions for turning your web site visitors into paying customers...

Music to Their Ears

There are certain marketing buzz words that, by their very nature, draw attention to themselves. One of those is the word FREE. Free Music, Free Downloads, Free Trial, Try it Free, Free Stuff Here, Free This, Free That, you name it. People like free stuff! Just having the word somewhere on your web page will draw your visitors' interest. So, if you want to sell your music, incorporate that word into your marketing strategy on your official web site, your targeted web site, social networks you're involved with, and any other web site you promote your music on. Here's how:

Win Free Music!

As previously mentioned, John, our Flamenco guitar player, created a topical web site about Flamenco music to attract a specific target audience. Wouldn't you think those targeted visitors might like a chance to win a free Flamenco CD (or the entire album in MP3 format)? Yes! Contests are a great way to publicize your music and build up a database of interested customers. Here's how you do it:

First, create a link to your contest from your main pages. It might simply say something to the effect of "Win Free Flamenco Guitar Music!" This link will lead to your contest page. On the contest page have complete information about the CD/MP3 package as well as sound samples of your music that your visitors can listen to. On this contest page, give your visitor the option to either a) buy the CD/Album download now (with a link to your order page) or b) enter their name in your *monthly* drawing for a free CD and/or MP3 package. Make a big deal of the fact that once your visitor enters your contest, they are *automatically entered in the contest* every month thereafter increasing their chance of winning.

Next, use a web form (or an email link if you prefer) to take your visitor's information. Get their full name, address and email address. Their email address will be *required* because you will use that method to notify them if they win the contest. I also suggest you use the form to take a very brief survey. Ask simple questions like, "How did you find our web site?" or "What's your favorite and least favorite thing about our web site?" You'll find out a lot about your audience that way, as well as get some useful data that may influence how you market or design your web site. Don't ask more than two or three questions, however, or else you'll discourage people from entering.

Once a month, pick someone randomly from your contest list to receive a free copy of one of your CDs (I found a great random number generator at http://www.random.org/sequences). Notify your winner via email and ask them to respond to you to verify their physical mailing address and email address. When (if) they respond, send them the CD (or the link to the MP3 downloads) and a nice thank you note with information on your other music releases. The reason you wait to send the information until they respond is so that they will be watching for your CD to arrive in the mail. You'll create a bit of anticipation and excitement this way. You also verify that you have your winner's correct contact information. Do NOT send a CD out until you get a response from your winner.

Next, send an email to every person that entered your contest to let them know who the lucky winner was, and within that email include information on how to preview/buy the CD/MP3 package and let them know they will be automatically entered in the next month's drawing. You can also use this opportunity to highlight any other specials you have, or point them to reviews of your music, YouTube videos of performances, or anything else that specifically encourages them to *listen* to your music.

What you've done by offering this contest is given yourself an excuse to advertise your CDs via email to a growing list of potential new customers every single month. The first month you may only have ten or twenty entries. But the next month you may have forty, then a hundred, and eventually thousands. While you may give away a free CD/MP3 package every month, you'll more than make the difference up in paying orders as people are repeatedly exposed to your music. Repeated exposure is important, as not everyone is going to buy your music the *first* time they hear about it. In fact, most people *won't* buy your CD the first time, so this style of advertising keeps reminding them, and reminding them, and reminding them every single month.

I've seen statistics stating that the average person has to see an advertisement seven times before they'll actually respond to it. I don't know if this is exactly true, but I know that with my own buying habits it *does* often take more than a single prodding before I'll purchase something. I recently purchased a CD by artist Cheryl Bliss (http://www.cherylbliss.com) who I first discovered over *three years* ago. It took me that long to finally get around to buying her CD! It was repeated exposure to her name that kept prompting me to finally go ahead and do it! After a while something clicked in my head that said, "I might as well." I'm glad I did, too, because it's one of my favorite CDs in my collection.

NOTE: Don't forget to include an unsubscribe option from your contest list! That way if someone decides they no longer want to be included in your contest, they can easily remove themselves.

The "Best Of / Music Sampler" Effect

If there is one thing I've noticed in my marketing experiments over the years, it is the effectiveness of the term "Best Of" or "Music Sampler" when promoting music. It's another one of those buzz words. For quite some time I'd been selling one of my CDs, a solo piano project called "While the Trees Sleep" at a reduced price from my targeted web site. I did so in an effort to further entice visitors to take a chance on buying the album since, from my experience, many of those buyers would come back and purchase other my CDs and/or downloads at full price.

One day, on a whim, I decided to promote this album as a "sampler" of my music. That was, after all, an accurate description of my intent, which was to offer potential buyers the opportunity to sample my music in its entirety for a very low price. I was surprised by the result. The use of the term "sampler" nearly doubled the number of visits to my sales promotion page for that album. From there I was able to further interest my visitors with streaming sound files and details about the CD. The effect on sales was quite noticeable. In fact, sales improved so much that it encouraged me to create an actual "Best of" album called "Whisperings: The Best of David Nevue." I released that album in 2001 and guess what? To this day, that is my best selling album, not only from my web site, but also on iTunes, Amazon.com, CDBaby.com and even at gigs.

Why is having a "best of/sampler" album important? While folks might like the music they hear on your web site enough to keep on listening, they may not be convinced to actually purchase your music. But if you offer them a "best of" album of your best songs, that might just be enough to encourage them to go ahead and buy it. If you offer this album of "favorites" at a discounted price, that gives them *yet another reason* to pull out their credit card.

The point is, if you have multiple albums of your music (at least two) or a great number of tracks to sell (at least 20), you absolutely should consider creating a "Best of" compilation – even if it's just the equivalent of a 5-8 song EP. What's great about living in this day and age is that you don't even have to manufacture a formal CD if you don't want to. You can just create a package of MP3s, put them into a single zip file, and sell it that way. Or, you might offer your MP3 package as a free download to entice folks to try out and (hopefully) buy your full length album titles.

"Best of/Sampler" albums give your visitors one more reason to TRY your music and even pay for it. Give your visitors *as many reasons to buy* as possible, because the more reasons you give them to buy, the more likely you are to overcome their natural resistance to actually making a purchase.

The One-Two Punch: Combining Samplers and Coupons

Purchasing an album containing your "best" music will definitely motivate some folks to take the plunge and buy your music. Even so, some customers need a bigger push to get them to finalize their purchase. So offer your visitor a "coupon." Tell your customer that if they buy your CD/MP3 sampler, you will give them a special gift coupon for "X Amount" off any other full-priced CD in your catalog. The bigger the coupon, the more likely your visitor is to accept your offer. This in effect gives your customer the sampler CD/MP3 album for practically nothing if they make use of your coupon. You've given your web site visitor *one more reason* to purchase. If they don't use the coupon, you lose nothing. If they do, you make a few more bucks, and you are turning your onetime visitor into a repeat customer, who will be likely to purchase more of your product later.

The "Toss-In"

One of the great things about creating a "best of" sampler album is that it costs very little to do so. The music, after all, has already been recorded so there's no new studio time to pay for. If you choose to manufacture an actual CD as I did, the only costs you have are possible mastering costs (to equalize your tracks so they better complement one another) and package design. You just have to decide on your track list, create the mix, and put it on a CD.

This is probably as good a place as any to recommend a CD manufacturer. If you want a company that's both fast and inexpensive, check out Kunaki (http://www.kunaki.com) . While there's nothing fancy about their web site, the quality of their product (and the turnaround time) is superb. You can order short-run CD quantities (as few as you want) or huge bulk runs (thousands). Either way, the price will run you between about $1 and $1.30 per CD. Better yet, once you place an order, your finished CDs will ship out to you within 24 hours. The only drawback... you're limited to a two-panel insert for your CD art. Kunaki keeps it simple, and that's why they are so very fast at what they do.

If you want a complete CD package, you might consider NW Media (http://www.nwmedia.com), based out of Portland, Oregon. This is the company I have been using for manufacturing for several years now. They can do virtually *anything* for you, not only CDs, but DVDs, poster printing, mastering and so on. My contact there is Josh Sustarich. You can email him at josh@nwmedia.com .

Should you need CD package art design (or poster art, logo art or anything else of that nature), check out the work of Matt Strieby. See http://www.musicbizacademy.com/artdesign/artintro.htm for more information and to view some of his portfolio. He's done my design work for years and you'll get an amazing price on professional art design. He's a super easy guy to work with and he'll make your product look fantastic!

If you want short-run CDs, but aren't keen on Kunaki, the company I mentioned above, there are other options. DiskFaktory (http://www.musicbizacademy.com/diskfaktory.htm) can provide you small quantities of retail-ready CDs for a reasonable price. Another interesting option is Mixonic (http://www.mixonic.com) where you can literally design and create your own CDs online. Other places to investigate that are similar include CreateSpace.com (http://www.createspace.com), Disc On Demand (http://www.discondemand.com) and the aforementioned AudioLife (http://www.audiolife.com).

Finally, you might consider creating your sampler in a small compact package, such as a "CD Jacket" style package. See http://www.discmakers.com/products/jackets.asp for an example of what these look like. A CD Jacket package makes your sampler very easy to toss into a package you're already mailing, which makes it a fantastic promotional tool. That way, if a customer orders one of your products, whether that's a CD, DVD, a tee shirt, or anything else, you can "toss in" your CD Jacket sampler into the package for free. Your customers will love you for it, and this will give them *one more reason* to purchase your music!

Another toss-in option: Give the customer a duplicate CD of one or more CDs they purchased and encourage them to *give away* that CD to a friend, coworker or loved one. This encourages your buyers to share your music (and their enthusiasm for it!) with their friends.

Have I Got a Deal for You...

If you have more than one album to offer your customers, give them the option to buy your entire collection for a special, low price. In late 2001, I began selling all five of my CDs as a collection. My headline read "Buy 5 CDs for $50 Bucks!" The result was quite amazing. In fact, I could hardly believe it! Almost half the CD orders I received were for the entire collection! It's the "Costco," buy-in-bulk mentality. People are willing to spend more money if it means a good deal! This change alone greatly increased the volume of my album sales online.

I now have 11 CDs in my catalog, and offer a "11 CDs for $100 Bucks" option which many people go for. I also offer "Any 3 CDs for $35 Bucks." I sell more CDs in bulk than I do singles. In fact, it's pretty rare that a customer buys just one CD from my web site. If you have more than one album, give this strategy a try. For me, just doing this one thing increased CD sales greatly from my personal artist web site.

By the way, this strategy also works *very* well when selling CDs at gigs! When I perform live, I offer a "3-pack" of my CDs for $35 and almost half my orders are for the 3 CD special. Do the math. If, for example, I sell CDs to 50 customers at a gig, and half of those customers purchase the 3-pack, that means that while 25 people only bought 1 CD each (at $15), 25 bought 3 CDs each (at $35). That adds up to 100 total CDs sold, with 75 of those sales coming from those that purchased the 3-pack. So, my total sale for 50 customers, based upon these figures, is $1,250, which averages out to $12.50 for each CD sold. Not a bad profit at all.

Free Shipping!

This is fairly self-explanatory, and another great way to boost your sales. For example, "Purchase our 3 for $35 CD pack and shipping is FREE!" It's just *one more reason* for your customer to make the purchase. Do you see a theme evolving here?

Free Bonus Offer!

I've already talked about this option a bit, but let me get specific: tell your visitor that if they order your CD and/or MP3 package RIGHT NOW, they'll receive something else, a "bonus" item, for free. What might that be? If they buy a CD, how about free MP3 downloads from the album they purchased? That way they can start enjoying your music right away and they don't even have to wait for the CD to arrive. Or, perhaps you could offer a free e-book of poetry you've written which they can download after their purchase. I occasionally run a special where if someone buys one of my CDs, they get the sheet music of their choice (in PDF format) from my sheet music collection for free. One artist I know targets her music to environmentalists and she includes small packages of tree seedlings with CD orders. Any time you give your customer a bonus item to go along with their purchase it increases the perceived value of what they are buying. It makes your customer happy, and increases up front sales. Plus, if what you offer for free is in digital format (like PDFs or digital sound files) it doesn't cost you anything extra to give out, and your customer will love you that much more for it.

NOTE: Whatever your bonus offer is, put an implied time limit on it. Tell your visitor that the offer is only available for a limited time. This will create a sense of urgency, knowing that if they don't buy your music today, they might lose the opportunity to receive your free bonus.

"Fear is the Mind-Killer" (and a Sales Killer Too!)

The number one thing between you and making a sale from your web site (aside from a simple lack of interest) is fear. Your visitor has learned *not* to trust strangers. They've been burned by scams and shams and as you yourself well know, buying *anything* over the Internet can be risky. You just never know who you're giving your personal information to and what they might do with it.

Even if your web site visitor *wants* to purchase your music, they might find an excuse not to. Perhaps they simply don't know you well enough to trust you. Maybe the web site design looks a bit amateur, and so they question the integrity of your order system. They might be wondering, "If I place an order, is my credit card information safe? Will I start receiving phone calls from telemarketers, or spam in my inbox?" I'm sure you can relate to these concerns. It is an absolute *necessity* that you address any and all fears your customer may have up front. The better you do this, the more likely you are to close a sale.

Take a look at the promotional page I put together for this book at http://www.promoteyourmusic.com. You probably read through that before buying this book. But now, read through it again, carefully, and note how the text of the entire page is designed to address any possible fears my potential customer might have.

First, there's a personal message from me to the reader. I use this to establish trust and to talk directly (in a manner of speaking) to my visitor. I want my visitor to know that I'm a real person, not just some faceless entity. Next, I specify my intent with this book and "cut through the hype," addressing (and relating to) the skeptical nature of my visitors. I follow this by stating what the book is NOT, directly addressing common fears. The more you read, the more I establish trust. After establishing that trust, I show the many benefits of the book, and offer testimonials from happy customers. I want the reader to know that my book will make them happy too!

After all this, I provide a "questions" link so my visitor can *easily* get answers to any other question (or fear) they might have. This is a great sales tool because when I respond quickly (as I try my best to do) to the visitor's question, they realize just how accessible I am. That almost *guarantees* me a sale. Nine out of ten times, if someone sends me a question I know they will buy the book if I just give them my personal attention.

Finally, in the sales copy I guarantee the quality of the book, and tell the customer what they can expect when reading it. I give them a variety of order options, including a mail order option for those afraid to purchase online. I also assure my customers that their personal information is totally and completely safe.

As you can see, I use *every opportunity* to put my visitor's fear to rest. I do this same type of thing on my artist web site using an order FAQ. See http://www.davidnevue.com/questions.htm for an example of how I do this. The latter is considerably shorter due to the nature of the product, but serves the same purpose.

To sum it all up, if you address your visitor's fears up front, you'll sell more of your products because you aren't giving them more reasons *not* to buy. The reasons to buy should outweigh the reasons not to buy.

Check out this great article:
20 Tips to Minimize Shopping Cart Abandonment, Part 1 & 2
http://www.clickz.com/clickz/column/1707845/tips-minimize-shopping-cart-abandonment-part
http://www.clickz.com/clickz/column/1711012/tips-minimize-shopping-cart-abandonment-part

"Can We Talk?"

Another way to ease your visitor's fear is to *talk* to them. It's a well-known fact that if a web site visitor can see your face and/or hear your voice, they are *much* more likely to trust you. Create a short video clip with you talking to your potential customer and embed that video right on your order page. In that video clip, let your customer know who you are and how much you appreciate your business. Invite them to email you with questions or concerns. And as you do, smile, make eye contact, and be likeable.

Damaged Goods or Best Buys?

Remember the first time you ordered CDs from a manufacturer and how excited you were when those boxes of CDs finally arrived? Then you opened up the first box... only to discover that every so often you'd find a CD with a cracked case, bent artwork, shredded shrink wrap or some other such thing. It seems inevitable, that when manufacturing CDs in bulk you get a few bad apples. I've worked with four CD manufacturers over the years, and I've encountered this with every single one to greater and lesser degrees. Of course, if you have too many bad CDs, you ought to return them, but if you have only a few here and there, sometimes it's just easier to hang onto them and use them for demo purposes. After all, you can't sell them, right?

Why not use these CDs in your online marketing efforts? Most of the time, all you need to do is replace a cracked case or another easily replaceable component to make the CD as good as new. All you are missing at that point is the shrink wrap. Here are some suggestions for using your "damaged goods:"

1) Once you've replaced the broken parts, use these CDs as giveaways in your online contests or even at shows. Since you are giving away CDs for free as part of your marketing strategy anyway, you might as well use these. As they are giveaways, no one will care that they are not shrink wrapped.

2) Use the repackaged, unwrapped CDs to make you MORE money. How? Sell "personally autographed" CDs for a couple bucks more. You can refer to these CDs as your "Signature Series," which sounds very impressive. Naturally, to autograph your "Signature Series" CDs you need to remove the shrink wrap, and since the shrink wrap has already been removed from these formerly damaged (but now repaired) CD cases, it saves you the trouble.

3) Offer the repackaged, unwrapped CDs to benefits, charities or other causes you care about. This is a fantastic way to get your music out there! I have had my piano CDs included in gift packages for Valentine's Day benefits, as well as used in "grab bags" that were auctioned off to raise money for a cause.

4) Don't want to bother with taking apart and repackaging your CDs with cracked cases? Then how about just selling these CDs "as is" at a "scratch and dent" discount? This is really easy to do. Just add a link on your order page (right beside the price) that says "find out how you can save $5 on your CD purchase!" This will take your web site visitor to a page where you can explain the situation. Tell them you have CDs direct from the manufacturer with slightly damaged cases, but that the CD itself is fine. Assure them that these CDs have never been played - you simply can't sell them as "new" because of the slight damage to the case. You'll be surprised how many people go for this. If you'd rather, go ahead and repackage your CDs with new cases but don't bother with the shrink wrap and make the same offer. If you sell the CDs at a discount, you are still making money, and that discount might be the very thing that encouraged your visitor to buy. A "scratch and dent" sale is better than no sale at all!

DIY Shrink Wrap: You may be interested in knowing for that just $245, you can purchase your own shrink wrap machine designed specifically for CDs. So if the issue is one of a cracked case, just replace that part, rewrap and you are set. For more information on this shrink wrap system, visit CDPro at http://www.stevensonind.com/cdpro.cfm . You can also buy shrink wrap systems and supplies from ULINE (one of my favorite office supply companies) at http://www.uline.com/cls_16/Shrink-Wrap?desc=Shrink+Wrap . Finally, my CD manufacturer, NW Media (see http://www.nwmedia.com) has offered to re-shrink wrap my own "scratch and dent" CDs for just .10 cents each. So, you might contact them.

NOTE: One of my readers pointed out that most print shops will shrink wrap CDs as well. She suggested Office Depot, which charged .50 cents per CD to rewrap hers.

Turn Your Visitors into Long-Term Customers

The absolute best way to increase sales from your web site, iTunes or anywhere else you sell your music, is to turn your one-time visitors into *long-term* customers. You can't grow your business without repeat customers. Repeat business is an absolute necessity; because it's those repeat customers who will go on to become your most enthusiastic fans. If those fans are coming to your web site often, you know they are into you. And if they are into you, they'll tell others about you. And if they tell others about you, they become a walking advertisement for you and your music.

The moment your visitor comes to your web site they will start making judgments about you. Knowing that, when a potential fan visits your web site, what kind of impression are you making? If your web site had "body language", what is your web site's body language saying? Is it impenetrable? Obstinate? Indifferent? Full of itself? Just in it for the money? Or is it inviting, friendly, smiling, offering to help, and ready with open arms?

Get Friendly!

I really can't believe how many musicians keep their fans at an arms-length distance. Some artists are so full of themselves! That's fine, I suppose, if you're a mega-superstar and have people stalking you and going through your trash. In that case, being anonymous is a necessity for mental and emotional survival! However, if you're like me, a simple musician who *needs* his fan base, getting downright friendly with your fans can make a real impact on your sales.

My music can be found all over the Internet. As a result I receive messages every day (via email, Facebook, MySpace) from people who are discovering my music for the first time. The moment someone I've never met contacts me about my music, I take advantage of it. It's a sales opportunity! I befriend the person, thank them for their encouragement, and ask them if they have questions about my music. I *encourage* a continued conversation, and use the opportunity to find out a little bit about this potential customer. "How did you find my music?," I'll ask. "Do you have a favorite song?" "What other kinds of music do you like?" Remember the earlier chapter on getting to know your street team members? You can apply all that information here. Ask those kinds of questions of new fans you meet.

A fan's message to you also gives you the perfect opportunity to invite them to join your *Fan Newsletter List*, which is an important thing (more details on that shortly). Below is a boiler plate newsletter invitation I use for all my new-found Internet friends. As you read it, note how *personal* it sounds. And yet, this is the same "template" I send out to pretty much everyone. I may alter it slightly for a particular situation, but it doesn't take much to copy and paste this template at the end of a response I give to a fan...

<body of the personal message> and then...

"I want to thank you very much for your encouragement. I really appreciate your support for my music! You made my day!

Would you be interested in my email newsletter, *Notes from the Piano?* I send it out once every month or so. Subscribers get access to special discounts on my CDs as well as all the latest news on future CD projects. I also ask my subscribers for feedback on new songs, as well as take votes for what sheet music to release. I also give away a free CD to a random subscriber every issue. So, there are a lot of good reasons to sign up! :)

You can find more information on my newsletter at http://www.davidnevue.com/subscribe.htm . If that's something you think you might be interested in, just click the link below to subscribe or, if you'd rather, just let me know and I'll add you. If you join, but later decide you want to be removed from the list, that's easy to do as well. You won't hurt my feelings! :) You can unsubscribe any time you want.

Anyway, I'd love to have you on the list so I can more easily ask your opinion on future projects. Either way, thanks for your email today. It's good to know my music is getting out there where people can enjoy it!

Best regards,

David Nevue
http://www.davidnevue.com
http://www.facebook.com/davidnevue
http://www.twitter.com/davidnevue

Now, doesn't that email make you feel all warm and fuzzy inside? Imagine receiving an email response like that back from your favorite band! Doesn't it make you want to tell your friends later that day about the conversation you had with your new, favorite band? That's the point. Get friendly with your fans and potential fans, and they will carry your message and music to other people in their social circle. Even more importantly, if your fan feels like they have a relationship with you, they will *remember* you. That's helpful, because when Christmas comes around, you'll use your newsletter to encourage them to purchase ten copies of your CD to give out to their friends and family!

At this point, I'd like to include a large portion of an article called *Making Your Fans Your Closest Allies* by Kenny Love. Kenny submitted this to me for use at the Music Biz Academy and he really hit the "Get Friendly" nail on the head.

You can read the entire article at http://www.musicbizacademy.com/comment/klovefans.htm .

Making Your Fans Your Closest Allies
by Kenny Love

Artists should learn to not distance themselves from their fans, who are their careers' life blood. If fans are not buying your music, you are not an asset... you are a liability, even unto yourself. Hence, do anything you can, and as much as you can to forge the closest relationships possible. And, a perfect example is a family.

I believe you will agree that, relation aside, the closest family members are the ones who see and interact with each other often, as opposed to members who simply show up at graduations, weddings, reunions or funerals. Hence, as an artist, *you* are the head of a "family," of which members include your fans. And, as all members must be nurtured and cared for by the heads of households, as the figurative head, it is your obligation and responsibility to touch base with your family members (fans) as often, and in as many ways as possible.

This can include:

1) **Mailing List**
   A regular mailing list to keep them apprised of news and career developments. If your career is highly active, a bi-weekly list will probably be appropriate. If your career is less active, then a monthly list is acceptable. In both cases, always insure that you have something new to say about what you are currently doing.

2) **Discussion List**
   A discussion list, whereby, you establish a one-on-one contact and actually participate with your fans a few hours per week, as opposed to your list being one of many fan lists hosted by an unfamiliar party. Fans, generally, understand that you probably lead a fairly busy life. However, your personal participation will go far in guaranteeing a lifelong allegiance to you and your music.

3) **"Fan" Discounts**
   Special "fan" discounts to them on new music.

4) **"Fan" Songs**
   Songs created especially for them in an effort to show your appreciation for their alliance with you. Now, this need not be brand new music, but music that you have, possibly, placed on the "back burner," so to speak.

5) **Customized Fan Press Kits**
Personally sending them a sort of press kit that has been customized for fans. This might seem slightly expensive at the onset, but will pay for itself many times over in the course of your career and life.

6) **Contests & Giveaways**
Holding special contests and giveaways exclusively for them. Be sure to make your prizes worth their attention, value-wise.

7) **Gift Certificates**
Providing them with the opportunity to win gift certificates, both related and unrelated to your music.

8) **Raffles**
Holding raffles exclusively for your fans and, again, that come with value-perceived prizes.

9) **Area Car Washes**
Work together, with your fans, to raise money for a local cause or charity.

10) **Mall Signings**
How about hanging out in the mall for a day, and doing a signing? Even better, hook up with a mall music store to get even better exposure during your signing by passing out flyers on your music.

11) **Mall Giveaways**
Personally give away FREE copies of your singles for a day at a mall, directing mall patrons to stop in at the mall music store and pick up your CD. Make sure your single (which you can either have made at your manufacturer or burn yourself) has your web site and contact info on its label.

12) **Poster Mail-Out**
Do a poster mail-out campaign to fans who bought your CD.

13) **Fan Birthdays**
Put a form on your web site that asks for your fans' name, mailing address and birthday, while assuring them that you will keep their personal information private. Then, on their birthdays, surprise them with a gift. You could also send your fan a cute song specifically customized for them. Think that won't be memorable and make a lifelong customer?

14) **Fans As Street Teams**
Why not turn your fans into promotional street teams? After all, besides you, who knows you and your music better? And, who would ever be more passionate about it than you?

Above all...don't sell your CD for $18.99 (I've even seen some for $22.99), especially in today's market. Plain and simple...it just won't work. Price? $9.99-$11.99 TOPS! And, even at $11.99, you had *better* have some bonus track *and* some serious multimedia happening.

I'm sure you can dream up even more ways to reach out to your fans in the interest of sealing a lifelong relationship with them. Everyone, regardless of their status in life, appreciates recognition to some degree. Your fans will dearly love you for showing them you care about them.

The point is to get your fans to feeling that they truly know you, and that you are not simply interested in the amount of money you can make off them with your music. In other words, don't allow them to feel as though they are being used and that, outside of their parting with their money, they are of little or no consequence to you...that the only time they will hear from you again, is when your next CD is released.

Above all, forging a warm and honest relationship with your fans, while also providing them with some, all or even more of the above elements, will pay off far more via word-of-mouth exposure than you can possibly ever imagine. And, it is certainly something that fans are unaccustomed to receiving from artists or labels. But, you have the opportunity right here...right now to change their perspective. After all, since most artists are *not* involved with their fans to the degrees above, your being one of the first to do so could, eventually, make you one of your genre's most pioneering and prized staples.

Great article, huh? By the way, be friendly at concerts and performances, too. Don't take the attitude that you're something special just because you're the artist. As Kenny mentioned, this is, in most cases, the way your fans *expect* you to act, but just think of the impact you'll make if after the show you take the time to come out, introduce yourself, and hang out with them. Remember, these are the people who are going to help bring you more sales in the future!

How to Build a Powerful (and Effective!) Mailing List

Mass Mailing in a Social Media Age?

I have made reference several times in this book to the concept of building and managing a mailing list of your fans and customers. So let's talk about that for a chapter or so.

A successful, long-term marketing campaign *demands* you build and maintain a mailing list. I know, I know… the focus in today's world is all *social networking*. An actual newsletter sent via email seems *so yesterday*, right? Wrong! Social networking is not enough. While posting status updates via Facebook is an *immediate* form of communication with your fans, delivery of that message is sporadic. Not everyone on Facebook is going to see every status update you post. By comparison, if you have a regular email list of fans to send updates to, that message actually resides in your recipient's inbox. So the chances are better your message will actually be seen and read by your fans and followers, even if it isn't as immediate. Plus, keep in mind that there are a lot of folks out there who are *not* using Facebook yet! Shocking, but true!

As I emphasized in the previous chapter, *repeated* exposure to your music, month after month, even year after year, will result in sales for you. For every fan who buys a CD or MP3 package, there are likely ten more who, for various reasons, have put off buying your music. A mailing list allows you to kindly, gently remind each of them that your music is still out there, waiting for them to add it to their library.

I have found great success selling music through my *Fan List*. As I demonstrated in the last chapter, one of the ways I encourage people to join this list is to offer them incentives available only to subscribers. This includes not only discount prices on CDs and download "packages," but the opportunity to provide feedback on new songs, help with promotion (yes, I solicit fans to help with both Internet and concert promotion!), or vote for songs they'd like to have transcribed into sheet music. I also give away CDs and sheet music to random subscribers to encourage them to not only remain on the list, but to actually take the time to read the newsletter. I offer my subscribers *amazing deals* they just won't find on my web site.

Your mailing list is the lifeblood of your relationship with your buyers and fans. As you write your newsletter, let your excitement about new music projects you're working on come through. If you do, your fans will share in that excitement. Solicit their feedback on a regular basis, and when a fan emails you, respond to them and acknowledge their value to you. While your fans think YOU are important, when you respond to their emails and comments, let them know how important THEY are to you! Let your fans ride the wave of your successes with you, and give them easy access to you. By doing this, you can be assured that no matter what happens, you'll always have a mailing list full of people who will not only support you financially, but will also be a constant source of encouragement to you.

This is why one of your biggest goals should be to not only sell your music, but to motivate fans to subscribe to your newsletter. Once they've signed up, you have a connection to them that will last as long as they hang on to that email address. Your fan list becomes a pool of resources for you to draw from for so many things: promotion help, booking, networking, marketing data, advice, fan feedback and, of course, sales! Your subscribers are the people who will help you succeed!

You should make your newsletter sign-up form a primary function of your web site. Not only by having an obvious "subscribe" page for your newsletter, but also by adding a newsletter signup option to your order process, so that when a customer places an order, they choose right then and there, whether to subscribe to your mailing list. If you are using your own shopping cart system (I described some options earlier in this book), create a field or a checkbox on your final order page giving your buyer the opportunity to opt into your mailing list. I do this by adding a simple drop down menu to my order page that includes this text:

> "Would you like to receive David's email newsletter? It's sent about once every two months to announce new sheet music releases, concert events, and album project updates. If you do NOT wish to receive that, choose 'No Thanks' to opt-out here..."

Folks have three options to select from: "Yes, Please.", "No, Thank You." or "I'm Already Subscribed." But they always have to choose an option. So for every order that comes through, there's a good chance I'm adding a new fan to my mailing list.

Aside from your web site, the best way to promote your newsletter and start building your mailing list is to include your newsletter sign up information in virtually every conversation you have online. That includes email conversations, responses to comments/messages people send you via the social networks, and in any messages you post to forums or discussion groups. At the end of every message I write, I include this simple statement:

"Sign up for my newsletter, 'Notes from the Piano', at http://www.davidnevue.com/subscribe.htm" .

I just add it to the bottom of my "signature."

TIP: In the last chapter I talked about addressing the *fear* your visitors may have about buying online. People have fears about joining mailing lists on web sites, too. So on your newsletter sign up page, assure your visitors that their email information is private, won't be given or sold to anyone else and that they can remove themselves from your list anytime they want.

Tools of the Trade

I've talked about why you should start an email list and how to motivate people to subscribe, but how do you actually manage your list? There are a number of software programs available to make managing email lists easier. The two discussed the most are Constant Contact (http://www.constantcontact.com) and Campaign Monitor (http://www.campaignmonitor.com). I use the latter.

With Campaign Monitor, you can create your email list (just give it a name) and set it up to accept data entry from your web site "subscribe" form that includes pretty much anything you want. My newsletter sign-up form requests the visitor's first and last name, as well as their email address and physical mailing address. The only fields I *require* be filled out are the name and email address fields, but I tell subscribers that if they include their physical address, I'll send them specific notices (and even a postcard in the mail) when I play concerts in their area. Having the physical location of your customer is important, because it makes targeting specific regions for concert booking and promotion so much easier. When the customer fills out the sign up form and submits it via my web site, that data gets automatically entered into my Campaign Monitor database.

Side Note: If you're interested in sending out postcards to customers to advertise concert events, new album releases or anything else, check out Vistaprint (http://www.vistaprint.com) and Overnight Prints (http://www.overnightprints.com). Both services let you design your own postcards, either by using their pre-made templates (customizable with your text) or letting you upload your own artwork to their service. In just a few days, those sharp looking postcards will be delivered to your door. If you prefer, these services will even mail the postcards out to your mailing list for you, saving you the hassle of applying labels and postage! I have used both services and can recommend either one.

Once a customer signs up for your mailing list using either Constant Contact or Campaign Monitor, their data is kept in that database. You can export this data anytime for marketing purposes. If you want to keep the information in your own database program, something you use on the side, you can do that. In fact, that is what I do and what I recommend. I use Campaign Monitor, and when someone subscribes, their data goes into the Campaign Monitor database online, but I also take those subscribers and import them into my own database software. I feel more secure having my customer data in more than one place. I would hate to build up a huge mailing list of 10,000 fans and then have it destroyed or compromised by some fluke virus or web site hacker! Always keep a local backup of your mailing list!

You'll notice that both Constant Contact and Campaign Monitor charge fees for their services. With Campaign Monitor, you only pay when you actually send out an email. They charge $5.00 + 1¢ per recipient. So a message sent to a mailing list of a thousand people will cost you $15.00. Constant Contact, on the other hand, charges monthly and based upon how many email addresses you send to. You'll always pay at least $15.00 a month, and that will allow you to send to up to 500 recipients. As the number of people in your list grows, your price grows too, but on a monthly basis. Personally, I prefer Campaign Monitors pricing model, and that's why I use them. I only pay when I actually send out an email to mailing list subscribers.

I am sure at this point you are asking, "Why pay? Can't I just send an email to my fan list using my email account?" The answer is yes, you can do that, but the larger your email list becomes, the more difficult it is to manage in this way. Plus, most email clients, like YahooMail, Google's Gmail, Hotmail and so on, really frown on seeing one message sent to a huge list of people. They just assume you are using your email account to spam others and if they think that, they'll shut you down.

Another reason to go with a professional list management service is the "spam" factor. Campaign Monitor and Constant Contact are both respected email services, so most spam filtering companies allow messages from these services through their filters. That means that when you send an email blast to your fans via Campaign Monitor, your message is much more likely to actually get past all the spam filters out there and make it into your fans' inbox. It's not guaranteed, but it does make a difference.

Finally, both Campaign Monitor and Constant Contact provide some great stats about your mailings. You can see how many were received, read, bounced and who unsubscribed or even flagged you as spam. You also get some great reporting tools with those accounts, so there are many good reasons to pay for the service.

I would be remiss if I didn't recommend you check out FanBridge (http://www.fanbridge.com) also. FanBridge is a list management service designed specifically for musicians to help them build a fan base using the current social networking trends. The whole point of FanBridge, really, is to make list management and social network communication fun and easy. FanBridge gives you a mailing list sign-up form that you can put just about anywhere, not just your web site, but also MySpace and Facebook. Using their service you can send out some really nice looking newsletters with links built right in to purchase your music. It's free to try, but if you decide to stick with it, pricing starts at $9/month for up to 1,000 messages sent.

If you want to try something that's free, there are options out there. I've had good luck using Yahoo's Group list program in the past. You'll find this at http://groups.yahoo.com/ . The service is somewhat outdated, but still works well and makes it quick and easy to set up your own mailing list. You can call your list whatever you want, for example, mylistname@yahoogroups.com . Yahoo Groups will provide you the HTML to add to your web page to allow your customer to subscribe to your mailing list directly from your web site. Once your list is created and you have subscribers, all you need to do is send your email to the address you created (mylistname@yahoogroups.com) and your message will be distributed to every subscriber. It is as simple as that.

The disadvantage of Yahoo Groups (and others like it), however, is that your subscriber has to go through a third-party system to sign up for your list. In early 2002 (yes, it was that long ago that I was using this service!), I was curious how many potential subscribers I was losing due to that additional step and I set up a system to track the sign-up rate. Guess what? I found that 50-60% of potential subscribers dropped out after arriving at the Yahoo Group sign-up form. Yikes!

So, I decided to investigate email software, something I could purchase and set up on my own server to eliminate the Yahoo "middle man." For a while, I settled on Group Mail (http://www.group-mail.com) . My subscriber sign-ups doubled once I got this set up on my own server. I was really excited about it! So, I switched to this program for several months, but in doing so I learned a very big lesson: managing your own email list server is a huge amount of work! Although my sign-ups doubled, many of those extra sign-ups were bogus email addresses. So, I was constantly dealing with bounces, lost emails and other irritating hassles. One of my targeted email lists grew to over 20,000 subscribers very quickly, but I was pulling out my hair with technical problems every time I sent out a newsletter. In the end, I returned to Yahoo Groups. Life was easier that way!

In the fall of 2003, I discovered another email software program that is free and hosted entirely online. It's called Dada Mail, and you can find it at http://dadamailproject.com/ . I used it for many years and liked it very much. It made for a nice compromise between Yahoo Groups and Group Mail. There is some configuration involved in the set up, including some cgi script stuff that isn't too terribly difficult to figure out. The installation instructions at the Dada Mail site are fairly simple and straightforward to follow. I was able to figure it out, and I'm not exactly a programming wiz. If you can't figure it out, the Dada Mail service will install it for you for $100.

Dada Mail is a very easy mailing list manager to use, and I used it for years. I found, however, that I wanted more advanced features, like the reporting Campaign Monitor provides, and I found, over time, that more and more of my emails were getting flagged as spam. These two factors are what finally drove me to switch to Campaign Monitor. I've been with them for two or three years now, and am very pleased with their service.

If you'd like to find out more about *free* email list managers out there, once again, just Google it. You'll find lots out there to read and research. Here's a short list:

MailChimp: http://www.mailchimp.com/
ListPower: http://www.listpower.com/
Freelists: http://www.freelists.org/
phplist: http://www.phplist.com/

In addition to everything I've described above, it's entirely possible that your web hosting company offers some kind of free list management software with your hosting account. CD Baby, for example offers a great email management system as part of their hosting program, which you can find at http://www.hostbaby.com. Be sure to consider that possibility. It may save you some money.

Email Confirmations = Missed Opportunities

Whenever someone subscribes to your newsletter, you should be sending them some kind of email to confirm their subscription and to thank them for subscribing. Guess what? This is another opportunity to market your music.

Why not advertise your music, your CDs and/or other products in your subscription "thank you" email? It may be that you just had this great conversation with a fan, and they signed up for your newsletter. Isn't the email confirmation they receive after subscribing the *perfect* time to offer them a special discount on your music or other merchandise?

You don't even have to get verbose. It can be as simple as including a message that says, "Thank you very much for subscribing to my newsletter! I promised you a special discount on my CDs if you subscribed, and here it is! Order my latest CD using the link below and get 20% off the regular price..." You get the idea. You can use the subscription confirmation email to give your subscriber discounts on your music, booking information, or a link to contests you're running. Think of the possibilities! If you are going to send out email confirmation messages, you might as well use them to their full potential.

The same is true, by the way, for "unsubscription" confirmation emails. If someone unsubscribes from your email list, it may be your last chance to pitch your music to that customer. Don't miss that opportunity.

13 Rules for Sending Successful Emails & Newsletters to Your Fans

When You Send Out Your Newsletter…

1) **Make it count.** Don't send out a newsletter unless you have something newsworthy to share, something your fans will care about. *Say something important!* Don't just blather on about random stuff, and don't send out the same newsletter copy over and over again for the solo purpose of "advertising" without having some kind of tangible reason for it. Your fans don't want to feel like you're just hitting them with ads. Make each newsletter interesting and new. Surely, each and every month you can find at least one thing to say about your music and/or music career that's important, exciting and newsworthy? If you don't have something newsworthy to share, that's an indication that you're not doing enough to

further your music career. You're stagnating. Kick yourself in gear. Stop watching TV. Shut down those video games. You're wasting time!

2) **Use a killer subject line.** The subject line of your email has incredible influence over whether your recipient actually opens and reads your newsletter. Yes, true fans will read just about anything you send them (so long as you don't abuse their email address and start spamming them… see #1 above and #7 below), but most of the folks who sign up for your mailing list will be casual fans at best. Whatever the main point of your newsletter for that particular issue, call that out in the subject line. For example, if you're sending out an email to announce a concert event, put the basic event information in your newsletter subject line; "Pianist David Nevue in Concert in Your Town - May 15th." The subject line might also be a call to action; "Pianist David Nevue on Tour Near You… Book a House Concert!" If you've got a new CD release, call that out. "David Nevue's New Album Just Released!" Use your subject line to get your fan's attention and give them a clue as to the content of your newsletter. Give them a taste of what's inside, and if they're interested, they'll read it.

3) **Remind your recipient why they are receiving it.** In your newsletter introduction, remind your reader that they are receiving your newsletter because they signed up for it either via your web site or at a concert event. State that you never add anyone to your mailing list unless they specifically signed up for it (this is true, right?) and then give your reader a link to opt out of future emails and unsubscribe if they so desire. This is a courtesy.

4) **State your most important news first.** People are busy and in a hurry. Get to your biggest news first, so that if the reader only reads the top third of your newsletter, they'll see it! If you have a main point of the newsletter, say a big concert coming up, a new album release, a TV appearance or you want feedback from your fans, get to the point quickly.

5) **Keep it short.** Don't overwhelm your reader with *too much information*. The reader isn't going to read every word you write and *the more you write the less your recipient will read*. It feels exhausting to open an email and see paragraph after paragraph of text. If you have articles or blogs you've written that you want to let your fans know about, don't include the entire text of the blog in your email! Just give them the title of your blog and include the link to the blog/article on your web site. That's one of the primary purposes of your newsletter, after all – to drive people back to your web site. Be concise.

6) **Ask for feedback and/or help.** Your newsletter is a communication tool, so encourage two-way communication! Ask fans to give you feedback on your web site or new music you're working on. Do they have a favorite song or album of yours? Ask them what it is and why. Do they want you to tour their area? Find out, and if so ask if they can help you find a venue. Need help promoting a show? Ask. Your fans will help you if you give them a chance.

7) **Don't annoy your fans.** You don't need to send your newsletter out every day or every week. Keep it to once a month at most unless there is *really big news* that just can't wait. If your messages show up in your fans' inbox too often, they may begin to feel like you are abusing their email address. You don't want to annoy your fans. Again, when you send out a newsletter, make it count. Say something important. Your fans have trusted you with their email address. Don't make them regret it.

8) **Don't be selfish.** Yes, your newsletter is primarily about "you," but give your newsletter the appearance of being "others oriented" as well. Talk about charities you support and are involved with.

Share opportunities you've had to help others. If you put on a successful benefit concert recently, talk about it, and show how it helped others in need. Encourage fans to contribute to a cause.

9) **Give something back to your fans.** In each of your newsletters, feature a "goodie" of some sort, something cool that's only for your newsletter subscribers. Maybe that's a "sneak peak" at an upcoming album release. Perhaps it's a big, big discount on purchases. Those kinds of things motivate your readers, and if you do it consistently, your fans will be eager to read your newsletter as soon as they see it in their inbox.

10) **Be funny (if you can).** People like to be entertained. Make your newsletter enjoyable to read.

11) **Check your spelling!** Typos make you look lazy and sloppy at best, and stupid at worst. *The more typos you have, the less forgiving people are* when they see them. Use a spell checker, but don't rely on it entirely as many "typos" are actually words that are mistyped or misspelled. For example, perhaps you meant to write the word "your" but you wrote "you," leaving off the "r." Or you wrote "their," but the grammatically proper word to use is "they're" or "there." As you can see, these words would all pass a spell checker, but they are wrong. I will never forget the time I sent out a newsletter containing the phrase "pubic download" instead of "public download." Just imagine my horror when a fan pointed that out to me. Proofread your newsletters! Even better, have someone else (who is a good speller and understands grammar) do it for you. Writing intelligently is important and if you don't, it'll cost you readers.

12) **Consider the spam filters.** There are certain words that you can bet spam filters are going to key in on, and if you include those in your email, there's a good chance your newsletter will never even be seen by many of your intended recipients. Don't overuse words like "free," "buy now!," "money back guarantee," "limited time only," or "Call now!" Never use any of those phrases in your subject line and DON'T OVERUSE CAPS. Consider this: if your newsletter reads like an advertisement, a spam filter will probably decide it *is* an advertisement.
Read this: http://www.mailchimp.com/articles/how_spam_filters_think/
and this: http://www.trumba.com/help/email/watchwords.aspx

13) **Use a unique "from" address, just in case.** Create a special email address that serves only as the "from" address of your newsletter. Why? Because inevitably your email will get flagged as spam by someone (it happens!) or the spam filters themselves may eventually blacklist you (it's possible.). If that should ever happen, you want the email address that gets blacklisted to be one that you don't use for any other purpose. Do NOT use your primary business email address as your "from" address!

Tip: On both your newsletter sign up page and your subscription confirmation email, inform your subscriber what your newsletter "from" email address will be and request they add it to their approved "whitelist" or "friend lists." That way your newsletter will always get through.

Royalties: Getting What's Coming to You

Before I head into the last third of the book, I need to address the subject of royalty payments. Did you realize that if your music gets played *anywhere* – including Internet radio – you may be due royalties? If you don't have your music registered with the appropriate organizations, you could very well be leaving money on the table.

If you reside in the United States, you are probably already familiar with BMI, ASCAP and perhaps even SESAC. All three are Performing Rights Organizations (PROs) that monitor royalties due songwriters and publishers from "public use" of their compositions in the U.S.. This includes the monitoring of song plays on cable television, traditional broadcast radio, background music services like Muzak, web sites, clubs, restaurants, hotels, hold music and so on. Legally speaking, any organization that plays a song you own the copyright for should be reporting that fact and paying a royalty to your PRO organization for use of that music.

Another royalty organization you may or may not be familiar with is SoundExchange (http://www.soundexchange.com). SoundExchange is different than the PROs in that they monitor royalties due not to the songwriter, but to the copyright holder of the sound recording itself… that is, the actual recorded performance. If you, as the artist, have copyright ownership of both the song (the composition) and the sound recording (the recorded performance), you should expect potential royalties from two places. First, as the owner and/or publisher of the song, you receive royalties from the PROs. Second, as the copyright holder and/or publisher of the sound recording, you receive royalties from SoundExchange. Two different copyrights, two different organizations.

To get what's coming to you, royalty-wise, you need to register your music with not only the PRO of your choice, but also with SoundExchange.

Let's first discuss the PROs; BMI, ASCAP and SESAC. Many artists struggle with deciding which organization to choose. You can only register with one PRO at a time, and once you affiliate yourself with a PRO, it's difficult to undo that and switch to another. So who should you go with? BMI, ASCAP or SESAC?

If you're a relatively unknown artist, you can eliminate SESAC (http://www.sesac.com) from the running. SESAC is difficult to get into and very selective about who they let in. They are the smallest of the three PROs (by choice) choosing, to quote their web site, "quality over quantity." However, if you do manage to get in, SESAC takes an active approach to working with the artists they represent. If you are an established professional artist without a PRO, or if you're an artist with a PRO who wants to change your affiliation, SESAC would be a good choice to look into. If you're an up-and-coming artist, however, you will likely need to choose between ASCAP (http://www.ascap.com) and BMI (http://www.bmi.com).

Which is the better organization? I've read all kinds of debate on this. You'll find artists arguing for and against both ASCAP and BMI for a variety of reasons; some complain that they never get paid, others complain they can't get anyone at their PRO to talk to them. I've also read comments from artists on both sides who are quite satisfied with their PRO of choice, whether that be BMI or ASCAP. It is difficult to get a feel for which is really "better." Everyone seems to have a different experience and opinion. I will say this; ASCAP is the largest of the PROs and is owned by songwriters, publishers and composers. BMI is a corporation and is owned by broadcasters. So you could say, theoretically, that ASCAP, being owned by artists and publishers, should be more "on your side" and sympathetic to you than BMI is. However, I have heard as many artists complain about the service they receive from ASCAP as I have the service at BMI, so I don't know that that really matters.

Personally, I chose BMI. Why? Because when I first started my career, an independent artist I respected recommended them. I have never regretted my choice. I receive royalty checks on a quarterly basis, and some very nice ones at that. What would have happened if I had chosen ASCAP instead all those years ago? Who knows? Maybe I'd have received more royalties… or maybe far less. There's no way to know. When it comes to you choosing for yourself, just read up on both services and go with your gut. It costs $35 to join ASCAP. Joining BMI is free.

How do BMI and ASCAP determine royalties due you? Both use different methods and formulas, but it basically comes down to a combination of sample surveys and data retrieved from play logs and cue sheets provided by the stations, broadcasts and services that report to them. In other words, the PRO organizations rely on not only the reports provided to them from broadcasters, but also on findings from any data samples they gather as they police various services and organizations that might use your music.

What that means, in reality, is that you may or may not get paid a royalty if your music is played somewhere. If your music is used by a company, and that use is reported to the PROs, then you'll get your royalty. However, if the company in question doesn't report the use of your music to the PROs, or if they have a *blanket license* to use music from the PROs, then you won't see a dime from that. The only way you'd see a royalty is if your actual song was reported or if your PRO happened to see your music used on one of the data samples they receive. This is true regardless of which PRO you sign up with.

The *blanket license option* in particular is frustrating in terms of how it affects artists and the royalties due them. PROs offer smaller media organizations, including most Internet radio broadcasters, the option of paying a blanket license fee to stay "legal." Once they pay this blanket license fee, the organization can play whatever music they want to. This is an easy, hassle-free option for the broadcaster because they don't have to worry about monitoring, logging and reporting every single song they play. For the PRO, it's easier as well, as they don't have to worry about tracking songs from a million small broadcasters. Once the media company pays the blanket license fee, the PROs take that money and distribute it however they see fit. Everyone is happy with this arrangement – except the artists, of course – whose music is being played but who never see a cent of royalties because the use of their music is never actually reported.

So why bother registering your songs with the PROs at all? Because if you become a successful artist and your music does get played in larger markets or by any of the larger media companies, you will, eventually, see some royalties. In other words, there's really no good reason NOT to register your songs with a PRO. You register, then wait and hope. Perhaps one day you'll see a nice check in the mail. When I first registered with BMI, it was quite a long while (2-3 years?) before I ever saw a check. But now I receive checks every single quarter without fail.

Here's some reading for you on this topic…

How Music Royalties Work:	http://entertainment.howstuffworks.com/music-royalties7.htm
ASCAP vs. BMI Commentary:	http://www.musicmarketing.com/2004/08/ascap_vs_bmi_th.html
BMI vs. ASCAP (CD Baby forums):	http://cdbaby.org/stories/06/08/10/4085523.html
ASCAP vs. BMI (TAXI forums):	http://bit.ly/9K0VPi

Now let's discuss SoundExchange (http://www.soundexchange.com). If you're doing your job promoting your music online via Internet radio, Pandora.com and other such places (which I will be discussing shortly), there is great potential for you to earn some very nice royalty checks from SoundExchange.

SoundExchange administers royalties from the music played on streaming digital music services, which includes digital cable companies, satellite television services (like Music Choice and MUZAK), satellite radio (Sirius XM), and most Internet radio networks (including Pandora). As an Independent artist, you are much more likely to get airplay via the Internet than via traditional broadcast media and so you are more likely to earn royalties via SoundExchange than you would via a traditional PRO. In fact, if you've had Internet airplay in the past and have never signed up for SoundExchange, you probably have royalties waiting for you right now. By the time I got around to signing up for SoundExchange several years ago, I had accumulated over $1300 in royalties. I was pleasantly surprised to receive that first check and I've received payments each and every quarter since. Is SoundExchange waiting for you to claim your money too? Maybe. As of this writing, SoundExchange is holding over 100 million in unclaimed funds by artists. A statistic recently posted on the SoundExchange web site stated that nearly 25% of all the royalties they collect remained unclaimed by artists. That's an amazing amount of cash just sitting around waiting for someone to claim it.

Here are more articles and web sites I recommend you visit:

The Top 10 Reasons Artists Don't Register With SoundExchange
http://soundexchange.com/2010/04/23/top-ten-reasons-artists-dont-register-with-soundexchange/

Take Your Royalty Check, SoundExchange Begs…
http://articles.latimes.com/2010/mar/12/business/la-fi-ct-music13-2010mar13

Does SoundExchange Have Money For You?
http://soundexchange.com/performer-owner/does-sx-have-money-for-you/

Signing up for SoundExchange is free. If you haven't done it yet, do it now. You can sign up at http://soundexchange.com/performer-owner/performer-srco-home/

Now, let's sum up everything we've talked about in this book so far...

13 Things to Do Right Now to Improve Your Internet Sales!

As you can see, there's a lot involved in designing and marketing a web site designed to promote and sell your music. There's enough work here to keep you busy for several months! Not everything has to take a lot of time, however. Here are 13 things you can do right now to increase your Internet sales.

1) *Clean Up Your Keywords and Page Titles*
Your page title is the most important part of your web page as far as the search engines are concerned. Make sure your title contains your most strategic keywords but as you do so, remember that your page title must be attractive to a human being as well as the search engine, so keep it short and to the point. Your title should be a brief, concise, one-line ad that will attract your target audience when they see it in a search result.

2) *Submit Your Most Important Pages to Google*
Submitting your web pages to Google is fast and free. Don't wait for the robots to come to you, submit every major page as soon as possible. As you add new pages and or blog postings to your web site, vary your keywords and page titles as appropriate for that page. Use each additional page to target a specific topic of interest to your potential customer. The more pages you have indexed by the search engines, the more likely it is your target customer will find you.

3) *Simplify Your Web Site Design*
Nothing is worse than making a visitor wait to load your page... except perhaps blinding your visitor with animations, killer backgrounds and overdone graphics. Take another, objective look at your web site design. Is it too cluttered? Do an overwhelming number of animations, buttons or links discourage your visitor from spending time on your site? If so, plan a site redesign that will narrow your focus and keep it simple. Remember to limit your visitors' options. Make it *easy* for them to navigate your web site. "More text, less graphics" should be your guide. Use javascript, flash and animated icons with restraint to keep your site fast loading.

4) *Make it Easy to HEAR Your Music*
Make sound samples of your music readily available and obvious. When a new visitor lands on your home page, make that "Listen" link or button easy to find and be sure your sound samples or flash music players are fast loading.

5) *Make it Easy to BUY Your Music*
The more options you give your customer for purchasing your CD and/or downloads, the more likely they are to do so. Accepting credit cards is an absolute must, but beyond this, let them order by phone (a toll-free number if possible), PayPal, send you a check by postal mail, or order by any other means your customers are likely to make use of. Provide easy links to your music on iTunes so that with a click of a button, visitors familiar with iTunes can immediately purchase it.

6) *Make an Offer Too Good to Refuse*
Give your customers a "push" to buy your CDs and or MP3 packages by adding value-added incentives. Offer your customer free stuff if they order your music. Think of who your target audience is and consider what added value item would appeal to them. What would close the deal? The more perceived value you pack into the items you are selling, the more likely you are to make the sale. Also, offer visitors unbelievable deals on your CDs or download packages. If you have more than one CD to sell, offer your visitors a fantastic package deal so that they will be motivated to buy multiple CDs. Finally, make your offers "for a limited time" to encourage your customer to buy NOW, rather than putting it off until later.

7) *Overcome Fear with Desire*
What excuses might your visitors have for NOT buying your music? Address those concerns up front on your sales page and provide a means for your visitor to contact you directly to ask about their concerns. When they do contact you, respond immediately.

8) *Create More Product*
The more product you have to sell, the more *opportunity* you have to sell. Keep working on that new album project, but in the meantime, consider selling sheet music, guitar tabs, album lyric sheets, signed photos, ringtones, signature CDs, band merchandise (tee shirts, mugs, mouse pads, etc.,) live and "bootleg" albums, digital downloads, e-books you've written – anything you can sell.

9) *Stay in Touch*
Use your web site to collect your visitors' email information and make use of it, whether that be via a monthly contest on your web site or via a newsletter that they've subscribed to. Send out a newsletter every month to stay fresh in your customers' minds.

10) *Become Part of Your Fan's Daily Routine*
Be accessible and easy to contact, not only via email, but via the social networks, *especially* Facebook. When a fan or visitor to your web site emails you or comments on a status post you made, respond quickly and pleasantly. Have regular online chat sessions with your fans and get them *involved* in what you're doing by soliciting their feedback and opinions. Work hard at developing that long term relationship because if you do, you'll turn your fans into walking billboards. The more your visitor feels they *know* you (and like you), the more likely they are to support you.

11) *Update, Update, Update!*
Give your visitors a reason to come back to your site again and again. Make visible, weekly updates to your web site and provide readers with information they will be interested in. Consider starting and maintaining a blog or, at the very least, a Twitter account that you update daily. Then embed your Twitter updates into your web site home page to keep it fresh and current (you can do this at http://twitter.com/goodies/widget_profile). Do whatever you can to make your web site "alive" and interactive to keep your visitors coming back.

12) *Use the Microphone*
If you are a performing musician, don't be afraid to make use of the microphone. Fearlessly promote your web site/blog/newsletter/album/contest/whatever from the stage whenever you have the opportunity.

13) Get Your Royalties in Order

There's nothing better than getting an unexpected check in the mail, especially when it happens every three months. Register your songs with a Performing Rights Organization (BMI or ASCAP) and do NOT put this book down for the last time without having signed up for SoundExchange. Any airplay you get *anywhere* online may result in royalty payments you. If you don't register, you'll never see that money. What are you waiting for?

The Best Places to Promote, Sell, and Distribute Your Music Online

Targeting through Product Placement

Having talked extensively about how to promote your music using your own web site, a targeted web site, blogs and newsletters, I now want to branch out into a promotion strategy that works very much like product placement does in film and television. That is, rather than promoting your music on just your official home page or your targeted web site, you strategically place your music on third-party web sites and services where people are already hanging out and discovering new music. To put it another way, you're going to be a musical parasite that feeds on the popularity of other web sites and uses that popularity to your own promotional advantage.

A Thousand Points of Light

To this end, there are tens of thousands of music-related web sites and Online Music Distributors (OMDs) where you can upload your music, set up shop and sell and advertise your CDs and downloads. If you really wanted to, you could find a thousand different web sites to place your music online. But ask yourself, do you really want to manage CD stock, sales, stats, inventory, keep track and stay on top of all those web sites? No, of course you don't! It's just too much. It boggles the mind.

Consider my earlier chapter on search engines. There are *thousands* of search engines on the Internet, but only two of them really matter. So why bother optimizing and submitting your web site for every possible search engine? That's a lot of time and energy used up for very little gain. The same is true for online music promotion and distribution. Though there are a multitude of web sites, OMDs or other "exposure points" where you can promote your music, only a few of those have a large enough user base to generate significant sales and exposure for you. Those are the places you'll want to invest your time.

In this chapter, I'll give you my recommendations for what I consider to be the best places to sell, promote, and distribute your music online. These are the web sites and services you'll want to attach yourself to and create a presence at. I base my choices on three important factors. First, which of these "exposure points" (for lack of a better term) are creating a buzz on the Internet? That is, who has the attention of the press? Secondly, which web sites draw the most traffic from visitors looking for new music? Finally, which of these services are musicians talking about and recommending to one another? All of these factors have influenced my selections.

Setting Up Shop

Before I list my selections, I want to give a strategic overview of how to use these exposure points to draw visitors to your own official artist web site. Understanding this will help you organize your thoughts as you read through this material.

Many of the web sites and services I will suggest give independent artists the tools necessary to create their own artist or product page within their web site. This is really common with OMDs like CD Baby, Amazon.com and ReverbNation.com. You get your own little corner of their store to add your content to - a "mini-store" of sorts. The flexibility you have with your mini-store varies from place to place, but most will allow you to upload audio samples of your music, a photo, and a link to your official web site at the very least. Some offer additional options, such as the ability to offer digital singles or albums which customers can purchase and immediately download. I recommend you first create a presence on the top five or six sites on my list. Later, as you gain time, confidence and experience, you can experiment with the others. That way the process, which can be time consuming, isn't quite so overwhelming.

Your task, as you promote your music to the online world at large, is to use these points of exposure to attract visitors to your music, redirect them to your own official artist page, and once you have them there, encourage them to purchase your music using the marketing methods described in previous chapters. At the very least, you want them to subscribe to your newsletter.

I created the crude diagram below to illustrate the "big picture," which is actually quite simple in concept. Go to where your potential audience hangs out, get their attention, draw them in and pitch your music. Notice how visitors are directed to your web site from all the various targeting points I've discussed throughout this book.

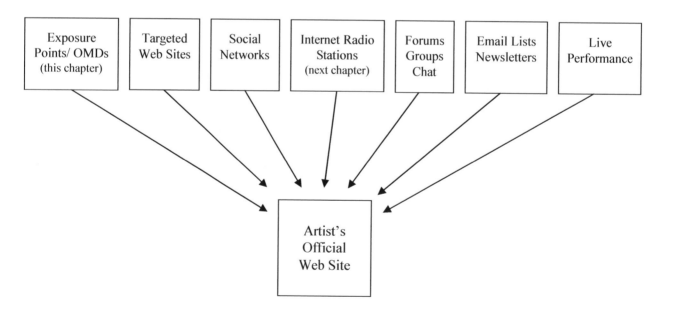

Having prepped you with the general marketing concept, here are my personal picks for the best places on the Internet to promote, sell and distribute your music online...

The Top 12 Places to Promote, Sell and Distribute Your Music....

#1) iTunes - (http://www.apple.com/itunes/) : In terms of digital music distribution and sales in general, iTunes is the #1 place to sell your music. It's the most popular digital music store in business right now, with nearly 70% of the total market share and represents 25% of all music (digital or CD) sold in the United States. With that kind of market share, getting your music on iTunes is a must. One great thing about iTunes is that they give independent music the same respect as major label music. They don't care if you're signed to a label or not, only that your music *sells*. If your song sells better than a song by a major label artist, their song charts will reflect that, regardless of your signing status. In that sense, iTunes offers a level playing field for everyone.

So what's the easiest way to get your music on iTunes? That depends. If you already have an account with CD Baby (http://members.cdbaby.com), the quickest way to get your music on iTunes is to simply opt into CD Baby's digital distribution program. Since you already have your CDs in their catalog, the only additional charge to you for the service is when you make a sale. CD Baby takes 9% from your digital sales as a "maintenance fee." Since iTunes pays out .70¢ for each song sold or up to $7.00 for each album sold, you'll profit roughly .63¢ per song and $6.30 for each album sold on iTunes.

The downside of that 9% fee, however, is that the more sales you make, the more money you're paying into the fee. If you make $2,000 in digital music sales in a given month, CD Baby's 9% fee for that month would amount to $180. Yikes! That's a lot of money to be giving away.

Fortunately, there are other options for distributing your music to iTunes. Of all the services out there, the one I most heartily recommend (aside from CD Baby) is TuneCore (http://www.tunecore.com). They have a great reputation and have been fine-tuning their service for several years now. Plus, digital distribution is their main business, so that's what they focus 100% of their time and resources on.

Getting an album distributed through TuneCore is a simple matter. Just sign up for an account and you'll see how easy it is. They've done a great job of streamlining the process. Best of all, they don't take a percentage of your sales like CD Baby does. They *do*, however, have an annual fee. Your initial cost at TuneCore is $49.99 per album, and then $19.98 per year after that (per album) to continue. For singles, the cost is $9.99 to start and then $9.99 annually per single. So while you're not paying a percentage, you are paying a yearly fee for each album or single you distribute.

Here's a side-by-side comparison of CD Baby and TuneCore's digital distribution services and their cost:

	CD Baby Digital Distribution	TuneCore
Setup Fee:	One-Time fee of $35 per album or $9.00 per single to get an album/single into CD Baby's catalog. After that, submission to all digital music stores is free.	$49.99 per album $9.99 per single (Plus an annual fee each year See below)
Number of Stores Delivered to:	18 different stores listed as of this writing. If new stores are added, there's no additional cost to you.	16 different stores listed as of this writing. If new stores are added, you'll need to pay an additional $1.98 per album to include your music on them.
Percentage of Your Cut Taken:	9%	None
Annual Fee:	None	$19.98 per album per year. $9.99 per single per year.

The bottom line: if you do very little in digital music sales (less than $500 your first year and less than $200 per album per year after that), it's less expensive for you to go through CD Baby. However, if you do more than $500/year in digital music sales, you're going to save a *lot* of money using TuneCore's service. You are planning on *succeeding*, right? I presume so, and if so, TuneCore is probably your best choice in the long run.

Now this doesn't mean you *shouldn't* sign up for CD Baby (see #4 below). It simply means that TuneCore may be a better financial choice when it comes to managing digital music distribution.

Once your music is on iTunes, how do you promote it? Obviously, you want to make your music as easy to find on iTunes as possible. One way to do that is to send out an email to your fan base and ask them to do you a ".99¢ favor" and purchase one of your best songs via iTunes during a pre-determined time period. If you can get 100 people to buy your song during a short span of time, that's going to boost you up the iTunes charts for your given genre, which will improve your chances of being found by new listeners when they are searching and/or browsing the iTunes store looking for music. Just about every time I send out a newsletter, I feature one particular track and encourage my fans to support me with that ".99¢ favor." In this way I keep sales moving and important songs selling.

You can also make your iTunes downloads available to your existing fan base by linking to them directly from your own web site. Apple provides an "iTunes Link Maker" just for this purpose. You'll find that at http://www.apple.com/itunes/linkmaker/ . Just search on your name, click a couple buttons, and iTunes generates the links for you. They'll look something like this:

http://itunes.apple.com/us/artist/david-nevue/id6233886?uo=6

Go ahead. Click the link. Make my day! That link will take you right to my iTunes page.

Using that linkmaker, you can link to your "artist" page, an "album" page, or one particular track on iTunes.

If your fans are prone to buying downloads, chances are excellent that they are already familiar with iTunes and will gladly make use of your iTunes links to buy and download your music. So putting a link from your web site to your downloads on iTunes is something you simply must do. Also be sure to include a link to your iTunes artist page in your newsletters and when you do, encourage your fans to share your iTunes links with their own friends on Facebook as well (in the iTunes music store, click the down arrow beside the buy button of any album and/or song and you'll see a "Share on Facebook" option.) That's a great way for your fans to help you spread your music!

Finally, song titles and album titles are key, much in the same way page titles are key when promoting your web pages on the search engines. If you play cover tunes, especially, iTunes can be used to your tactical advantage as iTunes users are searching, in large part, based on song title. Recording and selling cover songs is a great way to promote yourself in the digital music stores (be sure you acquire the digital licensing rights to the cover songs in question - see the note at the end of this section.) People searching for a particular song may find your arrangement of their favorite tune, preview it, and if they dig it, buy it. That might just result in your making another fan. The best selling tracks on iTunes by independent artists are cover tunes.

iTunes "Bonus" Check: Did you know that iTunes has an affiliate program? It's true. Sign up at http://www.apple.com/itunes/affiliates and you'll earn 5% on every sale coming from your web site links. In other words, you get paid not only when someone buys your song via iTunes, but you get another 5% if that buyer comes from your web site!

Note on Digital Licensing Rights: In order to sell any song via iTunes (or any other digital music service), you must first own all the copyrights to it. If you do not, such as is the case with a cover song, then you need to get a license from the publisher to sell your arrangement of that song. How do you go about doing this?

The simplest way is to visit RightsFlow's Limelight licensing product (see http://rightsflow.com). Just search for the cover song(s) you want to license, enter the details, pay and you're done. It couldn't be easier. You can use Limelight to acquire licenses to sell and distribute both digital and physical products.

Another option is to go through the Harry Fox Agency (HFA) via their licensing web site at http://www.songfile.com . Once you create an account, you can purchase licenses for digital sales and distribution as well as CD sales and distribution.

The cost for both services is about the same. Each charges a processing fee of about $15 per song. In addition, you'll have to pay the current statutory rate of 9.1¢ per digital download you want to sell. So, if you create a license to sell 200 digital downloads, your cost will be about $33.

There is an important difference between the two systems, however. Licenses acquired through RightsFlow never expire. However, licenses purchased through the HFA last only a year, and so must be renewed each year. Overall the RightsFlow Limelight option is more musician friendly.

If you cannot find your particular cover song in the HFA database or via Rightsflow, CD Baby has a well-written explanation of how to acquire digital licensing for cover songs on your own at http://members.cdbaby.com/whatwedo/faq.aspx#faq29 . Follow the directions in that document to proceed.

#2) **Amazon.com** - (http://www.amazon.com) : Amazon.com is by far the Internet's biggest and most popular all-around store. In addition to selling books, electronics, toys and even cheese (yes, you can buy cheese at Amazon.com), they provide a music distribution outlet for independent musicians. Amazon.com offers what it calls the "Advantage" program, allowing independent artists to sell and distribute their CD catalog in the Amazon.com store. You can read all about the Advantage program at http://www.amazon.com/advantage

Once you sign up for Amazon Advantage, you'll need to submit your CD(s) for review. Once your CD(s) are approved (be sure your CDs have bar codes as they are required), Amazon.com will give you a dedicated product page from which you can, to a limited degree, edit your content. You can include your bio, CD descriptions, short editorial reviews and artwork. You can also assign your music to two browseable categories in Amazon's catalog, meaning you have some ability right out of the box to target visitors browsing Amazon.com for a particular style of music. When Amazon.com's stock of your CD titles get low, they'll email you a request for more. Finally, you are paid once per month via an electronic funds transfer directly into your bank account.

The benefits of the Amazon.com Advantage program are obvious: you get to sell your CD on an extremely high-traffic web site, one flowing with people who have money to spend. Also, having your CD on Amazon.com makes it easy for people to find you. Most everyone who shops online knows and trusts the Amazon.com brand. So, if a new fan heard your music somewhere, wants to buy it online, but doesn't know where to look, chances are good one of the first places they'll go to search for your music is Amazon.com.

All this being said, there are some *disadvantages* to Amazon's Advantage program (pun intended). First, there's a $29.95 *annual* fee required to participate. On top of this, Amazon.com takes a whopping 55% of your retail price. So if you sell one of your CDs retail for $12.99, your cut is a meager $5.85. Plus, you never see the customer details, so you have no idea who purchased your CD.

There are ways to *somewhat* overcome these disadvantages, however. In addition to the "Advantage" program, Amazon offers another seller program called "Marketplace" (see http://www.amazon.com/marketplace). Participation in this program is *much* less expensive than Advantage, in that your cost per sale is only 15% of retail plus .99¢ (as opposed to 55% overall). So, from that same $12.99 CD, your cut is $10.05 (you have to do your own shipping, but Amazon compensates you for that). Since you are shipping to the customer yourself, Amazon.com provides you with your customer's shipping information, so you know who purchased your album and where they live. You can also email the customer a shipment notification giving you the ability to not only contact them directly about their order shipment but also to encourage them to sign up for your mailing list. Sounds great, right?

Well, here's the tricky bit: in order to make use of the Amazon.com Marketplace program, your product has to *first* be in Amazon.com's catalog. So you're back to square one. You have to first sign up for Advantage, pay the annual fee, get your CDs approved and in stock, and *then* sign up for Marketplace.

Those of you familiar with CD Baby may be aware that you can have them distribute your physical CDs into Amazon.com's catalog through CD Baby's partner, Super D Distribution. However, I don't recommend you do this. You'll actually make less money if you go that route as Super D buys your CDs from CD Baby at a discount... and then Amazon takes their percentage as well. So your cut gets split twice. You're much better off signing up for the Advantage program and distributing your physical CDs to Amazon.com directly.

Once you have your CDs in Amazon.com's catalog, sign up for Marketplace and set up your CDs to sell for a price that is significantly less than the "new" price you're charging through Advantage. That will encourage buyers to purchase your CDs via Marketplace rather than Advantage. You'll make more money per album that way. For example, from a $12.99 CD you sell via Advantage, your cut is $5.85. However, sell that same CD via Marketplace for just $10.99 and your cut is $8.35. So, as you can see, your earnings per CD sale are significantly more through Marketplace, even if you discount it. However, even if you do this, realize that a vast majority of your Amazon.com buyers will opt to pay full price and buy direct from Amazon rather than clicking on the "Used and New" option to purchase from you via Marketplace. So, even though you make more profit selling through Marketplace, the large bulk of your orders will still come through Advantage.

Does this all sound complicated? Yes, it is a bit. Amazon's system takes a bit of getting used to. It's worth it, however. You really must make your CDs available in the Amazon.com catalog.

If you'd like to see how a completed product page looks, just search for "David Nevue" at Amazon.com under the "Popular Music" category and you'll see my CDs and MP3 albums displayed.

Tip: While Amazon.com's product administration system is confusing at first, its shopping system is quite amazing and very customer-friendly. When you search for an item to buy and view the details for it, Amazon.com will recommend other products to you based on the purchase history of other customers who have bought the same item. You can use this feature to *your* advantage. Encourage your fan base as well as the folks on your street team (see chapter on *Targeting Your Customers to the Max!*) to purchase some of their favorite CDs at Amazon.com, and while they're at it, buy a copy of your CD as well. This way, your CD registers in Amazon.com's database as having been bought in tandem with other music your target audience is likely to search for. As a result, when targeted visitors at Amazon.com are searching for their favorite artists, there is a chance your products will be recommended to them.

Other Ways to Promote Your Music on Amazon.com: Aside from the *Advantage* and *Marketplace* programs, Amazon.com offers these opportunities:

Get Your Music in the Amazon.com MP3 Store: Yes, that's right, you can distribute your digital albums and singles through Amazon's MP3 store at http://mp3.amazon.com as well. How? Sign up for either CD Baby's or TuneCore's digital distribution plan. Either one will get your albums for sale on Amazon.com in MP3 format. I love that Amazon.com sells actual MP3 files as well. It makes it a nice alternative to the iTunes AAC format. I give my buyers a choice for purchasing digital music downloads. They can purchase via iTunes or Amazon's MP3 store, whichever they prefer. So if they prefer a straight MP3 format, I make it easy for them to purchase that through Amazon.com

Sign Up for Artist Central: Signing up for Artist Central allows you to create your own artist-themed page on Amazon.com. You can include a photo gallery, your own banner, upload videos, add MP3s to a player for listening, link to your web site, and add a bio. Once completed, your Artist Central page will show up when people search for your name on Amazon.com. You can also promote your Artist Central page link to your fans, giving them one page on Amazon.com to go to purchase your music. You can sign up for Artist Central at https://artistcentral.amazon.com . For an example, you can view my Artist Central page at http://www.amazon.com/David-Nevue/e/B000APOX12 .

Add Sound Clips for Your CDs: Obviously, having sound clips of your CDs available on Amazon.com is optimal so that people who stumble across your music on the site can preview it. Here's how to submit your sound clips per the Amazon.com web site:

- CDs must be submitted in a jewel case or other sturdy packaging to protect them from damage during transit.
- CDs must have a printed UPC, a barcode for scanning, or both, as well as a complete and accurate track listing, included in the CD jewel case or packaging.
- CDs cannot be sealed, have any plastic or shrink wrap packaging--they must be opened and easily accessible.
- You may not submit homemade copies of CDs--no "burned" or duplicated CDs will be processed.
- Please send one (1) copy of each Advantage album to:

  Amazon.com Advantage / Sound Clips
  701 5TH AVE
  SEATTLE, WA 98104

- CDs submitted for sound clips cannot be returned.
- Do not send any correspondence, orders, or review copies to this address.

To view the most current information about adding sound samples to your CD pages, login to your Advantage account, then click on the HELP link in the upper right, then simply search the help pages for "Sound Samples" to bring up a link describing the current submission guidelines.

Recommendation Features: Amazon.com has many "Recommend-it" style features that you can utilize to promote your own CDs within the Amazon.com store. For example, you can use Amazon.com's *Listmania!, Make a Search Suggestion* and *So You'd Like to...* guides to recommend your music to visitors searching for other items in the store. To make use of these features, search for products (not just music) on Amazon.com that you believe your target audience may be searching for. As you do, keep an eye in the left and right columns (as well as below the product listings) for opportunities to offer your advice and suggestions to other buyers browsing these particular products.

Ask Fans to Add Reviews: One of the most popular features at Amazon.com are the reviews left by people who have purchased CDs from them. These reviews can greatly influence whether someone commits to buying your CD. To populate Amazon.com with good reviews of your music, email your fan list and ask them to go to Amazon.com, view your CD/MP3 album product pages and add positive customer reviews. The more positive reviews you have, the more likely potential buyers are to go ahead and buy your CD.

While the costs of putting your CDs on Amazon.com may be a bit discouraging to you (a 55% cut feels huge, I know), music lovers *will* find you there. Lots of them. Of all the places I sell my physical CDs on the Internet, I sell more CDs on Amazon.com than anywhere else, even my own web site. So for me, it's well worth the cost of putting my CDs there. And as for MP3 sales, while my #1 source of digital music income is iTunes, the #2 payer is Amazon.com. It's significant.

#3) Pandora Radio - (http://www.pandora.com) : If you spend any time at all online, you are probably familiar with Pandora radio. If you aren't, many people you hang out with are. It's that big. The gist is this; as a user, you can create your own "radio station" based upon your favorite artists. For example, if you're a fan of the band Dire Straits, you can create a "Dire Straits" station that features music from Dire Straits while also playing songs by other artists of a similar style. You can create a multitude of "stations" based on your favorite artists. As you listen, you can give "Thumbs Up" to songs and artists you like and want to hear more of, or "Thumbs Down" to songs you never want to hear again. It's radio customized to your specific musical tastes. The more you listen, the more you love it.

As an independent artist, you can submit your own music to Pandora, and if you're accepted, Pandora will begin recommending your music to listeners who enjoy your particular style of music. So, for example, if your music sounds like Usher and Pandora classifies you in that vein, fans with an "Usher" station will be introduced to your music. There's really no better way to get your music out to new listeners on the Internet.

How do you benefit from this? Two ways; first, listeners can purchase your music through "Buy" links that give them a choice to purchase your song on iTunes, Amazon.com (CD) or AmazonMP3 (MP3). The second benefit is even better: royalties. Here's an incredible statistic: If you take all the royalties paid out to artists from radio – whether that be royalties paid for traditional radio or Internet radio – 40% of all the royalties paid to artists comes from plays on Pandora radio. Yes, you read that right. That's how huge it is. If you are registered with SoundExchange and get significant play on Pandora you'll see some very nice royalties.

Promoting your music on Pandora is somewhat automatic once it's on there. If folks like your music when they hear it and give it a thumbs up, that impacts the extent to which your music gets introduced to new people. Beyond that, just let your fans know your music is on Pandora. Have them create stations based on your name, and then ask them to share their stations with their friends on Facebook and other social networks they are involved with.

How do you submit your music? Take a look at Pandora's submission guidelines at http://blog.pandora.com/faq/#31 . Read them carefully. You'll notice that not only do you need a bar code on your CD(s), a physical CD version of your album must be available for purchase on Amazon.com as well. So take care of those requirements first if you haven't already. You'll also need to sign up for a Pandora account if you don't have one already. If you do, just log into Pandora, and then submit your CD under that account.

Finally, you are only allowed to submit one album at a time to Pandora, and you can only submit two tracks from that album for the initial review. So if you have multiple CDs in your catalog, submit your two best songs from your best album first. Then wait for that to be approved before attempting to submit anything else. The approval time to get in Pandora's database is quite long – a matter of months – but once you do get in, you're going to get a lot of exposure from that.

Once your album is approved, Pandora will send you an email notification with instructions on where to send in your CD for full consideration. At that point, Pandora will consider your entire CD in order to select tracks to put into rotation.

#4) CD Baby - (http://www.cdbaby.com) : I've referred to CD Baby numerous times in this book. There's good reason for that. If you're an artist selling music online, this is one web service you must be hooked into.

CD Baby was started in 1997 by Derek Sivers, an independent musician who designed the site as a means to sell his own music on the web. He opened the store up to his fellow musicians and they joined in droves. It became a HUGE success. By 2002, Derek had stopped working on CD Baby full-time, letting his capable employees handle much of the day-to-day routine. Over the course of the next few years, Derek found himself wanting to do other things. So, in 2008, Derek sold his company to Disc Makers who, in my opinion, have taken the CD Baby storefront to a whole other level of cool. They made a huge investment in time, money and resources and completely revitalized the site, all the while retaining the original indie-music-friendly feel. Derek may be gone, but CD Baby is still a company run predominantly by independent musicians. And you can tell.

Today, CD Baby is the second largest seller of independent music on the Internet, second only to Amazon.com. Boasting over 200,000 artists, CD Baby is the best organized, most talked about Internet storefront for musicians. As of this writing, CD Baby has paid out $157 MILLION dollars to independent artists! That alone should be motivation enough for you to sign up.

There is a setup fee of $35 per CD to get your music on the site. From that fee, CD Baby creates a beautiful page for you in their store complete with sound samples for your visitors to stream. You can use that page to take CD and music download orders, link to your official web site, include any sales copy you want, and solicit CD reviews from visitors. Also, once your CD is in CD Baby's catalog, you can opt to make it available for order at a wholesale price to retail stores nation-wide. CD Baby has a partnership deal with Super D One-Stop distribution (http://www.sdcd.com), which means that virtually any retail store can now order your CDs wholesale from Super D and CD Baby. Fans can go to their local record store, request your CD, and the store can get it in stock.

But that's not all. As I previously mentioned, CD Baby provides its members free digital music distribution to stores like iTunes, AmazonMP3, Rhapsody, Napster, Last.FM, Spotify and others (you'll find a complete list at http://members.cdbaby.com/digitaldistributionpartners.aspx). You have to opt-in to get this service, but once you do, CD Baby will take your CD, digitally encode it, and submit it to all of these digital music stores for you at no additional charge.

That's one of the nice things about CD Baby. Aside from the $35 per CD setup fee, you don't pay anything else until you actually sell something. Once you do make a sale, CD Baby does take a portion of that. Here's how it breaks down:

For CDs: CD Baby takes a $4 cut from each CD you sell via their web site. So if you sell a CD for $12.95, you'll see $8.95 of that. Note that CD Baby keeps your CDs in its warehouse, so they handle the shipping and order fulfillment. When your stock gets low, CD Baby will notify you so you can send in more. You get paid for sales by check, PayPal or direct deposit as often as once per week if you wish.

For In-Store Distribution via Super D: If you opt to have CD Baby distribute your physical CDs to stores via Super D One-Stop (which you should), you set your own wholesale prices for that. Keep in mind that the lower you set your wholesale prices, the more likely it is that stores will be motivated to stock and/or order your CD. You can set your wholesale discount to whatever you want, anything from 0% to 50%. I have mine set to 40%.

For Digital Downloads: CD Baby keeps 9% of the *profit* from any download sold to help offset their costs. Refer to my earlier comments about distributing music to iTunes (see #1 on this list) for my thoughts on that. CD Baby provides an excellent service, but that 9% fee does add up, especially if you start making a good deal of money on sales.

The one caveat to distributing music digitally is that you must have permission from the copyright owner to do so. If you're the copyright owner for all the songs on your CD, that's no problem, but if you're selling a cover song, you must obtain a digital product license from the publisher in order to sell that song. I addressed this in detail in the iTunes section above also, so if you need more info on that, check that out.

Note on Digital Singles and CD Baby: For those of you who wish to sell digital singles rather than albums or physical CDs, you can sell those via CD Baby's digital distribution service as well. CD Baby's fee for a single is $9 (rather than the $35 it costs to set up an entire album.) For that one-time setup fee, CD Baby will distribute your single to all the major digital music stores. From that point on, they take their usual 9% of the profit on sales. You can read more about this at http://members.cdbaby.com/whatwedo/sellsingles.aspx .

The administrative tools CD Baby provides to manage all this are detailed but very easy-to-use. When I first signed up, I was amazed that something that looked so good could be so simple! CD Baby's service is, simply put, amazing.

CD Baby Affiliate Program: Sign up for CD Baby's affiliate program and earn $1 for every CD your link sells and 5% on all downloads sold over $5.00. Details at http://www.cdbaby.biz/ .

Quick Note: Would you like to accept credit cards at gigs and performances, too? CD Baby members have the option of leasing a Credit Card swiping system for just $30. Once you have the card swiper, you can keep it as long as you're a CD Baby member and sell your CDs anywhere. After shows, mail in your swiped credit card slips and CD Baby sends you a check for the total sales amount minus 12.8% (on swiper sales, CD Baby takes 12.8% rather than $4 per CD). If you're interested in this, log into your CD Baby member account and then visit https://members.cdbaby.com/Swipers/AddSwiper.aspx for details.

Also: See https://squareup.com and http://www.innerfence.com for two other ways to accept credit cards at gigs and performances!

***#5)* Facebook** - (http://www.facebook.com) : Having talked about Facebook in depth in this book already, I don't want to spend too much time in this section dwelling on what it is and why you should be there. That should be fairly obvious by now. Aside from Google, Facebook is (as of June 2010) the most visited web site on the planet. If you, as an artist, have fans, then it's pretty much guaranteed that you have fans who are active on Facebook. If your fans are there, you need to be there, because every time you post a status update, active fans on Facebook will be reminded of you and your music.

Facebook isn't so much a place to sell music (although that can be done) as it is a place to develop an ongoing relationship with your existing fan base. So developing a presence on Facebook alone isn't, on the face of it, going to drive up your sales. What being on Facebook will do, however, is allow you to be forefront on the mind of your most dedicated fans who *already* buy your music and give them an easy means by which to *share* you and your music with their Facebook-connected friends, family, and acquaintances. That can, of course, lead to more sales for you. However, if your only reason for getting on Facebook is to sell music, you will likely be disappointed in the result.

Think of it this way... Amazon.com, iTunes, CD Baby... those are all places whose purpose it is to *sell music*. Being online stores, that is their function. Facebook is *not* an online store, so if you try and make your Facebook fan page just another storefront, you're missing the point. If all you do on Facebook is pitch, pitch, pitch your music, folks who follow you will see that, sense that, and unfollow you, because following you won't be very interesting. Think about it. People don't sign up for Facebook to buy music. That's not why they spend time there. They are there because they want friendships. At the core of it, people sign up on Facebook because they want interaction with other human beings and Facebook helps them feel more connected to people they care about.

Your best means of selling music via Facebook is by *developing relationships and friendships* with fans, and then making it easy for your fans to share you and your music within their own Facebook networks, if they so choose. That's how you make sales and new fans on Facebook, through *networking*, not by a hard sales pitch. Got it?

OK, let's get to it. Before we really dig into the subject of how to best promote your music on Facebook, you need to understand that there are basically *two types* of Facebook pages. There are *personal* pages – which is what you'll get when you sign up for a generic Facebook account – and there are "Official" pages (usually referred to as Fan Pages) which are typically set up for businesses, organizations and celebrities. There's a lot of confusion out there about the difference between these two types of pages, so let me try and clarify them for you.

Your *personal page* is about you, "the person." On it you talk about your likes and dislikes, your day to day life, what you're doing now and what you're thinking about and concerned about. It's something you cater to your friends and family especially, though many of your fans will be interested if they want to know you on a more *personal* level. One thing to consider is whether or not you want to open up your personal Facebook page to fans. Sometimes it's good to have something that is just *yours*, so you can post what you want without feeling the need to please people who don't really know you (but still have expectations of you). On the other hand, if you allow your fans into your "personal space" they'll feel more like they are your "friends" and may be more motivated to share your music-related posts with their own friends on Facebook.

Your *fan page* isn't so much personal as it is *business,* focused on your brand and your music. Its purpose is to *promote* you and your brand, plain and simple. You can use your fan page to post concert event listings, news pertaining to your music career, links to music downloads, videos and other items all catered *specifically to your fans*. You can even use your fan page to send targeted messages to followers located in specified regions of the country. That's a great feature when you need to target fans in one particular area. Finally, your fan page (and anything you post on it) are things your fans can very easily share within their own network of friends on Facebook.

That's a brief overview of the two types of Facebook pages. More than likely, you'll want one of each.

To sign up for a basic Facebook account, just point your browser to http://www.facebook.com/ . Signing up is quick and easy. Just follow the directions. Facebook will take you step by step through it.

To sign up for an "Official" fan page, point your browser to http://www.facebook.com/pages/create.php . Once there, create a page for an "artist, band or public figure" and then enter your "page name." Your page name should be your band or artist name, though I do recommend you differentiate the name of your fan page from your personal page (especially if you're a solo artist and your "band name" is your actual name). That's important, as it may impact how easily people find you on Facebook. This is especially true if you have a name that is common, one that many other Facebook users share with you. So for your Fan page, give it a name that includes your artistic title, for example, "John Smith, Flamenco Artist" rather than just "John Smith." *Be careful what fan page name you choose because once you choose it, you can't change it later!* Once you've decided on a name, enter that, check the box that you officially represent yourself and then click on the "Create Official Page" button. Follow the directions from there.

Now, if you've spent any time researching how to promote your music on Facebook, you've undoubtedly seen a lot of focus on spicing up the design of your Facebook fan page. While having an attractive fan page is a good thing (you do want to look interesting, after all), keep in mind that the only time most people will visit your fan page is when they initially visit to click on the "Like" button to follow you. That's because once your fan has "Liked" you, they'll see all your wall posts and status updates in their Facebook feed and will have no real reason to return. Anything you post on your fan page will show up in their feed reader. So while you should make your Facebook fan page attractive and functional, it's not something you need to spend gobs of time on once you have it set up.

The primary purpose of that fan page is to make a strong first impression. This is especially important when people who aren't familiar with your music visit your fan page for the first time. This will most likely happen as a result of your existing fans "sharing" your music and/or fan page with their own friends, families and Facebook networks. So for those folks who are just getting to know you, you definitely want your Facebook page to stand out. You want to come across as a professional artist, and while you can use the standard, default Facebook fan page, if you spice it up – even just a little – you'll make a better impression on those folks who are visiting you for the first time.

So how do you spice up your Facebook fan page?

The first tool I'd suggest you to look into is the RootMusic.com BandPage service. BandPage allows you to create a custom tab on your Facebook fan page that contains your photos, music, videos, bio, concert calendar and more. The basic service is free and the "Plus" version of the service, which gives you a lot more control over the design, is only $1.99 per month. Read more about BandPage at http://www.rootmusic.com/ . Once you've created your BandPage, you can make that the default page for your Facebook fan page if you wish. You can see my own BandPage at http://tinyurl.com/234r5jg

Another option to look into, though it's not quite as cool or customizable as RootMusic, is the iLike application (http://www.ilike.com). It's basic, but it's free, and fairly fast to set up. Take the "Artist's Tour" of iLike.com at http://apps.facebook.com/ilike/artist_tour_1 . Once you do that, sign up at http://www.ilike.com/account/artist_signup . Once signed up, you can add/upload your songs, photos, video, blogs and so on, and the info will display on a "Music" tab on your Facebook fan page. It's not beautiful or stylish, but it's functional. Here's an example of what my iLike generated page looks like on Facebook: http://tinyurl.com/29jz8e6

If you'd like something a bit more complex, check out Nimbit's "MyStore" tab feature which allows you to not only post your general artist info, but actually sell your CDs and downloads right from your Facebook page. You can read more about that option at http://www.nimbit.com/what-is-nimbit/sell/ . Click the MyStore Facebook logo on that page for a video showing you how it works. It's very impressive. The MyStore feature is offered free from Nimbit, though you can only use the free version to sell digital goods. If you want to sell CDs and merch, you need to upgrade to their "nimbitIndie" plan, which is $129/year. Nimbit does take 20% from any retail sales you make.

If you really want to take charge of customizing your fan page, research a Facebook application called FBML which allows you to create custom pages on Facebook using HTML. If you know HTML, creating your own fan page on Facebook isn't all that difficult. I won't cover the FBML app in this book, but if you want to learn about it, visit YouTube.com and watch some tutorials on the subject. Here are a couple I recommend:

How to Create Custom HTML on Facebook Fan Pages
http://www.youtube.com/watch?v=VNxE3REU_e4&feature=related

How to Add a Welcome Page to Your Facebook Business (or Fan) Page
http://www.youtube.com/watch?v=icQYHYv7qYg&feature=related

Of the "spice it up" options listed above, the simplest and most straightforward is RootMusic BandPage. So if you want simple, yet stylish, that is your best option.

If you want to go for the bare minimum, you can just add a music player to your Facebook page. There are lots of widgets that will help you do that. ReverbNation.com, Audiolife.com and Bandbox.com, all of which I discussed earlier in this book, offer music widget applications for Facebook.

You'll find other apps to help you customize and utilize your Facebook Pages at http://www.involver.com/start . And there's the Facebook Application Directory at http://www.facebook.com/apps/directory.php .

Here are some additional articles you may want to read on this subject:

How Top Musicians Are Utilizing Their Facebook Pages
http://www.insidefacebook.com/2010/04/30/how-top-musicians-are-utilizing-their-facebook-pages/

How to Use Facebook for Business & Marketing:
http://www.techipedia.com/2010/how-to-use-facebook-for-business-and-marketing/

How to Create the Perfect Facebook Fan Page:
http://www.techipedia.com/2009/create-facebook-page/

Having covered the issue of spicing up your Facebook, let's move on....

How do you actually promote your music on Facebook? As I mentioned previously, once someone follows you on Facebook, they are unlikely to visit your Facebook fan page again... or at least, not frequently. Instead, they'll be monitoring you via their news feed. Any status updates and wall posts you add to your fan page will appear in their feed. That mean you'll want to use your status update posts not only to keep your fans informed about your music and career, but also to encourage interaction with your fans. You want them to talk to you, because if they are talking to you, they are paying attention to you! And if they are paying attention to you, your fans are more likely to share your wall posts, updates, and anything else you post within their own network of friends.

How can you encourage interaction with your fans? You build those relationships. Here's how:

- **Post daily.** Post something new and interesting to your wall every day if you can. Let fans know what projects you're working on, where you're performing, what you're thinking, what makes you laugh. You can post links to articles and blogs you write, links to your songs, videos using your music on YouTube, professional reviews of your music, photos you like, quotes you like, other artists whose music you enjoy, your own book and movie reviews... the options are endless. The more active you are, the more often your fans will be thinking about you.

- **Post status updates that include a question.** Request fan feedback. For example; "Here's what I think, what do you think?", "Here's my situation, what would you do?", "What's your favorite *whatever*?", "What do you think of this song?", "Where should I go on my next tour?", "I'm deciding between this photo and that photo for a cover shot, what's your opinion?" You get the idea.

- **Post status updates that are a call to action.** Request fan assistance. For example; "Want to help me promote my music? Please add a review for my CD on Amazon.com and/or iTunes," "I need help understanding what's important to YOU, my fans. If you have a few minutes, please answer this poll question..." "Which songs should I submit to Pandora Radio? Vote Here!"

- **If a fan responds to you, respond to them.** You want your fans to feel connected to you, so let them know you're listening. If a fan responds to your post, thank them and thank them *by name*. Encourage a discussion. Make it personal. If other fans reading along see you're active with your fans, they are more likely to jump in as well.

- **Give your fans free stuff now and then.** Surprise them with goodies, maybe a free music download or special contest just for the folks following you on Facebook. If you pique a fan's interest, and they know you're giving stuff away on occasion, they are more likely to pay attention to your updates. If you're not sure what to offer, *ask your fans what they want!*

- **Post status updates when people are active on Facebook.** Most folks browse Facebook while they are at work (much to their employer's chagrin). So the best time to post your status update is between 11 am and about 2 pm EST. If you post during that window, people are more likely to be monitoring Facebook and you'll be more likely to get a response to your post. Also, studies show that the best day to post is Tuesday, with Wednesday being a close second. So plan on posting your most important status updates on Tuesdays between 11 am and 2 pm to make the biggest impact.

- **Keep your posts relatively short and to the point.** Most people will skim, and even pass over, status updates that are too long. Most folks won't commit the time. Make your point quickly.

Here are other ways to promote yourself on Facebook:

When they "Friend" You...: If you're doing your job, folks will request to add you as a friend on Facebook on a regular basis. When they do, approve them, then send them a personal message, via Facebook, thanking them for their request of friendship. Let them know you've approved them, then invite them to visit your web site, check out your music, subscribe to your newsletter and tell them about any specials you have going on. Don't forget this critical part of your Facebook marketing strategy!

Create a Facebook Event and Send it to Fans: If you don't have it already, install the Facebook Events app. You'll find that at http://www.facebook.com/apps/application.php?id=2344061033 . Add that to your Facebook Page. Then, from your fan page, take a look at your wall tabs. You should see a tab for Events. Click on that to go to your Events page and post details about your event. Anything you post here will be sent out to your followers. The obvious Events to post are your concert performance dates, but there are other types of Events you can schedule as well. How about scheduling an actual phone conversation with your fans as a group in a conference call (see http://www.freeconferencecall.com)? Or, a CD or digital single release date can be an Event. Interviews you do on the air (or live via the Internet) can be an Event. Any time/date you want to draw attention to is an Event you can call out to your Facebook followers *and* ask them to share with others.

Send a Message Update to Your Facebook Fans: Facebook includes a "Send an Update" feature that goes beyond just your posting your regular status updates. Your regular status updates only appear in your fans' Facebook feed, but you can actually "Send an Update" that goes to wherever your fan receives their Facebook emails. To find this feature, log into Facebook, go to your Fan page, click the "Edit Page" link under your photo, then click the "Marketing" link on the left. On the right, you'll see a link to "Send an Update to Fans." Click on this to send an email direct to all your fans! Note the cool "Target this update" option. That allows you to send email updates to your fans in specific locations, or even to limit your recipients by age or sex. Pretty slick! Be conservative when using this feature. Don't spam your fans! Just use this for very important updates you want to be absolutely sure your fans don't miss.

Use Photos to Tag Your Fans: If you have photos of yourself with fans, friends or other artists, be sure to post those photos on Facebook and "tag" the person in the photo with you. To do this, just login to your Facebook account, "Create a Photo Album," add photos to it and during the process, you can click the photo to add the name of the person on whose face you clicked. When you tag a person, they'll get a notification that they've been tagged, and that photo will appear in their own photo gallery. You can get pretty creative with this idea. If you're playing a concert, take a photo of your audience from the stage, then tell the folks you will post the photo on Facebook that evening and ask all the folks at the concert to visit your Facebook page and tag themselves in the crowd! That gets your fans involved, plus may get them talking about your concert on their own Facebook pages! Any time you can tag other people, do so, as that draws them to your Facebook page and photo galleries.

Jump on Targeted Groups and Pages: You may recall in the chapter on targeting your audience, I talked about getting involved in discussion groups and chat rooms where potential new fans may be active. Well, there are gobs of groups on Facebook. How do you find them? Just do a Facebook search for a topic you know your fans tend to have in common. That might be a band whose music is similar to yours, a hobby, a political or religious stance, a cause.. anything your fans gravitate towards. When you enter a search term in Facebook's search field (at the top of your Facebook home page), a list of matching pages will pop up as you type. You'll notice at the bottom of that list, there is an option to "See More Results for..." Select that. Once you do that, on the left you'll see that you can filter results by People, Pages, Groups and so on. View the Pages and Groups available for your topic. You want to get involved in the Groups and/or Pages with tens of thousands (or hundreds of thousands!) of fans. This is one way to put yourself in the path of potential new fans. Jump in the discussion. (To see a general list of all the Pages available grouped by topic, visit http://www.facebook.com/pages)

Create Your Own Group: Create a Group specifically for your fans, so that they can interact with you and each other. How? Login to your Facebook account, click on the Home link at the top of the Facebook window. In the left column, under your photo, you'll see a listing that includes the text "Create Group..." Click on that and you're off and running.

Create Your Own Shortcut: Once you have 25 fans, Facebook will let you create a Facebook shortcut to your fan page. For example, http://www.facebook.com/davidnevue . To do this, go to http://www.facebook.com/username and follow the directions. Choose your shortcut username carefully, as once you set it, you cannot change it! To read more about this feature, see Facebook's note at http://www.facebook.com/note.php?note_id=383008189821 .

Paid Advertising: In addition to all this, Facebook offers a paid advertising option. If you have a Facebook account, you've no doubt noticed the ads on the right side of the page as you're navigating the site. Anyone can create an ad, and when you do, Facebook gives you many options for targeting your ad viewers. You can advertise your fan page, your event, your group or even your web site.

Facebook ads are really nothing more than banner ads, though, and the effectiveness of banner ads is limited. I suggest you flip back to the chapter in this book on *Search Engine Submission*. At the end of that chapter, there's a section called *Should You Pay for Position*. Give that section another read. What I stated there applies to Facebook, too. In order for advertising to really work, you need to be selling something people want, and let's be honest... if a person doesn't know you or your music and they see your ad in their peripheral vision, they aren't going to take any notice of it. So if you do try running a Facebook ad, you need to use a headline and an image that will grab their attention. What might that headline or image be? As I've said so many times in this book, consider your target audience. What are they looking for? What are they interested in? Appeal to that interest in your ad.

Here's an article about targeting your Facebook audience I think you should read. While it's not written for musicians or about music specifically, as you read it you'll see how the writer used clever headlines and text in the ad to get folks to "like" his Facebook page:

How We Got to 40,310 Facebook Fans in 4 Days:
http://www.allfacebook.com/2010/06/how-we-got-to-40310-facebook-fans-in-4-days/

Obviously, they are selling something much different than music (it's the Facebook page for Weekly World News), but you can see the effect headlines and eye-catching images had on drawing attention to their ad.

As for the cost of advertising on Facebook, you have options. You can pay by impression (the number of times your ad runs) or by actual click-through. I would recommend you pay per actual click as then you are only paying for results. Facebook click-ad rates work much like Google's ad program does. You set your own desired ad rate (as low as .01¢ per click). The more you are willing to pay, the more exposure your ad is likely to get. You can also create a daily budget for your ad so that you can ensure you never pay more than you expect to in a given time period.

I've heard from several musicians who have used Facebook ads to promote their fan pages. Many have told me they felt the ads helped them generate more page "likes." That's great, but does a "Like" translate into a true fan or an actual music sale? That's very difficult to measure. Personally, I don't believe banner ads sell music especially well. I'd rather focus my time and money elsewhere. I do, however, believe Facebook ads may be useful for promoting concert events targeted to a very specific area if you can get folk's attention with the headline. In that instance, Facebook has the potential to be at least as effective as a blurb about a concert in your local newspaper.

As with any advertising program, you'll have to experiment to discover whether you feel the bang is worth the buck. With your particular act, you may have something unique or unusual enough to offer that will draw attention from casual Facebook users. If so, go for it. Nothing ventured, nothing gained.

For more information on Facebook advertising read:

Primary Facebook Ads Page: http://www.facebook.com/ads
Guide to Facebook Ads: http://www.facebook.com/adsmarketing/
Facebook Advertising for Musicians: http://tinyurl.com/2dpday2

Be sure you read that Guide to Facebook Ads. It's very helpful.

Facebook is a vast tool with lots of corners to explore. You can lose yourself in it just looking for creative ways to promote your music. Always keep in mind that *most* people use Facebook in the most basic ways... they post status updates and watch their news feeds for updates from folks they are following. Make the most of your Facebook marketing by posting interesting updates about yourself, your music and encouraging your fans to become involved by spreading the word about you and your music to their own network of friends. That's the best, most cost-effective way to use Facebook to promote your music.

#6) YouTube.com - (http://www.youtube.com) : YouTube is by far the most popular destination on the Internet for watching video. No other site is even close. Any video on the web that matters can be found there. As far as your music goes, YouTube can be a gold mine for creating new fans, especially if your video gains traction and goes viral. If it does, you may just get your fifteen minutes of fame.

The most popular videos on YouTube have been watched *millions* of times. It's mind-boggling. Just imagine how many fans that kind of exposure could bring you! So what's the secret to creating a video that goes viral? Well, there is no secret, unfortunately. It's just right place, right time, right content and right context. You can't manufacturer a viral hit. If you could, *everyone* would be doing it, and then nothing would stand out, right? The truth is, it's impossible to predict how well any particular video will do. Just look at the top ranked videos on YouTube for the current month. You'll find both strange and mundane stuff. What makes a hit? A clever title? Weirdness? Craziness? Emotional or romantic content? a Hot topic? Sexual innuendo? Cute animals? Celebrity name dropping? Yes, all of the above, and sometimes in odd combinations.

YouTube is very much like a lottery. You create a bizarre/interesting/stimulating video that highlights your music, put it on YouTube and hope it catches fire. Maybe it will, and if it does, you might be the next big thing. But even if that *doesn't* happen (which, let's be honest.... it probably won't), YouTube gives you a wonderful opportunity to connect with your fans. Videos featuring your music give you and your fans something to talk about and share on Facebook, on your blog, web site... just about anywhere. At the very least, your fans will watch, and if they like it, they may share your video with others. That's where potential new fans and sales are going to come from.... word of mouth. Word of mouth is always the best advertising.

As for how to create your videos and promote them on YouTube, I covered that to great extent in the earlier chapter, *Social Media: Marketing Your Life*. So, for detailed information about promoting videos to YouTube and other video sites, review that chapter. I won't take the time to cover it again here.

I will say this, however: if you have a video and you don't already have it up on YouTube, get it there ASAP. If you don't yet have a video featuring your music, it's time to start planning one. If nothing else, go to Animoto (http://www.animoto.com) and use that very simple (and excellent!) service to create a video for you using your still image photos. Then get that up on YouTube and get your friends and fans involved. Ask them to help you promote it. That means not only asking them to watch your videos, but also to rate them, comment on them and share them within their own social media circles.

Another way to get videos featuring your music up on YouTube quickly is to actively encourage your fans to do it for you. Invite your fans to create (and upload) videos that make use of your music in new and interesting ways. The videos can be anything from stylized music videos to slideshows, stories, documentaries or even videos of your fans performing your music. You can turn it into a contest. Let your fans know that if their video is one you select as a "winner," you'll do something really special for them. That might include free CDs signed by the band, a personal phone call from you, a "date" with you, a free guitar or piano lesson from you or any number of things that would motivate your fans to get interested in making videos that feature your music. Those fan videos you really like, you can share with your mailing list as well as on Facebook and your web site, bringing them further attention. This is one quick way to start populating YouTube with videos featuring your original music. Every video on YouTube that features your music is like one more buck spent on a lottery ticket. You never know when one of them might turn to gold.

I've been amazed at what folks have done with my own music on YouTube. It's been great fun to watch. It's free publicity! One video posted by a fan of my music has garnered over 2.5 million views! That's free promotion that I didn't have to pay a cent for.

YouTube is an incredible tool for promoting your music. The options are endless. Again, review the previous chapter on *Social Media: Marketing Your Life*. Then go for it.

Potential Money-Making Tip: YouTube offers a partner program that allows you to make a little (or potentially a lot of) extra cash from your video successes. If you have a video that goes viral especially, you'll really want to look into this. Here's more info on that

YouTube Answers: Partnerships: http://www.youtube.com/watch?v=7VN131tLEBc
YouTube Partners Program: http://www.youtube.com/partners .

#7) Last.fm - (http://www.last.fm) : If Pandora is the undisputed king of Internet radio (in terms of actual listenership), Last.fm is the queen. Last.fm doesn't have near the user base or popularity that Pandora has (in the U.S., at least), but there are several reasons some folks consider Last.fm superior. Here are a few of them:

- Last.fm is artist-friendly. While you can submit your music to Pandora, there's no guarantee Pandora will accept your music. According to a recent interview done with Pandora founder Tim Westergren, Pandora rejects about 70% of the music sent in to them. Pandora's playlist is more commercially-influenced, in terms of the artists on its roster. At Last.fm, however, all artists are welcome. You can upload all of your songs to Last.fm and get them immediately on the network. You can even set up your own artist page on Last.fm so that listeners can find out more about you when they hear your song (you can't do this on Pandora). Finally, Last.fm provides independent artists the option of advertising on their network.

- Last.fm is a user-centric community. The service, itself, *is* a social network. That means fans can share music and playlists with each other. People can create friends lists, join neighborhoods and groups. Friends can see musical compatibility, compare tracks, and interact with each other in the usual social network ways. So your music can actually go viral on Last.fm. There's no way for that to happen on Pandora. When you listen to music on Pandora, you're listening *alone*, but when you listen on Last.fm, you're connected to other users. Your musical tastes actually impact what songs are recommended to other Last.fm listeners who share your musical tastes on the network.

- When Pandora recommends a new song to a listener, it does so based on musical qualities… song tempo, rhythmic patterns, vocal harmony and instrumentation that are similar to the music the listener has indicated they like. So Pandora does not suggest new music to listeners based on *artist similarities*, but based on musical patterns. Last.fm, however, predicts what new music a listener will like based on what other users with similar musical tastes actually like. That means that if fans of ColdPlay like your music too, your music is more likely to be recommended to other ColdPlay fans.

- While Pandora has a much bigger audience than Last.fm, its listenership is limited by location and technology. Pandora can only be heard in the USA. Last.fm can be accessed from over 200 countries. If you're tuned in via a computer, Pandora forces the listener to listen at the web site. Last.fm listeners have their choice of client-based desktop apps to use if they wish. Pandora limits free listening to 40 hours per month. There's no such limitation with Last.fm.

So the long and the short of it is, if you can get your music on Pandora, a LOT more people will potentially hear your music. However, with Last.fm, you can essentially market yourself. Everyone has a shot to go viral. You'll get a more global audience.

All that being said, I have my music on both networks and I consistently (just about every day) see sales as a result of being on Pandora. I don't see as many sales from Last.fm listeners, but I do get a lot of listens there. It's well worth signing up. People will discover you.

#8) Twitter - (http://www.twitter.com) : I've talked about Twitter in passing many times in this book. Twitter is essentially a microblog. You have just 140 characters to write something meaningful. People use Twitter to tell the rest of the world what they are doing, feeling and experiencing *right now* in short bursts of text. It sounds silly, and it is, but the folks who actively use it, love it.

To set up an account, simply go to http://www.twitter.com . You'll see a link there to sign up. Click on that, and the first thing you'll be asked to enter is your name and desired username. As with Facebook, consider your username carefully. You might just use your band name or artist name, but you might also include a couple of important keywords to make it more unique. Once you've completed that and you're in, you can add your photo, bio, web site link and edit your Twitter page design to give it a bit of personality.

If you're interested, you'll find the Music Biz Academy page at http://www.twitter.com/musicbizacademy . My personal Twitter account is http://www.twitter.com/davidnevue .

You are probably very aware of the buzz Twitter created in 2009 and early 2010. The act of "tweeting" (that is, sending out a "tweet" on Twitter) became a sort of in-joke. Every late night show had a comic with "tweet" jokes. For a short while, talking about Twitter and tweeting was the rage.

During that period of time, millions of folks signed up for Twitter, partially out of curiosity. A lot of folks used it... and then got bored and moved on. Barely two years after its rise, Twitter has peaked, in my opinion. Unless Twitter makes some very meaningful changes to add to its cool factor, I suspect the site will be on a slow decline from here on out.

But here is why you should get on board and stick with it. Twitter is a *very* useful tool. The reason for Twitter's gradual decline is not for any reason within the tool itself. When Twitter came out, it was completely different than anything that had come before. It was simple, had a cute name, and folks by the millions jumped on board to try it. After they tried it, a lot of folks who didn't fully understand its value moved on. They saw no reason to stay with Twitter since they already had Facebook... and most of their friends were on Facebook. So Twitter, for many people, was redundant. But for those folks who really understood Twitter and made good use it, it became an essential tool they use all the time. That includes me.

So, what's Twitter good for? Let me speak as a Twitter user first, not a musician. As a user, I love it, because I can go to one place to get quick, short updates about the people, products, services and things I care about most. I don't have to read long expositions from people and companies who are trying to sell me their stuff. I don't have to read long ramblings that go on and on, using up my precious screen space. I get just the summaries all in one place. That makes it easy to keep up to date on the people and products I really care about in a short period of time. What kinds of things do I follow on Twitter? A few musicians, very close friends, products I want updates on, music industry news feeds, Oregon Duck Football news, a couple political news sites and another dozen or so random things that interest me. That's about it.

So now, think about Twitter as a music promoter. What good is it? Well, for your friends and fans who love Twitter and use it as an information sorting tool as I do, it's a great way for them to get your most important news quickly and to the point. Those friends and fans of yours who are really into what you are doing and who also make use of Twitter will appreciate that you're on it, posting updates. Twitter is a great way to stand out in a crowd, as well, because those folks who use Twitter to *receive information* are generally pretty selective about who and what they follow. Most folks that use Twitter for informational purposes (not for marketing) aren't following thousands of people. They just follow a hundred or so people/sites/services they really, truly care about. If your music matters to that Twitter user, you've got a solid connection with them there.

So for promotional purposes, the reason you should be on Twitter is to make it easy for Twitter-using folks who are also fans of your music to stay in touch with you. Twitter advocates read their feeds several times a day, and if you're on that feed, you're forefront on their mind.

How should you NOT promote your music on Twitter? By contacting a zillion strangers on Twitter and following them just so they will follow you back in kind. I see many folks with Twitter accounts who have 10,000 or more people "following" them. Do you know why they have 10,000 people following them? Most of the time it's due to the "you follow me and I'll follow you" mentality. There's no real interaction, no real sharing. It's all about increasing numbers. If you take this approach, you could soon be following 10,000 people and those 10,000 people could be following you. But do you think any of those 10,000 people really care about your music? No. They just want you to follow them. Do you think they really even read their own Twitter feed? Highly unlikely. You just can't read that much data. Following that many people makes Twitter, as a tool to receive information, completely useless. Are your really going to sit there and read 10,000 tweets a day? I think not. Neither are those folks who are following you and 9,999 other people. Am I saying you shouldn't have 10,000 followers? No. What I'm saying is, don't follow 10,000 people just to get them to follow you back. If you gain 10,000 followers, let it be because those followers care about you and your music.

This whole "You follow me and I'll follow you" mentality is what doomed MySpace, in large part. MySpace was full of useless friends and followers who were more concerned with ratcheting up their friend numbers than actually doing something useful. Don't be a useless friend, and don't acquire useless followers. Forget all the hype you read on the Internet about "getting more followers" on Twitter (this goes for Facebook too). And whatever you do, don't pay someone money to get you thousands of useless followers.

So here, my friends, are some ways to make the best use of Twitter as a tool for you:

Follow People and Businesses You Care About: Not sure where to start or who to follow? What are you interested in? Are you interested in the music industry? How to promote your music? Rap music superstars? The Pittsburgh Steelers? Marvel Comics? The giant heads on Easter Island? Just go to http://search.twitter.com and search for any keyword or phrase. The search result will list the most recent tweets on the phrase you searched for. Each tweet begins with the username of the person tweeting. If you like what the person said, click the username to view that user's page along with all their recent tweets. If you decide this is an interesting person to follow, click on the "Follow" button to start watching their feeds via your own Twitter account.

Want more? Check out Twellow at http://www.twellow.com/ . You've heard of the Yellow Pages, right? Well, this is the "Twellow" Pages! You'll find lots of Twitter users, all grouped by their subject of expertise. There's lots to explore there.

Want more? You probably have favorite web sites you have bookmarked that you go to all the time. If you visit those web sites, you'll more than likely find a "Follow" link for Twitter. Click that, and you can follow all these web sites in your Twitter account. Cool, huh?

However you go about it, if you start making use of Twitter, it won't take long before you'll be following a lot of folks. It can make for interesting reading. You'll also find that if you start following too many people, reading through those updates can become a chore. Don't let your Twitter account get to this point. Unfollow folks when they stop posting news that's interesting to you. It's easy to unfollow someone. Just go back to their user page and click "Unfollow."

Let Your Fans Know You're on Twitter: This is an obvious statement, I know. Most of your fans aren't going to be Twitter users, but several of your fans probably love Twitter and those that do will appreciate your being there.

Post Updates on Twitter Regularly: With Twitter, you only have 140 characters, so you have to keep your updates brief. Be concise, make your point, and provide necessary links to those readers who might want more information about what you post. What kinds of things should you post? The same kinds of things you're posting about on Facebook: concert news, tour updates, links to blogs or articles you write, requests for fan feedback, "works in progress" you want to share, photos, music, links to reviews of your music and, of course, personal comments about the things that are important to you.

Watch for People Discussing You and Respond as Appropriate: When you log into your Twitter account, if you look in the column on the right-hand side, you'll see a link that says @yourusername . Click on that link to view all references to you made by other people. This will include replies to you as well as folks who retweet (RT) things you say or who are simply discussing you. You can also visit http://search.twitter.com and search for your full name to see who's talking about you or your music. When you see folks making reference to you, if appropriate, respond to that conversation. In many cases folks talking about you may not even know you're on Twitter. Say hello.

Put the Twitter Feed on Your Web Site: It's easy to create a nifty little Twitter feed box to put on your web site. If you take a look at my web site at http://www.davidnevue.com and look toward the bottom, you'll see mine. I also have one front and center on the Music Biz Academy web site home page at http://www.musicbizacademy.com . I love it because any time I post an update, I'm updating the content on my web site too. It gives my web site the appearance of being alive, current and in use. Want a cool feed like that on your own web site? Just log into your Twitter account, then look at the bottom of your Twitter home page. You'll see a link for "Goodies." Click on that and you can create a Twitter feed widget to put on your own web site. Just follow the directions there. You can customize the size and color to match your needs.

Use Twitter to Monitor Your Competition: There's nothing more interesting than seeing what your musical competition is up to. Twitter is a great way to spy on them (warning, they are probably spying on you too!) Just search Twitter for them or for folks talking about them, and you'll probably find them. Twitter is a great way to follow other bands or businesses that affect your own business. Maybe your fellow artists will post some great marketing ideas that will work for you, too! Or maybe by touching base with another band via Twitter, you can network, find commonalities, and play a show together.

Your Twitter Posts End Up on Search Engines: Did you know that the text you post on Twitter gets sucked into the search engines? It's true. On more than one occasion, I've seen posts of mine turn up on Google. Remember the chapter earlier in this book about using keywords and phrases to target your audience? Twitter provides you another opportunity to do that. Provide links, commentary and short reviews on news and topics that your target audience cares about. That gives potential fans a way to "discover" you via the Twitter search tool or even Google. If they drop by your Twitter feed and find you interesting, they may start following you.

Get the Most Bang for Your Tweet Buck: When you have an important announcement to tweet, always consider the time of day you tweet it. Folks are most active on Twitter between about 10 am and 2 pm EST. That's your best window to ensure the most views. Also, stick with posting important tweets on weekdays, especially Tuesdays or Wednesdays, if possible. Finally, when you tweet something important, ask your followers to retweet your posts to their own followers. Studies show that if you ask folks to retweet your posts (and say please when you do so), you are much more likely to get word of mouth going.

Tweet Your Music: Did you know you can tweet your music? There are several online tools that make it easy to tweet your songs to your followers. One of the most popular is Blip.fm (http://www.blip.fm). To get your music on Blip.fm (if it's not already there) create an account, (or log in if you already have one), then click the "Settings" link in the top right corner (click on your username to show the Settings menu item). From there, click "Music." You can enter in as many URLs to your songs as you like. Blip will save them for you and they'll be available for you to tweet. You can send them to Facebook as well.

Another great app for tweeting songs is is Twiturm (http://twiturm.com). You first need to connect your Twitter account with Twiturm. Once you do, just upload your song, add your description and it's tweeted. Pretty simple... and fast. It works with Facebook as well. Finally, check out TinySong (http://www.tinysong.com/).

Learn the Language: Twitter has a language all its own. Here are some common terms...
To **follow** someone means you subscribe to their Twitter posts.
A **tweet** is an individual message, posted by you or someone else.
A **DM** is a direct message, that is, a private message you send to another user on Twitter.
To **RT** or **retweet** is when you repost a message someone else wrote to your own Twitter followers. It's like email forwarding. When you do this, always credit the original source by including their @username in the retweet.
Trending topics are the most-discussed terms on Twitter at any given moment. Just go to the Twitter home page to see a current list. You can also see them at http://search.twitter.com/
@username is a public message to or about another person on Twitter. If you want to write about someone, and you want them to see it, include their @username in your post.
A **hashtag** is typing the # symbol followed by a keyword term, and then including that in your tweets. It's a way to categorize all the posts on a particular topic to make them easier for others to find.
Shortened URLs make it easier to fit long links into your 140 character messages. Twitter shrinks some URLs down automatically. There are lots of URL shorteners out there if you want to use your own. I like bit.ly (http://www.bit.ly) or TinyURL (http://www. tinyurl.com)

Once you get going on Twitter, you might find it helpful to have a tool to organize your different feeds for you, especially if you end up posting the same thing multiple places (Twitter, Facebook, MySpace and so on). Hootsuite (http://www.hootsuite.com/) is great for this purpose! With it, I type a comment once, and it posts to all of those social networks at once. Well worth looking into.

Article of Note About Twitter:

Top 10 Twitter Tips for Beginners:	http://www.pcmag.com/article2/0,2817,2341095,00.asp
27 Twitter Tips for Musicians:	http://tinyurl.com/bmlewe
A Musician's Twitter Roadmap:	http://tinyurl.com/5tq2vg
How I Use Twitter (by Derek Sivers):	http://sivers.org/tweet
$11K on Twitter in Two Hours:	http://tinyurl.com/lb7kxq
100 Twitter Tools:	http://tinyurl.com/bbkxtb
Top 10 Reasons I Won't Follow You:	http://mashable.com/2009/01/06/twitter-follow-fail/

#9) Rovi / The All Music Guide - (http://www.rovicorp.com and http://www.allmusic.com) : If you're distributing your music to any extent, whether that be through iTunes, Rhapsody or even via digital radio services like Music Choice, getting listed with Rovi's All Music Guide is an absolute must. The AMG provides detailed artist information and metadata to hundreds of retailers and is one of the most complete repositories of musical information on the web. Search the site, and you may *already* be included. If not, you can submit your bio, discography, images and promotional materials to the AMG editors and they will add it to their database. Then, when people discover your music at an online retailer that uses AMG's content, they'll see any cover art, capsule CD reviews, or biographical information AMG has for you in their database. For information on how to submit your material, just email product_submissions@allmusic.com or visit the web site at http://www.allmusic.com/contact#productsub . There's no cost to submit your info to the AMG.

While you're at it, be sure you submit your CD material to Gracenote (http://www.gracenote.com) as well. Gracenote controls how your CD, artist and track info appears in players that make use of their database. You can submit your CD info to Gracenote via iTunes. See http://www.gracenote.com/about/faqs/#upload for information on how to do that.

#10) Live365.com - (http://www.live365.com) : Live365.com is the Internet's largest hosted radio broadcasting network, logging over two million *unique* visitors a month. Most of the 'radio stations' on Live365.com are owned by individuals, many of which will consider your music for their programs.

If you research the popular webcasts for other genres on Live365.com, you'll see some impressive numbers. The top "Rock" program on Live365 logged over 72,000 listening hours for December 2010. The top "Alternative" genre station logged just over 101,000 hours for this same period and the top "Jazz" station, 174,000 hours. That's a lot of listeners!

Promoting your music to these listeners is a simple matter. Just find the programs that are the most popular for your genre and drop them an email to inquire about submitting your music. You have an open door to getting a good deal of Internet radio play, which may in turn lead to more sales of your CDs and/or downloads. The Live365.com radio player is hooked directly into Amazon.com for sale of both CDs and MP3s. So, if someone listening to a Live365 program clicks your song link, they will be given the option of viewing your information at Amazon.com (another reason you need to have your music there.)

On top of all this, Live365.com provides you with the tools to set up and run your own radio program. It's quite simple to do and really amounts to nothing more than creating and uploading your own MP3 files. The cost to operate your own webcast starts at just $5.95 per month. I really recommend you do this as a means of promoting your own music to Live365.com's listener base. My own Live365.com program, *Whisperings: Solo Piano Radio* (http://www.live365.com/stations/pianoradio) logs over 144,000 listening hours per month (just on Live365.com). That translates to quite a few CD sales. I'll have more detail on all this in the next chapter, *Internet Radio: Tuning in to More Exposure*.

See *How to Broadcast* at http://www.live365.com/help/broadcast/index.html for information on how to set up your own Live365 station.

#11) **SHOUTcast.com** - (http://www.shoutcast.com) : SHOUTcast is the hub for a huge network of Internet radio stations and broadcasters. In that sense, it's very similar to Live365.com. With SHOUTcast you have, at your fingertips, immediate access to some of the most listened to radio stations on the Internet. To promote your music via SHOUTcast, browse the service for the most popular stations in your genre, visit the station web sites, and research how and if you can submit your music for consideration.

While many SHOUTcast stations play only commercial music, some will include music from independent artists as well. For example, Radio Paradise (http://www.radioparadise.com) broadcasts to well over a million listeners each month and accepts submissions from independent artists. Start with Radio Paradise, and use SHOUTcast to find other, similar stations that will help you promote your music to the listening public. If your music is well-targeted and catches the listener's attention, you should see some increased sales from this effort as well as some traffic to your official site.

The SHOUTcast network is much larger than Live365.com, but is not a *hosted* network. In terms of setting up your own station on SHOUTcast, you'll need to set up your own server from which to stream your broadcast. This can get expensive as well as very technical. If you're a broadcasting newbie, start with Live365.com and you can have your own radio program up and running in about an hour. I'll talk a bit more about this in the next chapter, *Internet Radio: Tuning in to More Exposure*.

#12) **MySpace.com** - (http://www.myspace.com) : I debated whether to even include MySpace on this list, but decided I ought to at least comment on it. The problem with MySpace is that, as compared to Facebook, few people care about it anymore. MySpace is stuck in the past, and though it has tried again and again to reinvent itself, few (comparatively speaking) are paying attention anymore.

That said, it's not a bad idea to have a profile page on MySpace. At the very least, set up a profile and upload songs that folks can listen to. While most folks are spending time on Facebook now rather than MySpace, my MySpace page still comes up near the top of the search results on Google when you search for my name. Also, surprisingly, fans still request to be my friend on MySpace. I still get lots of email from fans there, and I am able to convert a lot of those folks into mailing list signups.

In terms of promoting your music on MySpace, treat it like any other social network. MySpace has forums and discussion groups just like Facebook does. Find those forums/groups where your target audience in likely to hang out and respond to threads where you have something to contribute. When you respond, always include your signature and in that signature, link to your MySpace page and web site. When folks request to be your friend on MySpace, respond with a "Thank You" note and invite them to sign up for your mailing list.

One of the biggest negatives about MySpace is that most of the friend requests you receive won't be from fans, but from either a) businesses who want to sell you their services or b) other artists and musicians trying to increase their friend count. Those folks don't really care about you, they just want you to pay attention to them. This is one of the biggest reasons folks have left MySpace in droves… "friend spam." When you receive friend requests, use discretion as to whether you approve someone. I've reached a point where I only approve friend requests from folks who are obviously (or potentially) fans. I generally don't approve friend requests from other musicians who are just promoting themselves and certainly not businesses who are trying to make a quick buck off of me.

So MySpace has its good and bad qualities. Yes, it's definitely worth having a profile there and keeping it up to date. However, MySpace is a trend that is quickly fading into history. I expect it at some point to go the way of MP3.com .

In Closing...

Time spent promoting your music to the web sites and services listed in this chapter will increase your online exposure greatly, bringing in that many more CD and music sales. If you can get your music on all of these services, you're off to a great *start* promoting your music. As you can imagine, getting involved with each and every one of these services takes some effort. Just begin at the top of the list and work your way down. Those I consider the most important are listed first.

Internet Radio:
Tuning In to More Exposure

Clearly a Monopoly

Every musician instinctively knows that radio exposure is one key way to generate sales of CDs and downloads. However, many young musicians don't realize that it's practically *impossible* to get your music onto commercial radio. Why? Because the music on virtually every radio station on your dial is controlled by one company: Clear Channel. Clear Channel owns over 800 radio stations nationwide, and that includes stations in 89 of the top 100 music markets. They completely control what's played on your local radio broadcast, and with few exceptions, every mainstream commercial radio station you hear is programmed by Clear Channel. You can read more about Clear Channel at http://www.clearchannel.com/ , http://en.wikipedia.org/wiki/Clear_Channel_Communications, or view the Clear Channel Radio Fact Sheet at http://www.clearchannel.com/Radio/PressRelease.aspx?PressReleaseID=1563.

While Clear Channel owns and controls much of commercial radio, *Internet radio* is wide open. *Anyone* can start and run their web-based radio broadcast (or webcasts, as some call them), including *you*. And that means that there are *thousands* of independent broadcasts in operation who will consider your music for their programs. All you have to do is find them.

Where to Find Independent Broadcasters

Fortunately, finding broadcasts on the Internet that will play your music is a relatively easy thing to do. A significant percentage of independent broadcasters stream their music through one of two networks: Live365.com (http://www.live365.com) or SHOUTcast (http://www.shoutcast.com). Both networks host *thousands* of individual radio programs, most of which are independently owned. Many have large and devoted listening audiences, logging *tens of thousands* of listening hours every month.

Both Live365 and SHOUTcast organize their active programs into genre-based directories. To start your search, simply visit Live365.com or SHOUTcast.com and browse the directory for your particular genre. Click on that, and you'll be presented with a list of active broadcasts displayed in order of their popularity. The programs with the largest listening audience will be listed first.

Each program listed will include a hyperlink leading to more information about the broadcast (or a link to their web site), as well as contact information for the owner and/or program director. Simply go down that list, explore the broadcast's official web site, then contact the webcaster for each of the programs you think your music is appropriate for. Politely ask if you can submit your music for consideration. Many programs include submission information right on their web site, so do look for that.

Make it your initial goal to contact the top twenty Internet radio broadcasts within your genre. Create a simple spreadsheet to track the programs you contact, the responses you receive, and the shows you send your music in to. Then follow up with each of them to make sure they received your package OK. Once they confirm, thank them, and then ask how long the review process might take. Some broadcasts receive a large number of CDs to review, so it may take several weeks or months for them to get to yours. If they say it will be about six weeks, contact them again after eight weeks if you haven't heard back to see where you stand. Go through this process with each of the twenty broadcasts you included on your spreadsheet. Once you've received responses to ten of your queries, either positive or negative, go find ten more programs to send inquiries to, add them to your contact spreadsheet, and keep the ball rolling.

The process takes time, but if you're consistent in your contact work and follow-up, you'll eventually create a spreadsheet logging a large network of Internet radio broadcasts that are playing your music.

Setting Up Your Own Radio Station

Getting your music on a large number of independent stations is a relatively simple thing to do. You just have to take the time and effort to do the contact and follow-up work. But the *real* fun starts when you begin to manage and operate your *own* radio broadcast.

Both Live365.com and SHOUTcast offer the ability to create and manage your own Internet radio station. However, SHOUTcast requires you to run your program from your own server, while Live365.com does not. With Live365.com, all you have to do is upload your MP3 files to their server and build a playlist. Once your playlist contains all the songs you want, you can add a simple line of HTML to your web site to create a "Play" link from which your visitors can launch your broadcast. Live365.com has a really nice widget option as well, one you can easily insert into your web site. Once that's set up, visitors browsing both your web site and Live365.com will have access to your program.

What's the cost for this? You can sign up for Live365's "Personal Station" account for as little as $5.95 per month. Their most popular broadcast account, which gives you 750 MB of space, is only $29.95 per month. It's easy to do, and with just a single day's work, you can have your program up and running. As for SHOUTcast, it's free, but you do need your own server and the know-how to set it up. SHOUTcast provides documentation on how to do this at their web site.

Consider a few of the benefits of managing your own Internet radio station:

- You can add Live365's station widget to your official web site so that fans can listen to and support your program.

- You can add Live365's station widget to your *targeted* web sites to further familiarize those targeted visitors with your music.

- You can create a fan page for your radio station on Facebook and talk it up on Twitter, in newsgroups, discussion groups, blogs and in chat rooms.

- You can create a 'Play' link from your email newsletters.

- You can build an official web site for your program, and then optimize and submit that web site to Google to target new fans searching for your style of music.

- You can populate your official broadcast web site with genre-related articles, links, and stories to create even more targeted content to submit for inclusion on the search engines.

- You can create publicity for your webcast by submitting stories and press releases to the various press release outlets.

- You can use your webcast as a tool to network with other musicians sharing your style of music.

- If these same musicians wish to have their music included on your webcast and agree to help you promote the webcast to their own fan base, that creates the opportunity for you to promote *your* music to *their* fan base.

- Thousands of potential new listeners may find your broadcast while browsing or searching the Live365 and SHOUTcast directories

- You'll gain MORE FANS!

- You'll sell MORE CDs and downloads!

I'm sure I can come up with a dozen more reasons to start your own Internet radio station, but you get the idea. For more information on starting up a broadcast via Live365, see http://wiki.live365.com/pmwiki.php?n=Broadcasting.IntroToBroadcasting .

Now, to demonstrate the kind of exposure for your music you can achieve through your own radio program, I'll provide you with a real life example....

How I Play to a Million People a Month

In August of 2003, I created my own Internet radio station on Live365.com called *Whisperings: Solo Piano Radio* (http://www.solopianoradio.com). The primary purpose of the radio broadcast was, of course, to promote my own music. However, I wasn't so vain as to think listeners would want to listen to *just* my music 24 hours a day. People want *variety* in a radio station. So, to create that variety, I contacted a number of other artists whose music was similar in style to my own and invited them to be a part of the *Whisperings* radio project. As the station grew in popularity, artists began to send in their material without my even asking for it. Now, seven years after I began, there are over 200 talented piano artists (and more than 2,000 tracks) in rotation on the broadcast. That gives the Whisperings program a *lot* of musical variety. However, as I am the program manager (and the whole purpose is to promote my own music) I make sure my music is *very well represented* in the playlist rotation. One of my original songs plays at least once every hour.

My goal when I created the *Whisperings* program was to make it a broadcast unlike any other. I played quality music you wouldn't be likely to hear anywhere else. I aimed for a particular signature *Whisperings* piano sound so that when people tuned in, they knew exactly what to expect and were not disappointed. I made the broadcast something that became an *addiction* for our listeners. When they wanted quality piano music, something to calm their busy days, they'd come to *Whisperings: Solo Piano Radio*.

In December of 2005, after just two years on the air, *Whisperings: Solo Piano Radio* became Live365's #1 show. Check out the following chart, which shows how quickly the broadcast caught on with listeners:

	Total Listening Hours	Listener Presets	Rank in Genre	Overall Rank on Live365	Notes
Jul 2003	0	0	NA	NA	First Broadcast Aug 30, 2003
Sep 2003	8,372	783	9	271	
Dec 2003	31,383	3,050	5	89	
Jun 2004	64,509	8,189	2	23	
Dec 2004	117,717	15,279	2	12	
Jun 2005	138,392	22,490	2	8	
Nov 2005	171,923	28,052	1	3	Picked up by iTunes, Nov 2005
Dec 2005	643,317	30,300	1	1	

Total Listening Hours: This represents the total number of hours *Whisperings* has been listened to in a given month. The average listener tunes in for about 90 minutes at a time.

Presets: This number indicates how many people bookmarked *Whisperings* in their Live365.com presets - in other words, Live365 listeners who are regular, repeat listeners.

Genre Rank: This is *Whisperings* popularity rank for its primary genre (New Age). As you can see, it didn't take long at all to break into the top 10 for the genre.

Overall Rank: This is *Whisperings* popularity rank for ALL of Live365.com. In other words, *Whisperings* quickly became the most popular program on the *entire* Live365.com network for *all* genres.

Whisperings: Solo Piano Radio held the #1 spot on Live365.com for over four years running. The only reason *Whisperings* is no longer their #1 station overall (as of this writing) is because I stopped actively promoting our station link on Live365.com. Why in the world would I do that? Because the *Whisperings* broadcast outgrew them. I have my own streaming server now, my own software, as well as my own *Whisperings* player for listeners to enjoy. At the volume of bandwidth I'm broadcasting now, it saves me thousands of dollars a month to serve the stream myself. And while yes, it's cool to be #1 on Live365, it's even cooler to be heard by more people (overall), control my own stream, and save money while doing it. Even though I no longer push our Live365.com station link, we are still one of the top ten broadcasts on all of Live365 and the #1 broadcast for our genre.

How big is *Whisperings* radio now? On the average day, my Internet radio broadcast is launched over 50,000 times. That's a LOT of exposure for my music. That's like filling a 1.5 million seat concert hall each and every month! *Whisperings* has resulted in a *great* many CD sales for me as well as downloads from iTunes. By creating your own broadcast and promoting it as I have, you too can generate regular, daily exposure for your music to thousands of potential new fans.

The Cost of Growing Your Broadcast

As you can imagine, it costs money to grow an Internet radio broadcast. Bandwidth isn't free! At the introductory level ($5.95/month), Live365.com will allow just three listeners to tune into your program at any one time. Once those three spots are taken, any new listener wanting to tune in will be locked out until someone else drops off. As you can imagine, it doesn't take long to fill up those three spots. Once you get the hang of how to run your broadcast, you'll want to upgrade to Live365's $29.95/month service so that up to 40 people can tune into your show at the same time. As your audience grows, you'll find it necessary to upgrade your service periodically to support your increasing number of listeners. That's exactly what I did as the demand for *Whisperings* radio continued to grow.

Hold onto your seat for what I'm about to tell you: as of this writing, I'm consistently supporting over 6,000 simultaneous listeners to *Whisperings: Solo Piano Radio* (about 50,000 tune in over the course of the day). My total cost to support those listeners is over $5,000/month. Now I know what you're thinking – "There's NO WAY I can afford that kind of money!" Well, guess what? Neither can I. So how do I pay for it?

The first thing I did to raise money to grow the broadcast was to ask the artists participating on my program to pitch in. I set up a *Whisperings Artist Partner Program* whereby artists could voluntarily contribute anywhere from $10-$40/month to help grow our broadcast (I took payments for this using PayPal's recurring billing option). Artists who became "partners" received promotional benefits that non-partner artists did not. For example, partner artists would get links from our web site, CD reviews, "feature" shows and *guaranteed* daily play. Guess what? 70% of my artists contributed, and that contribution covered the costs of running and growing our broadcast for a long time. So aside from my time, the show cost me very little out of pocket to operate.

You can do something similar to help get your broadcast off the ground. Let your artists know that the broadcast is a *community* effort and that in order to grow it, you're going to need their help. You are, after all, a musician just like they are. You're not some huge corporation with sponsors and millions of dollars in government funding. Sell your broadcast idea to your artists and encourage them to work with you to accomplish the dream – and then reward those who do.

One concern you (or one of your artists) may have about this idea – if you ask artists to contribute financially, and then give them additional promotional benefits in return, isn't that *payola*? Payola's a big no-no!

The answer is, NO, it's not payola. Payola would be if you said to someone "I'll play your music if you pay me 'x' amount of money" or if an artist said to you, "Here's $30, please play my song" and you take it and it was done in secret. *That's* payola. So long as you are open about what you're doing, make your partner program available to *all* your artists, and are clear that financial contribution does *not* determine whether or not someone actually gets airplay on your broadcast, then what you're doing isn't considered payola.

If your artists believe in you and help support your broadcast, they will help you cover the financial burden. That's the model I used to grow *Whisperings* for over three years.

I did reach a point though, where in order to grow our show further, I had to come up with something else. Our artist contributions, even though they amounted to well over $1,000 a month, were not enough to keep up with the incredible demand for our show. So I spent nine months putting together the next step in *Whisperings* evolution – a subscription version of the program that listeners would actually pay for.

Figuring out the technology to create a subscription version of the show wasn't easy. I ran into technical obstacles that made me want to pull my hair out at times! But in the end, I got it together. In September of 2006, three years and a month after our initial launch, I made *Whisperings PureStream*, the subscription version of our program, available to the public. For as little as $5/month, a listener got access to a commercial-free version of our broadcast that featured CD quality music and an expanded playlist. Best of all, it gave our dedicated listeners a way to financially support the show at whatever level they felt comfortable with.

PureStream has been going strong for over four years now, and we have over 4,000 paying subscribers. I have phased out the *Whisperings Artist Partner Program* and the broadcast is 100% listener supported.

If you should actually reach a point with your own radio broadcast where you want to build your own subscription version of your show, here's what you'll need:

1) **SAM Broadcaster**: http://www.spacialaudio.com/
   SAM is the best (and easiest) tool I've found to stream a broadcast.

2) **StreamGuys.com**: http://www.streamguys.com/
   The folks at StreamGuys are experts in audio streaming. They can help you set up your broadcast or even a subscription system like mine. They've been great to work with.

3) **A dedicated server**: You'll need a computer that serves no other purpose than to run SAM Broadcaster to deliver your stream to listeners. I suggest you talk to Streamguys about this as well. They can set you up with a dedicated server just for this purpose.

4) **A PayPal account**: If you set up a subscription system, that system will work hand in hand with PayPal. StreamGuys works with PayPal to automate the subscription account and billing process. You will need a PayPal account customers can pay their monthly fees into. If your shopping cart system supports recurring billing, you can accept credit cards from subscribers as well.

Obviously, this stuff gets a little technical. When you get into serving up your own stream and attaching password protection to it, there's a lot more involved. Don't worry about doing all that until you're ready. For now, just sign up with Live365 and use them to host and stream your program. It's *simple and inexpensive*. And don't worry about going from 3 to 6,000 simultaneous listeners right away. Take it in small steps, as I did. Start with 3, 10 or even 40 listeners; build to 100, then 150, 300 and up. The more artists you can attract to your broadcast (and they will come to you in droves if your show is a success), the more financial partners you will have to help you to grow your station. And remember - the point of your broadcast is, ultimately, to promote your own music. Yes, you promote other artists, too, but as you do so, you reap benefits for yourself, as well as other artists, as your station grows in popularity.

Other Broadcast Tools:
Need a program scheduler? Check out the "Music 1" scheduling software at http://www.gomusic1.com . It takes a little time to learn it, but once you do, you can schedule an entire week's programming in just a few minutes.

Paying Royalties: The Financial Reality

If you're going to operate your own Internet radio station, you'll need to make some decisions about how you're going to handle royalty payments and licensing for the music you play on your program. This is a VERY important issue to deal with as the RIAA, SoundExchange and the PRO organizations (ASCAP, BMI, etc.) are really going after Internet radio broadcasters right now.

If you host your station at Live365.com, this process is made slightly easier as they cover all your royalty fees for you – up to a point. You don't need to worry about paying anything extra so long as you follow the "rules" listed at http://www.live365.com/info/rules.html *and* let Live365 control the advertising content (banner ads, song links and in-stream audio ads) on your broadcast. This is something Live365 does on your station by default so they can cover your royalty fees. So long as you allow Live365 to advertise to your listeners, you can play any music you want, even music from major label releases (so far as it stands at the time of this writing).

But what if you *don't* want Live365 to run advertisements during your program? Then things get more complicated. To remove those ads, you need to sign up with Live365 as a *professional* broadcaster. Doing so gives you a number of benefits. First, you can drop Live365's ads and run your own ads (or run the broadcast ad-free) if you wish. Secondly, listeners can listen to your program on a player that you can customize to your own liking (see http://www.live365.com/pro/embeddedplayer.html for some examples). Finally, *you* control where your listeners are directed when they click the "Buy" and song links in the broadcast player. Here's a simplified break down showing the differences between a "basic" and a "pro" broadcast:

Live365 Basic Radio Program
Includes Live365's audio ads, banners, etc.
Uses Live365's default station player
Player "Buy" buttons link to Amazon, iTunes
ALL royalties are paid

Live365 "PRO" Radio Program
Insert your own ads or broadcast ad-free
Launch your own customized station player
Player "Buy" buttons link to wherever you want
NO royalties are paid

The disadvantage of operating as a "professional" broadcast, as you can see above, is that Live365 will no longer pay your royalties for you at no extra cost. That being the case, you have two options. The first is to pay royalty fees directly to the PRO organizations; to ASCAP, BMI, SESAC and Sound Exchange, yourself. If you take this route, you will need to submit legal paperwork to Live365 stating that you will do so.

Your second option is to pay extra for one of Live365's "royalty-included" professional packages. Doing this is more cost effective and convenient than paying the PRO organizations directly, however, it will still cost you a pretty penny. A station that generates just 5,000 listening hours a month (which isn't much) will cost $297 a month to operate with the royalty-payment included option. That's for a 64kbps stream. You can find details on Live365's professional broadcast pricing, with or without royalties included, at http://www.live365.com/pro/pricing.html .

If you want to play major label music on your show, you have no choice but to go with one of the above two options. You either sign up as a "basic" broadcaster and let Live365 advertise on your program and cover your royalties, or you turn "professional" and pay your own royalties.

There is a THIRD option available to you, however, if you do *not* plan on playing major label music on your program. You can simplify everything by asking your artists to waive royalties. This assumes that you are only playing music by artists who own the copyright to their songs. This is exactly what I chose to do for *Whisperings: Solo Piano Radio*. I created a license agreement every *Whisperings* artist has to sign. In this agreement, the artist verifies that they own 100% of the copyright to their music, and then they *waive* their right to royalties or representation by BMI, ASCAP, SESAC and Sound Exchange as it relates to the play of their music on *Whisperings*.

I can guess what some of you might be thinking. "David, why would you ask your artists to waive their right to royalties from your radio broadcast? Don't you want to support independent artists?" Well, yes, of course I do! But if I pay royalties, I *can't* support independent artists. Here's why:

1) Our *Whisperings* broadcast generates over a million listening hours a month. Royalty payments on that would add up to *tens of thousands* of dollars each and every month under the current royalty rates. If I had to pay that, I'd be out of business in no time at all. I would be forced to shut down the program and there would be no station left on which to promote my artists.

2) Even if I *did* pay those thousands of dollars each month in royalties, the artists on my program would never see that money. Those fees would be included in a *blanket* royalty payment to the PRO organizations and *they* would decide who gets that money. So it's entirely possible that Mariah Carey would receive royalty payments indirectly from my program even though I've never played her music. Meanwhile the independent artists I do actually play would never see a dime. Nice, huh?

So I was left with one of two choices; I could pay the royalties, the artists I play don't see any of that money and I go out of business – or – I could *not* pay royalties and the artists I play on my show get an incredible amount of radio exposure to a huge audience that they don't get anywhere else. I chose the latter option.

In the seven plus years *Whisperings* has been on the air, I've only run into one artist who wouldn't sign the agreement. Every other artist has done so without hesitation (including two major label artists who had their attorneys sign off on our agreement so they could be on our program). Most artists are more concerned with getting their music heard by the public than earning a few extra pennies on their royalty statement.

The point of all this is that if you want to start your own radio program, you'll need to think about how to best handle royalties and licensing. I would recommend you take some time to read the information at http://www.live365.com/licenses/faq/abs/ . That's the best means of getting a grip on how all this works. You can then post questions and receive answers in the "Want to Broadcast?" community forums at http://forums.live365.com/ .

If you decide to do what I did and ask your artists to sign a royalty waiver, just realize that means you can only play *original* music by those copyright holders. You cannot play any cover tunes, just original tunes or songs in the public domain. The latter includes most traditional hymns, classical music and a wide selection of folk and traditional Christmas songs. Once you have your signed waiver forms from your artists, you can send those into Live365's legal department to show that your program is legal and in the clear.

Podcasting: Jumping on the Audio Bandwagon

Podcasting is something you've probably heard about. It was all the rage a few years ago and the subject of a lot of media attention, though that has declined considerably now. What's Podcasting? "Podcasting" is just a fancy name for downloadable audio files, only in this case, the audio files work a bit like a talk radio version of TiVo. In the old days, if your favorite talk radio show was on at 3pm on Tuesday and you missed it, well, that was just too bad. But now you can subscribe to your favorite podcasts, have each program automatically downloaded to your computer, and then listen to it whenever it's convenient for you. You can also sync your podcasts up to your portable music device (your Droid, iPhone or iPod - hence the term "*pod*cast" – get it?).

Virtually all the commercial radio and television networks, as well as the most popular talk radio shows, offer podcasts that you can subscribe to. There are a gazillion others too, most of which are produced by amateurs, on every possible topic. People use their podcasts to put a voice to their hobbies, politics, rants and obsessions. To put it in its most simple form, a podcast is an audio blog or commentary made available to the public.

How about getting your music on some of those? There are several web sites you can sign up with that market music to Podcasters. Just a few of those include Music Alley (http://www.musicalley.com), MagnaTune (http://www.magnatune.com), IndieFeed.com (http://www.indiefeed.com) and Podsafe Audio (http://www.podsafeaudio.com). The idea with those web sites is that you sign up, upload your music, and hope Podcasters come along, find you, and want to license your music.

Probably the most effective way of getting your music on a particular podcast, however, is to approach the Podcast producer directly. With all the legal hoops podcasters have to jump through to include music on their program, many are happy to hear from artists whose music they can use free and clear. How do you know which podcasts to contact? As I've said so many times in this book, consider your target audience and what they might be listening to. If the audience of a particular podcast would have a predisposition for your style of music, or might relate to the *message* conveyed by your music and lyrical content, go for it.

OK, so how do you find podcasts in the first place? Use a podcast search tool! One of the biggest search tools for podcasts is Podcast Alley at http://www.podcastalley.com . Pick a genre on Podcast Alley and you'll find hundreds of podcasts listed. Even iTunes has a huge list of podcasts accessible right from the software. Invest a little time to research what's available and you'll find plenty of podcast producers to offer your music to.

So what about starting up your own podcast?

If you're going to do a podcast and make it successful, it's something you need to commit to doing every day. Frankly, it's very time consuming and, this being 2010 (going into 2011), podcasting isn't all that hip anymore. It's a technology that caught fire a few years ago, but burned out quickly. Folks are into video now, not audio, and so if you're going to take the time to do something like podcasting, I really suggest you invest that time in video blogging or something similar.

However, if podcasting is an avenue you want to explore, here are a few places to start your research:

Creating Podcasts…

Podcasting 101:	http://www.podcasting-tools.com/podcasting-101.htm
Podcast Primer for Indies:	http://tinyurl.com/24y25lr
podOmatic:	http://www.podomatic.com/
Make Your First Podcast:	http://podcastingnews.com/articles/How-to-Podcast.html
Create Your Own Podcast:	http://tinyurl.com/cllak
How to Podcast:	http://www.how-to-podcast-tutorial.com/

Podcast Software…

Propaganda:	http://tinyurl.com/33848j2
FeedForAll:	http://www.feedforall.com/
ePodcast Creator:	http://www.industrialaudiosoftware.com/products/epodcastcreator.html
PodProducer:	http://www.podproducer.net/

Podcast Legal Stuff…

Podcasting Legal Guide:	http://wiki.creativecommons.org/Podcasting_Legal_Guide
Creating Legal Indie Music Podcasts:	http://alchemi.co.uk/archives/mus/creating_legal_.html

A Happy Hollywood Ending

All this talk of licensing, royalties, copyright and getting "legal" with Internet radio and podcasting is a bit overwhelming. So, let me end this chapter on a positive, feel-good note. First, don't forget that you can start your own radio broadcast on Live365 for very little cost. You don't have to start out as a "professional" broadcast and pay all the required expenses. If you stick with Live365's *basic* program, it's enough to get going, and your royalty payments are included. You can focus on the music, playing whatever you want, whenever you want, whether that be your music, major label artists, independent artists, talk radio or a combination of all of those. It's only when you go *pro*, if you choose to go down that road, that things get expensive and complex. My advice to you is to start a small radio program on the side and see how it goes. That's exactly what I did, and I must say this: of all the things I've accomplished on the Internet, the success of my *Whisperings: Solo Piano Radio* program has been one of my most gratifying achievements. And it all started with a little, $9.95/month radio show.

If I can do it, you can, too. What are you waiting for?

Beyond Cyberspace:
Using the Internet to Get Gigs

Crossing Over: From the Internet to the Stage

Five years ago I rarely played a live gig. Yes, I'd have the occasional booking, but those were few and far between. Once my *Whisperings* Internet radio station got off the ground, however, I took that opportunity to organize piano concerts around the country with other artists from the show. While doing that I discovered, to my delight, that I was able to use the Internet to book concerts for myself pretty much anywhere I wanted to. I'd have a *Whisperings* concert in one city, and while there, I'd play a few solo concerts in that and neighboring states. Basically, I'd book my own tour of shows at churches, colleges, fund raisers, house concerts and whatever else came up.

How did I manage to do that? I used my email list. One benefit of having promoted my music online for fifteen years is that over time I've been able to compile a database of thousands of names, addresses and email addresses from fans around the globe. When I want to play a concert in a particular area of the country, I just email everyone on my mailing list from that region and let them know I'm seeking performance opportunities. Within a week or two, I'll have five to ten concert performances in development.

Now I know what you might be thinking. I've had *fifteen years* to gather names. You're just starting out. How are you supposed to build a fan list big enough to make good use of it? Well, for one thing, you just start doing it. You might be surprised how quickly your list will grow if you put into practice everything I've taught you in this book. Also – and let this be an encouragement to you – of those fifteen years online, *more than half* the people currently on my mailing list signed up during the last three years. You see, the more successful you are, the easier it is to become even more successful because more people out there are talking about your music, visiting your web site, and signing up for your mailing list. What starts out as a trickle becomes a flood. With this book in hand to guide you, you can build your online support system much faster than I did. So while you might not have the fan support to start touring right away, keep building your mailing list. When you have a hundred or so people on your list from one general area of the country, you can start exploring your options for performing there.

Though I've been speaking on a large scale here, in terms of traveling across the country, don't forget about your *local* music scene. If you're just starting out, chances are you can get a hundred people on your mailing list from your local community faster than you can gather them from the other side of the country. So while you're building up your global database of names through online promotion, start performing in your local area by putting your local connections to use. Perform locally when and where you can, and use those opportunities to refine your act before you take it on the road.

In regards to touring, I have found it to be a self-reproducing thing. Once your fans see (via your newsletter and web site) that you're traveling around the country performing, they will start asking you when you're planning to come to *their* area. That gives you an opportunity to enlist their help setting up a concert in their own community. The more successful you are on the Internet, the more you can build your fan base, and the easier it is to create opportunities for yourself to perform. Not only that, but the reverse is true. The more successful you are as a concert performer, the more traffic and sales you generate for yourself online, and the more new fans you can add to your mailing list, your Facebook page, and so on. So the elements of live performance and online marketing feed into one another. You can use each one to make the other more profitable. Speaking of profitable…

House Concerts: Small Audience, Big Profits!

One of the easiest gigs to get is playing in the home of one of your fans. If you're like me, however, you may feel some aversion to doing a concert at someone's house. I remember a time when I wouldn't consider doing a house concert because I kept thinking of it in the same terms as a piano recital. I was of the mindset that a *professional* musician would never do a house concert. I had to get over that prideful way of thinking. I did, and after doing one or two house concerts, I was hooked. Now when a house concert opportunity comes up, I jump at the chance. It's my favorite kind of gig.

Look, your fans love you and want to help you. They want to share their love for your music with their friends and family. If you're willing to come play a concert in their home, that event becomes the highlight of their year. Just put yourself in their shoes. Imagine if an artist you greatly admired was coming to perform a concert in your living room. Wouldn't that get you stoked? Wouldn't you tell everyone you knew about the concert and move heaven and earth to make sure it was a big success? Of course you would! The same is true for your fans. Their enthusiasm will sell CDs for you before you even arrive to play the show.

When I talk to someone about doing a concert in their home, I ask for a couple of things. First, I ask that they commit to doing everything they can to bring *at least* 20-30 people to the performance. I even provide them with posters and flyers to pass out to help them advertise if they want them. Secondly, I ask them to consider either a) paying me $300-$500 up front (price depending on the night of the week and other considerations) or b) charging $10 a head and then paying the difference between the final total and that $300-$500. Either way, I end up with at least $300 for the gig (more often than not $500), not including CD sales. As I am a pianist, I also require a tuned, working piano be available. If you're a singer/songwriter/guitarist, you might be able to bring everything you need with you in your guitar case. If you're a band, you might put together an acoustic set explicitly for this purpose. If you're a rap artist, just bring your portable sound system and the necessary attitude. Regardless of the music genre, in most cases you don't need to worry about much in the way of equipment. That's one of the benefits of doing a house concert.

Because the venue is so small, the level of energy is very high. Your audience is, in a manner of speaking, *on the stage* with you. They can feel the music and they can feel *you*. Use the intimacy of the venue to captivate your audience by interacting with them. Tell stories about your songs and let them ask you questions about your music. If you can communicate the soul of your music effectively to this small audience, they will reward you with CD sales. I did one house concert where I brought in over $1,000 just in CD sales. Even if a small audience turns up, I can still do a couple hundred dollars in CD sales, and when you combine that with my fee, I'll do at *least* $500 a night (I average about $800 a house concert with CD sales). Plus, every time I've done a house concert, I've seen a noticeable increase in CD and download sales from that area immediately after the fact. So house concert attendees are telling their friends about the concert, sharing your music and basically selling your CDs and downloads for you. The next time you tour that area, you can expect to have a bigger, more enthusiastic audience waiting for you.

House concerts are so popular now that there are entire web sites devoted to them. Many of those list house concert venues across the U.S.. See http://www.houseconcerts.com for one example as well as http://www.folkmusic.org/shows/venues.html and http://www.concertsinyourhome.com/. Want more? Just perform a search for "house concerts" on Google and you'll find quite a lot of information.

Sharing the Gig, Finding Venues, Making the Rounds

I mentioned above how I teamed up with other artists from *Whisperings: Solo Piano Radio* to play concerts around the country. This has been an amazing experience as, not only have I met and played with some extraordinarily talented musicians, I've shared the stage with some of my own musical heroes. Starting your own radio broadcast is just one way to meet and network with other like-minded musicians.

Another way to meet your fellow-artists is through MySpace.com, which hosts the world's largest community of musicians. Visit http://www.myspace.com , click on the "Music" link, and you can search for musicians in any part of the world. If, for example, you want to see every band playing a show near you, just click on the "Shows" menu item and perform a search. Once you do this, you can "change" the city you're searching near. This feature becomes very useful when you know you're going to be touring a particular area of the country. Just enter the zip code where you plan to be, and then perform a search to list bands and the venues they are playing at. You can then follow up with the venues or hook up with the bands listed for gig sharing, networking, or to ask their advice about the local music scene.

Managing Your Travel Budget

Traveling and touring is expensive business, especially for a *band* when you've got several members to account for. Not all of us can fly across the country whenever we want. I'd like to offer a few tips to help you lessen, or at least streamline, your travel costs:

1) First of all, I don't travel to an area unless I can book several shows within a few hours' driving distance of each other. If I just played a single show, I'd lose money on the trip. It's not until the third show that I usually start to see a profit. If you get a booking offer from one particular state/province, start looking for other performance opportunities in that state/province and the surrounding ones as well.

2) When I travel to an area of the country, I'll fly into one city, rent a car, and then drive everywhere. That way I have only one airport and one car rental to worry about. I usually book it as a road trip that takes me in a big loop through several states. If I land in St. Louis, I'll start there, drive a few hours each day to each of my pre-arranged performance dates, and eventually end up back in St. Louis for my return flight home.

3) Rent an economical vehicle to save on gas. You don't have to rent an extravagant car to be comfortable in your travels. These days I rent my cars from Enterprise (http://www.enterprise.com). I have consistently had a good customer experience with them and they are very competitive on price. One thing to watch out for on car rentals – make sure you get unlimited mileage in all the

states you plan to travel to. Some companies give you unlimited mileage, but restrict you to just one or two states. If you go outside those states, they start charging you an extra 25¢ per mile.

4) Eat at the grocery store. You can save a lot of money buying groceries rather than eating out. If you do eat out, drink water instead of soda pop. Most restaurants charge over two dollars for a medium drink these days. You'd be better off putting that money in your gas tank. The cost of soda adds up fast! When you're on the road, rather than buying water in conventional bottles, by it in gallon jugs. You can buy a gallon of water for a buck or two, and that will last you a couple of days.

5) Sign up for Choice Hotels and the Choice Privileges Visa Card (http://www.choicehotels.com). I put all my business charges on this card and as a result I get most of my motel/hotel rooms (and my morning breakfast, which is provided) for free. This chain of hotel brands can be found just about anywhere in the world. You can book your rooms online and see pictures of the rooms before you book to ensure you get a room to your taste. More often than not, you'll have a dozen motels in the same city to choose from.

6) Stay the night with your host. If you're doing house concerts, church, college events or fund raisers, there's a good chance that someone can put you up for the night somewhere. Most people have a couch and who knows, you might even get a free breakfast out of it the next day. You can also use MySpace.com or Facebook to befriend local artists and perhaps get a room for the night with one of them while you're in town.

7) Sign up for airline frequent flyer programs. These points add up and eventually you can turn them in for a free flight.

8) Don't be afraid to ask the people hosting you for a show to help with travel expenses. If you're playing a club, you're probably out of luck getting help with travel costs. But if you're playing a private event, a church, a house concert, fund raiser or other such event, it's OK to ask.

9) Know where you're going so you don't waste time and gas getting lost. I use my Garmin Nuvi GPS to provide me step by step directions from one place to another as I drive. I love my Nuvi. I never get lost and I always know what time I'm going to arrive at my destination. But the biggest reason I'm glad I bought a Nuvi is that it's much safer to follow that when traveling than to try to read a map and drive at the same time. Doing the latter almost cost me my life three times while touring. Once I got a Nuvi, getting lost and in a panic was never a problem again. You can purchase a Nuvi for just over $100 at Amazon.com.

When planning your own concert tour, you'll want your concert schedule well-organized up front so you know exactly where you're going, how long it will take you to get there, what's happening, who you're meeting, how much you're making, and where you're staying. I have a spreadsheet that I use to log my travels. Here's an example…

City & Event	Gig Contact Name and #	Fee Promised	Expected Turnout	Accommodations Phone # & Res. #	Notes
Friday, Sept 8th St. Louis House Concert 345 Yeti Ave. Start at 7:30 PM	Teri Jones 555-777-1234 (cell) 555-777-9875 (home)	$10/person, $300 min. guarantee. Also agreed to contribute $100 for travel expenses.	20-30	Comfort Inn Suites, 7113 Douglas W. Res # 13234782093YH Phone# 555-777-0230	Pretty sure she can get 30 people, if not, she'll cover the difference.
Sunday, Sept 10th Kansas City Lutheran Church

Play special music for two morning services. Evening concert at 7:00 PM | Bob Smith 555-777-3942 (cell) 555-777-9234 (home) | No ticket sales for church event. Agreed to $300 to cover expenses. Plus CD sales table OK during morning services and for evening concert. | 400 combined at services

100 or so expected at concert. | Staying with Joni Welch, parish member. Offered free room plus breakfast. | Church will be putting up posters plus making announcements about the concert starting three weeks before. |
| Wed, Sept. 13th Clarke College Des Moines, IA 8:00 PM Start | John Campos 555-234-2343 | $1000 Fee (paid in advance) , plus $10/student (see notes) | 400-500 | Mainstay Suites 1275 Associates Dr. Res # 98F98L38 Phone # 555-980-9398

Clarke College is paying for the room. | Agreed to donate all ticket sales to student music scholarship. I keep 100% of CD sales. |

Having such a spreadsheet is useful when managing several gigs at a time. Otherwise keeping places, people, phone numbers and verbal agreements straight in your head can be difficult. There's nothing more awkward than showing up to play a concert and being unable to recall the name of your contact or the exact details of how much you're being paid.

So is your mind processing all this? Even if you haven't been a gigging musician to this point, I hope you can see how, using the Internet, you can become one if you want to. Your online success can have a very big impact on how often and where you perform live. The fans you make online are there to help you with this aspect of your career and they *will* help you if you develop a continued relationship with them. Get your fans involved and they will play a big part in your success down the road, whether that be by supporting you at a concert performance, joining your online street team, or simply talking your music up to their friends, family and online acquaintances.

How to Use Advertising to Pump Cash Into Your Music Career!

Secrets to Creating Cash With Advertising and Affiliate Programs!

Bonus Checks for Great Performance!

During the last ten years I've spent a great deal of time experimenting with advertising and affiliate programs. I have some great news to report - there's money to be made! Online companies are looking for successful web sites to advertise on, and once you've reached 100,000 page views per month you can make some decent pocket change selling ad space on your web site. How much? Just one of my affiliate programs brings in over $500 per month on a regular basis. Banner advertising and other programs bring in $1000 more. That's $1500 a month I can reinvest in my online business and music career.

This brief, but powerful chapter is here to give you some insight into how to make your ad space work for you. These tips are, generally speaking, intended to be applied to the topical web site you create to target your particular audience. Most of the ideas here are not something you'll want to implement on your "official" artist web site as once you have a visitor there, you don't want them going anywhere else.

Less is More

You may recall my advice to limit your visitors' options. This same advice should be applied to running ads on any of your targeted web sites. The more ads you run, the less effective they tend to be as visitors begin to tune them out. Even worse, if you put too many ads on your web site, your visitors will completely ignore any custom advertisements you create to promote your music. It's important to maintain a careful balance between running ads and giving your visitors the information they're looking for. You don't want to leave the impression that the only purpose of your web site is to push ads on people.

I recommend you limit yourself to two or three ads on a page and make each one a different ad style (banner, text and pop-under, discussed below). The use of different styles will keep the ads from dominating the page. Also, do your best to meld your ads into your web site's layout, color and design scheme. That way, they look like they belong there and don't become overly distracting to the reader.

Pay per-Click, Thousand, or Commission?

There are essentially three types of advertising programs: those that pay-per-click (generally referred to as CPC or "cost per click" ads by the advertiser); those that pay-per-thousand impressions (CPM or "cost per thousand"); and commission-based programs.

Pay-per-click (CPC) programs are the most common, particularly in banner advertising. This is because the advertiser doesn't have to pay you unless someone actually clicks on their banner or link. These ads typically pay anywhere from 5¢ to 15¢ per click. As you can imagine, it takes a while to generate much revenue when dealing with such small amounts. I have found that generally speaking, CPC programs are the least effective advertising campaigns to run. They are also the most widely available.

Pay-per-thousand (CPM) programs are less common, but are far more effective in terms of giving you a guaranteed payout. This is because your payment is based on how many thousands of visitors you have, not how many clicks are registered. As long as you keep the traffic coming in, you'll make money.

Commission-based programs are also popular, but their success depends entirely upon whether or not the products you advertise are of interest to your visitors. The negative side of commission-based advertising is that you only get paid when a customer buys, so if you have the wrong product, you may end up sending your traffic to another web site for nothing. However, if you have the *right* product, commission-based advertising can be lucrative.

Most banner advertising agencies use a mix of CPM and CPC banners. Most affiliate programs are commission based. First, I'll discuss banner advertising.

Banner Advertising: Everything You Need To Know

The easiest way to generate income using banner advertising is to sign up with a banner ad hosting agency that pays you, "the publisher," a set amount per thousand banner impressions. What you need to be aware of, however, is that while many of these services claim to pay up to $10 per 1000 impressions, the actual average is more like 25-50¢ per 1000 impressions. That means for every 1000 visits to your web page, you make around 25¢. If you have 100,000 page views per month, with one banner per page, you make $25.

Most banner agencies mix pay-per-click banners in with their pay-per-thousand banners, however. So your "thousand" ad impressions aren't all on that same payment scale. Pay-per-click banners typically pay 5¢ to 15¢ every time someone clicks on them. This is great if a lot of people click on the banner! However, statistics have shown that most banner click-through rates are less than .005%. That's 1 in 200 visitors, and I think that number is highly optimistic. The point is, you may not even make that 25-50¢ per 1000 impressions, but a number even lower than that.

I spent *years* trying to find a decent ad agency. In 2001, I finally settled on a company called ValueClick (http://www.valueclickmedia.com). ValueClick offers one of the most organized, user-friendly ad tools I've seen and allows you, as the publisher, to select the individual ads you want to display. You can also keep track of how much money each ad is making for you. If an ad isn't doing well and turns out to be a waste of space, you can drop it in favor of better paying ones. You can even include your own default banner ads (advertising your music or whatever else you want) in the ad rotation if you like. That's a really useful feature and ensures that your ad space never goes wasted on ads that aren't worth their low pay rate to display.

As much as I like ValueClick, I'm still only seeing about 40¢ per 1000 banner impressions from them. However, they do offer other advertising units that pay quite a bit more. Their pop-under ads, for example, pay about $3.00 per 1000 impressions on average (that's $300 for 100,000 page views). Normally, I hate pop-up ads, but these are fairly unobtrusive as the ads are displayed *under* your page when it loads. That means the visitor doesn't see the ad until after they leave your web site. Even better, ValueClick's pop-under code ensures each visitor only gets one pop-under ad per week. That keeps the visitor annoyance factor to a minimum, while still earning you some extra money.

A few years ago, I started implementing Google's AdSense program (See http://adsense.google.com) and I have been very impressed with them. Google's banner ad click-through rates are very good and I'm seeing better earnings from Google's ads than from ValueClick's. The only downside is that, in my opinion, the AdSense ad management and reporting tools leave something to be desired. Also, AdSense doesn't offer pop-under ads, which is where a good portion of my advertising revenue comes from. So, at the moment I am using ValueClick.com for my pop-under ads and Google AdSense for banner-style ads. That combination seems to be bringing me the best financial results overall.

For other advertising options, see the *Quick Reference Guide* at the end of this book. There you'll find links to other ad agencies, banner ad rotation software and banner-related articles.

Affiliate Programs

Another way to make money through advertising is to sign up for one or more affiliate programs. What's an affiliate program? Basically, it's when you sell a third-party product or service direct from your web site and/or newsletter. In most cases, rather than displaying a wide range of ads, you're promoting a particular product or service. Typically, affiliate programs work on a commission basis; that is, rather than getting paid per click or impression, you get paid a percentage of any product sales generated from your web site. If you can find the right program for your web site, there is a large potential for bonus income.

In order to have success marketing an affiliate product or service, you've got to offer something your web site visitors are likely to want. So again, you need to consider your target market. For music-related web sites, all kinds of product possibilities come to mind: books about the music business, sheet music and 'how to play' piano and guitar instruction DVDs are examples. If yours is a guitar tablature site, find affiliate programs for guitar tablature, guitar lessons, guitar gear and related accessories. If your web site caters to independent musicians, provide your visitors with books about the music business, recording, marketing and selling music. Give it some thought, because the sales are there if you have the right product and the right approach.

Where do you find these affiliate programs? Just perform a search on Google for the item you want to sell. Chances are, one of the first results returned will be a wholesale publisher or manufacturer for that product. For example, search Google for "sheet music" and the #1 search result is SheetMusicPlus.com, a store that will pay you an 8-12% commission on any sheet music sales generated through your web site.

If you can't find exactly what you're looking for, you can always sign up as an "associate" for Amazon.com (see https://affiliate-program.amazon.com/). Amazon sells virtually everything and they will pay you up to 15% on any item sold via a link from your web site. I've also included some affiliate program directories in the *Quick Reference Guide* at the end of this book to aid you in your research.

There's a *lot* of stuff out there to resell from your web site. Be prepared to go through a long process of testing and evaluating before you find a product that works for you. My general rule is that for every twenty sales and marketing ideas I try, one will succeed. So keep that in mind and don't be discouraged if it takes you awhile to find a product that generates any real income for you. You won't find success without first overcoming a long list of failures. That's just the way it works.

Two Secrets to Successful Advertising

Most affiliate programs give you the option of using either banner ads or text ads with a link to promote their product via your web site. My experience shows that text ads generate higher sales and click-through rates than do banner or graphic ads. This is because people are so used to seeing banner ads they tend to ignore them. If you instead integrate your affiliate link into a text ad that you write yourself, you can use your own words to sell the product. In other words, the ad isn't so much an ad as it is your *personal recommendation*. If people trust *you*, they are more likely to purchase a product you recommend, and that means more sales.

The second secret to successful advertising is that search forms of any kind have a very high click-through rate. People love to search! There are a multitude of search tools available that pay you every time someone uses them, including Google. Google's paid search tool (available through their AdSense program) is fantastic, because you can create a search form that not only matches your web site look and feel, but returns results from both your web site and the Internet. Whenever someone searches Google from your web site, you have the potential to make money.

When you begin combining two, three or even four successful ad programs, you really begin to benefit. $200 here and there, and soon you're bringing in an extra $1000 a month just for having a web site!

And So....

While banner advertising and affiliate programs won't advance your music career, they can provide you with some extra income from your targeted web site. That extra income can be invested right back into promoting your music or creating more music product to sell. The more your online presence grows, as will happen over time if you keep working on it, the more extra income those ads will bring in. Check out the *Quick Reference Guide* for recommended advertising and affiliate program resources to further research your options.

Speaking of Affiliate Programs…

If you think you might be interested in selling this book from one of your web sites, I'll pay you a commission on your sales. See http://www.musicbizacademy.com/bookstore/affiliate.htm for details.

Bonus Articles for Extra Credit...

There are several popular articles I've written that either don't quite fit into the topic of this book (such as my article on how to copyright your music) or else are just good summations of some of the topics already covered. So in the pages that follow, I've included a few of those articles here for your enjoyment. You can view these as additional information, a nice review of some of the material already covered or else just final words to encourage you to get out there and promote yourself.

If you're interested in reading more of my articles, I link to every article I've written about the music business at http://www.musicbizacademy.com/internet

Bonus Article #1:
How to Copyright Your Music

Why Copyright Your Music?

If you see yourself as a serious musician (and I presume you do), you would be wise to register your original songs with the U.S. Copyright Office (if you reside outside of the U.S., skip to the section on International Copyright below). This will protect you in the event that someone, somewhere, steals one of your songs and claims it as their own. Whether you want to copyright just one song for possible digital distribution or an entire CD of collected works, the process is the same.

How to Register Your Copyright

The U.S. Copyright Office encourages you to register your music via an online registration process called the eCO Online System. You'll find that at http://www.copyright.gov/eco/ . Once you go there, create an account for yourself, then log in and you're ready to start. Registering a copyright via this process is not all that difficult, but the technical language can be confusing. The online process does walk you step-by-step through filling out the document, but even so, take your time. Carefully read the help links (the underlined text) provided each step of the way. If you do that, it will help you understand what information goes where.

You'll find a tutorial for the eCO system at http://www.copyright.gov/eco/eco-tutorial.pdf . I recommend you take a look at that before you undertake the online copyright registration process to see what you're in for.

The filing fee for online song registration is $35.

A few tips regarding the eCO process that I think might help you:

1) You'll want to register your music as a "sound recording" as this kind of registration includes not only the performance, but the underlying music itself.

2) Under "Title of Work" add the name of your CD first and set the "Type" as "Title of work being registered." Then list your song titles and set the "Type" for those as "Contents Title." So the album name is the "Title", the individual songs are the "Contents."

3) If you have cover songs on your album, you'll exclude those under the "Limitation of Claim" section. For example, if track 7 on your CD is a cover tune, under "Material Excluded" check the boxes for "Music" and "Lyrics" (if you have lyrics) and then in the space for "Other" indicate "Track 7." Then under "New Material Included" check all the boxes and under "Other" list the track numbers for your original songs. So here you specify what tracks to exclude for copyright

registration (because they belong to someone else) and which tracks to register under your own name. If all the songs on your album are original, you can skip this section entirely.

Once you have filled out the form and verified all your information, add it to your cart, pay for it, and then you'll receive an email with instructions on how to print out your registration and mail it in with copies of your CD. You can also upload the files digitally, if you prefer.

If you don't wish to go through the online process, you can type all of your information in Form CO, print it out and mail it in. You can get Form CO at http://www.copyright.gov/forms/formco2d.pdf . And you'll find instructions for Form CO at http://www.copyright.gov/forms/formco2d-ins.pdf . Fill out the PDF file following the instructions and then print TWO copies. One copy for yourself, and one copy to mail to the Library of Congress to the address provided.

The cost to submit the form by mail is $50.00.

Either way you go, whether online or via mail, it will take six months to a year for the Library of Congress to process your registration. However, once you've submitted your work, you're *officially* protected. If you use FedEx to send your copyright forms (which I suggest you do), keep your tracking number handy and you can present this as legal proof of your effective date of copyright registration should you ever need it.

How Your Registered Copyright Benefits You

What does your copyright registration do for you? Well, if someone does steal your work, not only can you prove the work is yours by your registration, but you can also sue for damages (you can't legally sue for damages if your song isn't registered with the copyright office). If the copyright infringement is determined to be deliberate, your attorney can initiate a formal criminal investigation.

Registering your songs' copyright grants you these *exclusive* rights:

- The right to make copies and duplicate your music (in CD or other formats)
- The right to distribute your music
- The right to prepare derivative works (alternate versions, new arrangements)
- The right to perform the songs publicly
- The right to display the product publicly
- The right to perform publicly via digital audio transmission

Once you've registered your sound recording with the U.S. copyright office, these rights belong *exclusively* to you and you alone (provided, of course, that you are the actual copyright owner). No one can take those rights from you.

Once your song is registered, you no longer have to worry about someone stealing your song idea and taking credit for it. If someone does that, gets a hit out of it and you can prove the song is yours with your registered copyright, you are going to smile all the way to the bank when the court awards you damages, which can be very high for copyright theft.

Copyright of Individual Digital Creations: What if you only want to copyright a single song to prove it's yours? You might want to check out the service at http://www.myfreecopyright.com . With this service, you can upload your individual digital creations, be they music, video, lyrics or articles you wrote, and once you do so they are instantly copyrighted with a date/time of registration. The service is free, and it's a very simple way to copyright your individual music creations. Just so you know, however, even though you can use this digital copyright in a court of law to prove infringement, you cannot collect statutory damages from the infringer. You can collect lost profits that might be determined, but not statutory damages which is generally where the big money comes from. To collect statutory damages, you still need to send a registration form into the copyright office as stated above.

Creative Commons

There is an alternative means by which you may copyright your work called Creative Commons (http://www.creativecommons.org). What this does is create a copyright for your music whereby instead of all rights being reserved, only *some* rights are reserved. This invites others to use your work for certain purposes without having to get permission from you first. In theory, this means people searching for music to use in their products or digital creations are more likely to use your music since they won't have to jump through a lot of legal hoops to use it. So, for example, you might allow a song to be used in a non-commercial product (ie. no financial profit for the distributor) without forcing the licensee to get permission from you, but still reserve the right to collect a royalty if the product in question is a money-maker. The Creative Commons copyright is still a relatively new concept (compared to formal copyright registration), and there are many variations on it that may make the concept confusing for the potential licensee. Even so, this option is something to at least be aware of. For a list of the different Creative Commons licenses available, see http://creativecommons.org/about/licenses/meet-the-licenses .

International Copyright

If you are not a citizen of the United States, obviously the comments above do not apply to you as every country handles the copyright process a bit differently. However, chances are that your homeland is a member of the World Intellection Property Organization (WIPO). If so, you can start researching your copyright options at http://www.wipo.int/members/en/ . Select your country name from the WIPO list, follow the "contact information" link, and that will take you to a page that lists the web site address of the copyright office for your country.

For more places to research copyright and music law, see the *Quick Reference Guide*.

Bonus Article #2:
The "Secret" to Selling Lots of Music

My Biggest Payout Ever for Digital Distribution

I just recently received my biggest single payout ever for digital music sales from CD Baby. How much? Over $3,000 just in digital music sales. That completely blows my mind. Considering that I actually make .60-some-odd cents per .99¢ track sold on average, that means this single payment represents about 4,800 downloads sold.

It's amazing to realize that so many people are buying my music. Lest you think my success is the result of some gimmick, think again. I'm just a piano player. Nothing extravagant. I just play, write, and record my music. I have a few cover tunes, yes, but surprisingly that's not where most of my sales come from. A hefty portion of my digital music sales comes from my original music. In fact, my best selling song is an original tune called "No More Tears." If you look at my top ten best selling-singles, six of the ten are original.

I have been enjoying great digital music sales for awhile now. I typically average between $2,500-$3,500 over a month period. But to get one single payment of that size (CD Baby pays out weekly) is a marvelous thing. My lovely wife, the love of my life, is rejoicing.

I posted a simple comment about the event on my personal Twitter account (http://www.twitter.com/davidnevue) . Here's what I said:

> "I received my largest deposit ever from CDBaby. Record month for digital music sales! I'd do a happy dance if I wasn't so full from dinner!"

And that prompted this response from a fellow musician:

> "Hi David...to what do you owe your great digital sales success?"

Why People Buy Music

That got me to thinking. Why do people buy music, anyway? What is it that makes someone, a total stranger, actually go out and PURCHASE music? Especially when, in this day and age, people can find so much music for free on the Internet? *To what do I owe* my great digital sales success?

Now, I could get spiritually-minded here. I could say, *To Whom* do I owe my great digital sales success and then thank God for His great provision. That would certainly be correct and true. There certainly is a spiritual element to what I do. My music is faith-based. But there's more to it than that.

My response to my fellow musician was this; two reasons for my success came to mind:

1) I write music that some folks love so much that they can't wait to share it with others.

2) I have a large catalog. I have a discography of eleven albums now, containing somewhere in the neighborhood of 160 tunes. More product = more sales. It's easier to sell a little of a lot than it is to sell a lot of a little. When someone discovers a song of yours that they love, they'll listen to your other songs as well. And that single sale might turn into a whole lot more sales. The more products you have, the more you have the potential to sell.

I know what you're thinking right now… "Great… he has 11 albums of music. No wonder he makes so much money from digital distribution! I just have one album, so I can't make anything near that." OK, I want you to just take a moment and think that logic through. Yes, I have 11 albums of music. But how many albums of music did I *start* with? Just one. I started right where you are now. Building a career in music takes time. You start small, with one album. Then you take the money you make from that, reinvest it, and make a second album. Now you have two. Then you take the sales from both those albums and invest that money in a third. Now you have three, and you are making three times the sales and income. And on it goes. That's how you *grow a business*. One step at a time.

It's All About the Music...

When all is said and done, making significant income from your music boils down to the *music* itself. You can be the best Internet marketer out there, have a fantastic web site, twenty albums to offer, get widespread distribution and all the press in the world, and still not sell very much music. True, isn't it? Yes, absolutely. A great web site and publicity will help you sell *great* music, but it won't help you sell mediocre music, or even skillfully played music that people don't connect with. You can watch someone play at a concert and be amazed at their skill on their instrument, but is that what makes you break down and buy their music? No. You don't buy the music because someone is a great player, you buy the music because you like it and you connect with it. And even if you get caught up in the moment and buy someone's CD because you were amazed at their skill, what happened when you got home and actually listened to the CD? The excitement faded, didn't it? The skill didn't translate to audio enjoyment, because what you want to listen to for enjoyment is music that speaks to you *emotionally*, not technically.

Love at First Listen...

Music is all about emotion. For total strangers to buy your music online, especially if they are hearing it or sampling it for the first time, they have to fall in love with it in that very moment. Call it "love at first listen." They have to want it, to desire it, and then for you to find real success, your buyer has to love it *so much* that after experiencing it they can't help but to share it with their friends, family and co-workers who, in turn, fall in love with your music. That's how real success happens. That's how you grow a business based on your music.

At its core, music is more than just dials and buttons. It's more than good production. It's more than a great mix, more than a marketing plan, more than a skillfully played instrument. It's raw, untamed emotion. Capture that, and you just might have something.

1) Focus on your music and songwriting, first.

2) *Then* focus on the recording and production, taking great songs and making them sound the best they can possibly be.

3) *Then* focus on the marketing, distribution, and promotion.

A final word of advice: Never, ever, ever release an album or song before its time. Never be in a hurry to release your music. Make sure what you put out there is 100% what you want it to be, and that it represents you well. Once you put it out there, you can't take it back.

Do it right, no matter what it takes. If you settle for doing less than your best, then less than your best is what others will perceive as your "best." And is what you are about to release really your best work?

Make it your best. Do it right. And then enjoy life.

Bonus Article #3:
House Concerts: Be an "American Idol," One House at a Time

You Talk, You Share, You Play...

I'm a big fan of house concerts... when I go out on tour, about a third of the concerts I perform are in people's homes. There's nothing quite like it. I LOVE playing them. You meet so many great people on a one-to-one basis. You talk, you share, you play... and these folks love your music. So going in, you have that in common. Makes it easy to small talk.

Don't Scoff at the Size of the Audience

You may scoff at the idea of playing a concert in a person's home because you are concerned about SIZE. The size of the audience doesn't matter. In fact, you will likely find, as I did, that playing a concert to a small audience in a home is much more effective and financially lucrative than playing in a "typical" venue.

How much money do you usually command when you play a show in a club? $100 bucks? $200? I typically ask $500 for a house concert. I know musicians who charge as much as $1500 for an intimate home show. Now, I don't do that, because personally I want my concerts to be affordable to the average person. Most people won't and can't justify paying $1500 for a concert. But if someone is a real fan of your music, they'll find a way to come up with $500 for a show custom-tailored just for them – and they'll be even more stoked about it if you offer to play their favorite songs for them in their own home.

And what's even MORE fantastic about playing house concerts is how easy they are to do. All you have to do is show up and bring your instrument (if you are a pianist, as I am, you can play THEIR instrument. In that case, you just bring the clothes on your back and CDs and merch to sell). Your concert host does all the promotion, bringing in their friends, family and coworkers to show off YOUR music – which is among their favorite music – to their personal network of friends.

So you have no promotion costs to worry about. Oh, and guess what? The host provides the food, too. And they will probably even invite you stay the night at their home to save you that hotel bill.

How are CD sales? Ridiculous. At least, compared to playing a club.

When you play a club, how many fans are there to see YOU? Do you play and do your thing while people mill about talking, eating and drinking, hardly taking notice of you? Maybe you sell a CD here and there, but are you selling DOZENS of them?

At a house concert, you have a totally attentive audience. You can engage them, telling stories about your songs, laughing together, crying together, sharing not only your music, but YOURSELF with them.

If you're engaging, and if your storytelling and your music touches them, you'll sell CDs like candy.

When I play a house concert, I generally sell an average of 1 CD per person in the audience. There are always a few who don't buy, but those are more than made up for by those who buy multiple CDs.

So with one house concert audience of 30 people (about 15 couples), which is about my average, I'll sell 30-40 CDs. Let's say 35. At a $12 per CD average, that's $420. Plus my $500 fee. That's $920 for 3 hours of playing and hanging out with people who love my music. Oh, and they provide me a meal and a place to stay. What's that worth? Another $120 bucks?

So when I play a house concert I can make $1,000 profit a night. If you sell merchandise as well, you can do even better.

More Than Just Money...

Now that's great money, and if you're in it for the money, well, then, there you go. But I'm not in it just for the money. House concerts are a great way to develop relationships with your fans. It's about meeting and touching REAL people with REAL lives. Encouraging people who love your music. Exhorting them. Lifting them up. Helping them to get back on their feet. Making a difference, one home at a time.

But back to the money, because I know that's an important factor. We all have to support our families and our art. None of us want to lose money on a tour.

I've played to house concert audiences as small as seven people. Guess what? I still made $500 bucks plus a few CD sales. On the other side of the spectrum, I've played house concerts to over a hundred people – and sold well over a hundred CDs at a show. Almost $2,000 for 3 hours of work? That buys a lot of groceries. My wife loves that.

And it goes beyond that. Anytime I play a house concert, I see lots of follow up sales through my web site. Fans invite their friends to the concert, their friends buy a CD, love it, then buy more music via my web site or iTunes. They tell their friends. They are excited they saw me live, in person, and actually met me. They are jazzed. The next time I come to town, guess what? These new fans want their OWN concert. And they bring their friends, and now I'm playing to MORE people. Which leads to more OPPORTUNITY. Not only financially, but to build relationships that are lasting.

In today's connected world, with Facebook and Twitter being all the rage, setting up a house concert tour is easier than ever before.

Read the story of solo bassist Steve Lawson. You'll find his blog posting about his own house concert tour experience at http://www.stevelawson.net/2009/02/real-life-touring-a-social-media-fuelled-tale/. It's well worth reading.

Fill Those Empty Nights...

So the next time you're on tour and want to fill up those empty nights on your calendar, start talking with your fans in the area. Offer to play in their homes. You can ask your fee or even just ask for donations from the crowd. You might not make as much in donations, but playing a show in someone's home and making $200 from donations plus any CD sales you do is better than sitting at a hotel all by your lonesome eating pizza and watching American Idol.

Play house concerts and you can BE an American Idol, one house at a time.

Bonus Article #4:
Can You Help? And Please, No HYPE!

Here's an email I received from a visitor to the Music Biz Academy. It's short and sweet...

"Can you help? Please, NO HYPE. Either yes or no is fine. Would you GUARANTEE your success to me?"

I've been promoting my music on the Internet for over fifteen years now (since 1995), and for the last nine, I've been doing it full time, having quit my day job at Symantec Corporation in November of 2001.

I've worked really, really hard to get to this point. I've taken no short cuts, used no get-rich-quick schemes, just put a whole lot of hours into research and marketing to find ways to get my music out there using the Internet.

So, having reached this point, every once in a while I get a desperate email like the one above. The essential question being, "if I buy your book, 'How to Promote Your Music Successfully on the Internet', will you GUARANTEE me success?"

The answer is, **no, of course I can't**. I can't guarantee success to anyone. All I can do is share my experience with you, educate you, and present you with tools to help you attain your goals. It's up to you to take that knowledge, apply it, and find your own way. I can't do it for you.

Those who succeed will be those who are a) smart about how they manage their time and business, b) tenacious to no end and c) emotionally connected to their fans. It takes all three elements to succeed as a musician. Notice I *didn't* include "skilled" or "talented" on that list. You can be the best guitar player in the world, but if you don't connect with your fans emotionally, they'll have no reason to buy your music. On the other hand, there are artists who are not the "best players in the world," but connect emotionally with their fans, are incredibly tenacious, and know their business (that pretty much describes me).

When all three of those factors line up, success comes in time.

I can't make any guarantees you'll find the same level of success that I have, but I can say that if you apply yourself, using the tools I've made available in my book and at the MusicBizAcademy.com web site, you'll be a whole lot better off than you were before. You certainly should be able to sell a lot more CDs and downloads.

If you really want to succeed in this business, here's my advice:

1) Educate yourself by learning from those who have gone before you.
2) Follow through by applying what you have learned.
3) Realize real financial success may take YEARS to attain.
4) In spite of that, don't ever, ever stop.

Internet Resources for the Independent Musician!

The following pages include reviews of web sites and services that have received my highest recommendations at the Music Biz Academy. For a more complete list of resources, please refer to the musician's directory at http://www.musicbizacademy.com/directory .

General Resources for Musicians
Complete listing available at http://www.musicbizacademy.com/directory/indiemusic.htm

About.com: Musicians' Exchange - http://musicians.about.com/
About.com's *Musicians' Exchange* is a great place to just drop by and browse. There are gobs of helpful articles, along with a large number of useful links, resources, and reviews. You'll find information on promotion, legal advice, gear, labels, producers, and organizations. Virtually anything related to the music business that's of interest to you can be researched here.

Bandname.com - http://www.bandname.com/
This "Worldwide Band Name Registry" is basically a place to register your band name to ensure no one else is using it. In addition, you'll find a great selection of articles, a nice classified ad section, and a well organized link page to other valuable resources.

The Buzz Factor - http://www.thebuzzfactor.com
Bob Baker's "The Buzz Factor" is a must-see if you're an independent artist. While yes, Bob's web site is devoted primarily to selling his music and book marketing materials, you'll also find lots of great guerilla music marketing articles and tips. Check out his blog and while you're at it, sign up for the Buzz Factor newsletter.

Festivals.com - http://www.festivals.com/
At Festivals.com, you'll discover the latest details on festivals from all across America. Search by state, subject or keyword. A great research tool if you travel the festival circuit.

Festival Network Online - http://festivalnet.com/
Pick a date, a state, and see all the festivals happening within a particular area. Over 20,000 listings. You can view event listings for free, but need to join at $49/year to get the event details. Features include the ability to search by 24 types of music, perform a radius search, view festival ratings entered by others and perform keyword searches.

Magnatune - http://www.magnatune.com
Magnatune is probably the only "record label" we'd ever recommend you consider submitting your music to. Forward thinking, artist friendly, and totally aware of how music lovers prefer buying their music, Magnatune is making good use of the Internet to expose artists to new listeners and buyers. Their unique

business model has been featured in USA Today, the BBC, Time Magazine and others. Check out the information at http://www.magnatune.com/info/ for an overview of this fascinating music business model.

Talent Agencies and Music Promotion Services

Complete listing available at http://musicbizacademy.com/directory/talentagencies.htm .

As with record labels, talent agencies abound on the Internet. While I've reviewed the following web sites, I've not worked with many of these folks personally. If you opt to contact one of these companies, keep your head about you. If you have to pay an agency a fee before they will even listen to your music, be wary.

Ariel Publicity - http://www.arielpublicity.com/
If you're struggling in your effort to generate publicity for yourself or your band, stop by Ariel's place and see what she can do for you. Ariel's web site and credentials are most impressive. The list of bands she's worked with is as long as your arm and includes some big name acts. In addition to her PR services, be sure to visit her excellent SoundAdvice blog.

Buzzplant - http://www.buzzplant.com/
Buzzplant is an Internet marketing and promotion company focused on the Christian Music industry. It makes use of grassroots promotion as well as partnerships with Christian and music marketing web sites to promote its clients via the web, social networking, mobile marketing, viral video marketing, publicity and more. The emphasis at Buzzplant is to invest in developing relationships with potential buyers and then offering them the music they are looking for. Clients include some huge names; Sonic Flood, Delirious, John Tesh, Mercy Me, Michael Card, Ginny Owens, Charlie Peacock and many others. Visit the web site for examples of current promotions and case studies.

Concerts in Your Home - http://www.concertsinyourhome.com
There's nothing quite like a house concert - especially as a performer. They're simple to play, easy to set up, and the intimate setting makes an audience very enthusiastic about your music. "Concerts in Your Home" is a place you can go to find local house concert venues, or venues in areas where you'll be touring. House concert hosts are always looking for new talent to bring in, and unlike many venues, they're just normal folks who like good music. Check out the site to sign up as a house concert performer or to browse the house concert host listings. Membership is $148/year.

Evolution Promotion - http://www.evolutionpromotion.com/
Sting, R.E.M., Moby, White Stripes, Steward Copeland, Jane Siberry - these are just a few of the many artists who have made use of one of the many services provided by Evolution Promotion. Services include radio promotion, tour promotion, film and TV music placement, direct consumer marketing, Internet radio and marketing, web design and consulting. The Evolution Promotion team creates custom campaigns for clients designed to achieve breakthrough success at radio, on the Net and in the marketplace. The founder of Evolution, Karen Lee, was a national promoter for Elektra and IRS Records, where she promoted The Cars, Motley Crue, Metallica, 10,000 Maniacs, The GoGo's, Concrete Blonde, and others. Need a promoter? Get one with experience. Here's one place to start.

Goodnight Kiss Music - http://www.goodnightkiss.com/
Songwriters, check out Goodnight Kiss Music, a music publisher based in Hollywood, California. GKM specializes in placing songs within the film, television, and recording industry and they have a very

impressive list of credits. Goodnight Kiss is open to considering material from unknown songwriters for their projects, but they do have a strict list of requirements for submissions. Interested songwriters should check their web site to see what they are currently working on, and then contact them directly before submitting any material. A subscription-based newsletter is also available which outlines their current projects.

MusiciansContact.com - http://www.musicianscontact.com/
Over the past 30 years, managers, record company personnel, producers, booking agents, employers and production companies have used Musicians Contact to locate replacement musicians and singers. If you think you might be interested in putting your name in the pool, sign up. Clients using Musicians Contact seeking fill-in musicians include such big names as Glen Frey, Tom Waits, Warrant, Dishwalla, Herbie Hancock, Neil Diamond, Stomp, Gene Loves Jezebel, Ozzy Ozbourne, Billy Joel and others.

NOMA Music - http://www.nomamusic.com
NOMA Music is a multi-credited music licensing company and song publisher. They represent worldwide bands, songwriters, and composers who are interested in licensing, and of course, earning money and royalties from having their original music used in feature and indie motion pictures, television, and other multi-media projects. Some of their represented acts have songs currently heard in television shows airing on HBO, Warner Brothers, FOX, UPN, Touchstone, Paramount, Showtime, SyFy Channel, and FX Networks, as well as in motion pictures and commercial DVD releases. NOMA offers tremendous opportunities for the indie and established artist from the hundreds of production companies, directors and producers they have working relationships with, and as a client of theirs, your music will be made accessible to them. There are NO up-front fees, period. NOMA Music earns its money through licensing on a commission-only basis. Thus, the only way NOMA benefits financially is when YOU benefit financially.

Pump Audio - http://www.pumpaudio.com/
If you're in the market to license your music to TV, film, video games or other advertisers, check out Pump Audio. With your permission, Pump Audio will include your music in their database for promotion and possible licensing to their clients. You keep all copyright, ownership and publishing rights, and receive 35% of the licensing fees billed to their production clients if your music is used. There's NO submission fee, it's non-exclusive, and you retain 100% ownership of your songs. Based on feedback we've heard from artists, this is one of the best, most effective song licensing agencies around. However, the turnaround time to receive a response from your initial submission is quite long. Even so, well worth investigating.

Products and Services for Musicians
Complete listing available at http://www.musicbizacademy.com/directory/musicservices.htm .

ABC Pictures - http://www.abcpictures.com/
ABC is the premier photographic duplication company for artists looking to procure photo slicks or other promotional materials for your press kit. We have personally worked with ABC and can vouch for their quality, service and turnaround time. ABC offers glossy 8x10s, posters, postcards, business cards and specialty items. Call and request their free catalog or request free samples of their work from the web site.

BandPasses.com - http://www.bandpasses.com
At BandPasses.com, you can have some very cool laminated security and promotional backstage passes made for your concert or other event. The basic package, 25 passes with 1 side printed in color and lanyards, is just $99. Check out the sample gallery.

Bruce Miller Mixing and Mastering - http://bruceamiller.us/
We don't review many mastering services, but this service by Bruce Miller, who has engineered work for Miles Davis, Yes, Mariah Carey, Canibus, Lost Boyz, Dave Matthews, Luthor Vandross, Whitney Houston, and many others, really caught our eye. Bruce provides a number of services to musicians, including mixing, mastering, production, recording and editing. If you're in the market for any of these services, you simply must check out Bruce's prices, which include a $99 "Starving Artist Special" for one song.

CD Counter Displays
Looking for that perfect counter display for your CDs or DVDs at gigs? Here are four of our favorite web site resellers that together, give you about every conceivable display option for your product!

CD Counter Displays - http://www.counterdisplay.com/
MusicDisplays.com - http://www.musicdisplays.com/
DisplaysInStock.com - http://www.displaysinstock.com/
Displays2Go - http://www.displays2go.com/category.aspx?ID=1379

Cheap TV Spots! - http://www.cheap-tv-spots.com/
Want to make that "As Seen on TV" spot for your band or CD? Cheap TV Spots will help you come up with a concept, do all the scripting, filming, editing and even help you get your ad on television if you like. They can get you coverage locally, nationally or internationally. A complete, ready-to-air commercial runs $1,999. MUCH less expensive than many alternatives, and worth a look if you're in the market to do a TV ad. More details as well as plenty of sample ads at the web site.

FanBridge - http://www.fanbridge.com
FanBridge is a list management service designed specifically for musicians to help them build a fan base using the current social networking trends. The whole point of FanBridge, really, is to make list management and social network communication fun and easy. FanBridge gives you a mailing list sign-up form that you can put just about anywhere, not just your web site, but also MySpace and Facebook. Using their service you can send out some really nice looking newsletters with links built right in to purchase your music. It's free to try, but if you decide to stick with it, pricing starts at $9/month for up to 1,000 messages sent.

Indie Band Manager - http://www.indiebandmanager.com/
Indie Band Manager is a powerful database software that helps you manage your contacts and career. To quote the web site "Indie Band Manager is the complete and affordable way to manage a performing career. Musicians, agents, labels, comedians, dancers, film makers and publicists all over the world manage thousands of pages of information on fans, venues, media contacts, bookings, inventory, finance, content, and calendar all in one place." The PRO version comes with a database of thousands of contacts for venues, press, and radio stations included. The "Lite" version, which contains all Contact Management, Booking, and To Do List modules, but no financial, resource directory, or inventory modules costs $49.95. The full-featured PRO version costs $219.95. Download either version for Mac or PC to try out FREE to make sure it's right for you.

MasterLab - http://www.masterlab.com/
MasterLab is an all format CD, DVD and digital mastering and duplication facility, founded by former Marilyn Manson drummer Sara Lee Lucas and partner Trace, international computer whiz-kid. Aside from mastering and duplication, MasterLab provides graphic design services, video for CD & DVD, digital

photography, merchandising, and artist public relations. Partial Client List includes: The Rolling Stones, Prince, Snoop Dogg, Enya, Wu Tang Clan and Disney.

MP3Machine.com - http://www.mp3machine.com/
Need MP3 tools? Encoders? CD Rippers? Playlist managers? Skin makers? Editors? Whatever you need in terms of audio tools, you'll find options for in the MP3Machine.com directory. As of this writing, MP3Machine contains over 2400 software titles to help you get the job done.

Music Pro Insurance - http://www.musicproinsurance.com/
Founded by Phil Crosland, ASCAP's senior vice president of marketing, MusicPro provides insurance coverage for the music professional. Coverage includes instrument and equipment, studio liability, tour liability, special event liability, travel accident, health, life and long term care. Other insurance options are available depending on your state of residence. For more information, read the interview with Phil Crosland at http://www.musicdish.com/mag/?id=10191 about MusicPro.

TicketPrinting.com - http://www.ticketprinting.com/
Want to print up some quick tickets for your upcoming concert? Look no further. Just pick a template, enter your concert info and you'll have ready to use tickets in your hands in just a few days. You can also print raffle tickets, wristbands, posters, banners, badges and more. Request a free sample kit from the web site.

ULINE Shipping Supply Specialists - http://www.uline.com/
If you are looking for packaging supplies for your CDs or other products, ULINE is the place to shop. They have the sturdiest, most professional CD mailers I've seen and I've been using their products for over ten years now. I highly recommend the self-sealing multi-depth mailers for 1-4 CDs or the 10 CD tab locking box for large CD orders. Excellent customer service and fast shipping times.

Promotional Merchandise and Gimmicks

http://www.musicbizacademy.com/directory/musicmerchandising.htm .

Bandwear.com - http://www.bandwear.com/
Bandwear.com specializes in creating unique merchandise and specialty items for independent musicians. Using your own artwork, you can create shirts, caps, stickers, promotional items like mugs, keychains, matchbooks and lighters, promotional postcards and posters - just about anything. If you don't have your own art designer, their staff can help you with design and logos. Once your product is created, Bandwear can provide you with a custom link so you can sell your product from your own web site, making their store, part of your own store.

Branders - http://www.branders.com/
Branders, "The World's Largest Online Seller of Promotional Items" allows you to put your band logo or image on tons of cool products such as; mouse pads, lava lamps, calculators, hats, shirts, clocks, games, toys, magnets, notepads, chocolate bars, and more. You'll find more merchandising options at Branders than just about anywhere else.

CafePress.com - http://www.cafepress.com/
Create your own CafePress.com "shop" and you can sell T-Shirts, mugs, mouse pads and over 80 other products branded with your logo right from your web site. Simply upload your digital artwork, use their "instant design generator" to create the look you want, click "save", and you will instantly have your own "store" at CafePress.com. You sell the merchandise via a link from your site, then CafePress makes and

ships it. You collect the profit. The only cost to you is the wholesale cost of the merchandise you actually sell. You decide your own profit margin by adding your desired profit to the base price. For details specific to creating your own shop, see http://www.cafepress.com/cp/info/sell/index.aspx .

Flyadisc - http://www.discnow.com/flyadisc.htm
How about flinging your demo CDs and/or other CD media safely into crowds at concerts, festivals and sporting events - just about anywhere people are gathered. Here's a cool idea that will have curious strangers checking out your CD.

Identity Links: Light Up Promo Products - http://www.identity-links.com/light-up
Identitity Links offers an amazing selection of products you can put your brand, logo, or image on, but check out these light up promotional products, including necklaces, key chains, glasses, glow wands, fiber-optic hats, straws, pens and even ice cubes. Turn your club gig into a dazzling light show - worn entirely by your audience!

Stamps.com: Put Your Band on a Stamp - http://photo.stamps.com/
It's very expensive promotion (almost a buck per stamp), but a nice gimmick. Perhaps a good attention-getter for that press kit? Worth a look, if for no other reason than to know it's there.

Career and Music Business Help
Complete listing available at http://www.musicbizacademy.com/directory/musictutorials.htm .

FourFront Media & Music - http://musicbizacademy.com/knab/
Christopher Knab's huge archive of articles and how-to tips for musicians now has a permanent home at The Music Biz Academy.

HomeRecording.com - http://homerecording.com/bbs/
Are you a dedicated do-it-yourselfer who dreams of recording in your own studio? Then this is the place for you. HomeRecording.com is essentially a very active bulletin board forum where you can ask and get answers to questions on everything from recording and mixing techniques to DJ and Hip Hop production. For home recording newbies or wannabees, this fantastic resource should not be missed.

MyMusicJob.com - http://www.mymusicjob.com/
Looking for work in the music business? Join MyMusicJob.com to get access to job listings and internships, as well as post your resume. There are quite a few offerings here and all jobs are posted by the employers themselves. If you want a sampling of what's available, the best way to go about that is to use the free "Search Job" option to view "All Categories" and "All Locations." The cost for a 60-day membership is only $14.99, though you can still apply for any job posting over three days old if you're not a member. Members get the first shot at new job openings, however.

Rock Star Image - http://www.rockstarimage.com/
John Battaglia is an image and performance coach who's worked with some of the biggest names in the business: Usher, Beyonce, Jessica Simpson and others. He coaches emerging artists on how to build a Rockstar image to better attract industry attention. If you're uncertain about your "image" or "style," feel the need to reinvent yourself, or just need advice on how to better connect with your audience, John's your man.

Musicians' Communities

Complete listing available at http://www.musicbizacademy.com/directory/musichosting.htm .

In the Music Biz Academy resource directory I lump music hosting services right in with communities in general. However, since I've already addressed places to host your music in *The Best Places to Promote, Sell, and Distribute Your Music* chapter, I won't include them again here. Instead, I offer you some of my other favorite communities for songwriters and musicians.

Guitar 9 Records - http://www.guitar9.com/
Guitar 9 Records is a hosting service/online store/monthly e-zine for independent artists/bands that feature the guitar as their dominant instrument. If you're not already familiar with Guitar 9, I urge you (particularly if you're a guitarist with a CD to market) to take a look at Guitar 9's site. Guitar 9 Records has been around for years, and they have consistently stayed true to their purpose - promoting independent guitar music on the Internet (now over 1100 guitar artists). Some of the finest undiscovered guitar players in the world can be found here, and you'll find lots of articles on the music business from a guitarist's perspective.

Just Plain Folks - http://www.jpfolks.com/
JPF is a community of over 50,000 songwriters, recording artists, music publishers, record labels, performing arts societies, engineers, producers, journalists, retailers and just about every other type of member of the music industry. The idea, essentially, is that thousands of 'just plain folks' share ideas on touring, manufacturing, web sites, and organizations friendly to musicians. The entire community is centered on the idea of working together for the benefit of all. The forums, which are very active, are fantastic. Members include Grammy and Emmy winners, staff from BMI and ASCAP, TAXI, AFM, right alongside plain old street musicians trying to find a break. Membership is free.

The Muse's Muse - A Songwriters Resource - http://www.musesmuse.com
The Muse's Muse has, over its many years, become one of the most enduring and useful independent songwriter communities on the Internet. Songwriters will find a lot to peruse here, but I especially recommend checking out the 'Interactivities,' where you'll find chat rooms, as well as an active message board. I also highly recommend the writings of their columnists. Be sure to subscribe to the free monthly newsletter.

MusicThoughts Discussion Group - http://groups.yahoo.com/group/musicthoughts/
This very active discussion group was created by CD Baby founder Derek Sivers as "A popular, open place for musicians to talk to other musicians." It's a great place to hang out and get a vibe for what other musicians are thinking and talking about. If you need a place to get advice, receive feedback on your music, or find out whether or not a company is reputable, this is the place to ask.

The World Wide Songwriters Association - http://www.wwswa.com/
These folks have created a wonderful community just for songwriters. You can upload your songs to get feedback from other writers, get professional songwriting evaluations, collaborate and share ideas with other songwriters and so many other things. To quote the site, their "mission" is to "assist and encourage songwriters, both amateur and professional, in all genres of music around the globe." It's an "ever evolving community of songwriters around the world striving to further educate, evaluate and encourage the profession of songwriting." Membership to the site is free, so songwriters, sign up today.

Compact Disc Manufacturers

Inevitably you will be looking to produce your own CD of music, if you have not already. Like everything else, there are a large number of CD manufacturers represented on the Internet. Here's a short list of manufacturers worth checking out. All of these services are notable for varying reasons. Complete listing available at http://www.musicbizacademy.com/directory/cdmanufacturers.htm .

Café Press Audio and Data - http://www.cafepress.com/cp/info/sell/products/audio/
Café Press is known for their one-off merchandise printing, specifically, you upload your artwork and fans can buy t-shirts, mugs, hats and more with your band logo or picture on it. What you many not know is that Café Press offers one-off CD printing services as well. How does it work? Design your CD package on their web site (with full-color inserts), specify your track listing, mail in your CD master and they will create a CD for you that customers can purchase one at a time and have mailed directly to them from your own Café Press Shop. You keep whatever money you charge above their "base price." See the web site for further details.

CDFX - http://www.cdfx.com/
Here's a company to check out for not only CD manufacturing, but for all those odd-shaped, custom jobs. In addition to standard CD replication, CDFX offers manufacturing for business card CDs, DVD cards, shaped CDs, custom-shaped CDs, audio and data CDs, ticket CDs, flash drives, DVDs, eco-friendly packaging and, of course, traditional CD manufacturing. Good prices, a great looking web site and a very impressive client list (including Coca-Cola, the Dallas Cowboys, FedEx, Honda, NBC, United Way and even President George W. Bush.) Finally, CDFX offers fulfillment, inventory management, distribution and direct mail services for their clients.

CDS Group - http://www.cdsg.com/
While looking for a graphic designer, I stumbled across CDS, a company that specializes not only in graphic and CD packaging design, but also complete CD manufacturing services. Not only was I impressed with their design work (they have plenty of examples on their site), CDS can design and manufacture your entire CD package for you. While their prices are not the lowest you'll find, they are reasonable and this certainly is one case where you'll get the quality you pay for. If you're searching for a company to put it all together for you, and work side by side with you in creating a package that represents you and your music, CDS is certainly a good choice. 1-3 day turnaround on short-run CD duplication available.

DiskFactory: Short Run CDs - http://www.diskfaktory.com/enter/024/default.asp?AffID=024
DiskFactory came highly recommended for musicians who need a short run of CDs at really great prices and FAST. 100 CDs with full-color 4-page inserts is just $249. 5-7 day standard turnaround time, with a 3-day rush option available. I liked them so much that I invited them to partner with me. The link above takes you to our partner page.

DiscMakers - http://www.discmakers.com/
DiscMakers is arguably the most well-known CD Manufacturer marketing itself to independent musicians. If you know almost nothing about the CD Manufacturing process and don't have the time or desire to learn, DiscMakers would be a good choice for you. You can send in your photo or other art, and they will design your entire CD package for you and then send you a proof for your final approval. They have excellent customer service, a high-quality product and a fantastic, eye-pleasing web site. Yes, you can find less

expensive manufacturers and save a few dollars, but with DiscMakers, you've got that built-in trust that is so valuable. You know you're going to get a quality product.

Disc Wizards: Based in the UK - http://www.discwizards.com/
For our UK-based readers... here's a CD manufacturer close to home. CDs, DVDs, mastering and graphic design all in one place - and with a UK low price guarantee. To quote the site, "Ordering is as easy as 1-2-3." Used them? Let me know what you thought of your experience.

Front Porch CD - http://www.frontporchcd.com/
Front Porch CD takes the "guy next door" approach to CD manufacturing and duplication - their web site is very simple, but peppered with testimonials from very happy clients. The overall feeling one comes away with as a visitor to their site is that Front Porch CD takes very good care of their customers. The general consensus, from the clients quoted, is that Front Porch CD treats them like royalty. "It was good to finally find a company that treated us like real people," is one typical example. Front Porch's services include manufacturing, duplication, graphic design, and a promise of quick turnaround times. Their prices are very competitive. A large client list is available for reference.

GrooveHouse - http://www.groovehouse.com/
A slick, easy-to-use web site, great prices and an endless list of positive customer testimonials should make GrooveHouse a top contender for your next manufacturing job. Services include CD & DVD duplication and replication, traditional and alternative CD packaging, vinyl pressing, Digipaks, download cards, graphic design, posters and postcards. Short run duplication available as well with great pricing and shipping to you available as soon as two days! Their sole mission: produce the very best digital audio recordings while keeping competitive prices. The web site will wow you.

Kunaki - http://www.kunaki.com/
So many folks have recommended Kunaki to me that I felt obligated to include them here. The web site won't dazzle you, but if you want something quick, automated, simple and inexpensive for your short-run CD needs, Kunaki is an option. Prices are very good... $1.00 per disc for a basic, 2-panel insert CD for an order of 10 or less units. .75 cents to $1.75 per unit for 11 or more (the pricing varies day-to-day depending on the daily volume). How it works: you download Kunaki's software to design your CD package and send it to them (or optionally upload it or mail it in to them.). Once the CD is done, they can ship to you, drop ship for you to CD Baby, Amazon or anywhere else, or even ship direct to your customer. That's right, you can plug your web site right into Kunaki's credit card system... they'll take the order, make the CD, ship it, then send you the customer's info along with your money. Be sure you read through Kunaki's entire web site to get a feel for what they do. They beat to a different drummer, but for many folks, it's been a great solution.

Mixonic - http://www.mixonic.com/
At Mixonic you can create your entire CD, DVD, USB flash drive, posters, postcards or flyers from start to finish online. Just create an account, upload your files, and use the provided online tool to design your project. By the time you are done using their wizard-like interface, you've created your final work, which you can save (to finish later), or order for printing and manufacturing. Short-run orders or big orders, it doesn't matter.

Oasis Disc Manufacturing - http://www.oasiscd.com/
Oasis is one of the most highly respected independent music manufacturing plants in the business. You'll

find competitive prices on CD and DVD replication as well as posters, flyers, postcards, stickers, merch, download cards and custom USB drives. Lots and lots of packaging options to explore.

CD, Graphic & Web Design Services

If you need art designed for your CD, poster, logo, or anything else, let me first recommend Matt Strieby (stree-bee) at NewLeaf Design. I've been working with Matt for many, many years and you just can't beat his price for the service and creative design you receive. Read more about NewLeaf at http://www.musicbizacademy.com/artdesign/artintro.htm .

In addition, here is a short list of designers specializing in CD packaging, web sites and art design. A complete listing is available at http://www.musicbizacademy.com/directory/cdgraphicdesign.htm .

Auntie Momo Designs - http://www.auntiemomo.com/
If you're looking for someone to design (or redesign) a web site for you, here's an inexpensive option. Auntie's designs tend to be simple and classy, just as a web site should. View the online portfolio for some examples. Graphic and logo design is available as well.

CDDesign.com - http://www.cddesign.com/
CDDesign.com has an exceptional design portfolio and their design prices are quite good, especially for CD art packages that look as good as these do. My contact at CDDesign.com, creative director Eric Fritz, stated the following: "We provide flat-rate, per project quotes (no hourly charges) and we revise until the client is satisfied." If you need a designer, be sure to check out Eric's work. It's truly fantastic.

Digital Vista: Music Promotion Design Studio - http://www.d-vista.com/music/
Rich DiSilvio of Digital Vista specializes in what he calls "Visual Promotions" which includes web design, CD cover art and multimedia. Rich's artwork has a very unique touch, with a visually-stunning presentation. Those of you looking for a fantasy art/otherworldly/very colorful look for your CD covers, take note. Digital's CD cover artwork will make your album stand out, that's for sure. Additional services include computer illustration and graphics.

ProgArt - http://www.progart.com
If you're looking for a gothic, heavy metal-style design, don't miss the work of artist Mattias Norén at ProgArt. Mattias is without a doubt one of the finest artists I've seen in this genre. Fantastic designs for not only CDs, but also posters, shirts, logos and more.

Skyfall Media - http://www.skyfallmedia.com
Skyfall's designs are both impressive and affordable. Services include art design for CD covers, press kits, web sites, posters, logos, and more at a fraction of the cost of most designers. Hosting and registering domain names is also available. Be sure to check out the press kit designs for one-sheets in particular, which look really great. I've worked with Tiffany at Skyfall and she's a class act. Highly recommended.

Standard Design - http://www.standard-design.com
Standard Design offers stunning, stylistic design work. One thing's for sure; the images really pop out at you. Hand someone a "Standard Designed" flyer and you can bet they'll take notice. Whether you need flyers, postcards, posters, business cards, web design or CD artwork, SD's portfolio is outstanding. I'm not

sure why they call their company "Standard Design," though, as there's nothing "standard" about them. "Stellar Design" is more like it. Highly recommended.

Wix - http://www.wix.com
At Wix, you can create some pretty impressive Flash-based web sites with the Wix Web Site Builder, all point and click without having to know or understand Flash. They have many Flash templates that are music-based and already pre-made. If you want to hire a professional Flash designer, you'll find lots of links and portfolios here.

Music Law and Copyright Resources

Complete listing available at http://www.musicbizacademy.com/directory/copyright.htm .

The Future of Music Coalition - http://www.futureofmusic.org/
This fascinating web site features numerous articles and commentaries on the state of the music industry, technology and the evolving debate over intellectual property rights. One of the stated goals of the Coalition is to educate musicians about critical issues shaping the industry. You'll find a large selection of articles, a library of important books, research areas, newsletters, and ideas for how you can participate in the debate. Sign up for the newsletter to remain updated on what's happening on the legal side of the entertainment world.

The Harry Fox Agency - http://www.harryfox.com/index.jsp
Want to use a copyright-protected song but you're confused about who to contact and how to go about it? The HFA licenses the largest percentage of music in the United States for CDs, digital services and music downloads. Once you register, The HFA's easy-to-use licensing system takes you step-by-step through the process of licensing songs for use in recording, performance, film, or digital downloads, and tells you exactly what you need to do and what it will cost you.

MusicContracts.com - http://www.musiccontracts.com/
This site, an extension of the Law Office of J. Scott Rudsenske, offers an assortment of pre-made music business contracts for the artist, record label, manager, producer and publisher. Contracts are available in packages, or individually. Once you select and pay for the contract (most range from $20-$40), you may immediately download it.

Public Domain Music - http://www.pdinfo.com/
Need to find out if a song you want to perform or record is in the public domain? Then check out this public domain information project. You'll find numerous articles on public domain works and copyright information as well as public domain song lists, research resources, tips, and a well-documented FAQ.

Recording Industry Association of America - http://www.riaa.com/
The RIAA is a trade group that represents *most* of the corporate music industry. Its member companies comprise about 90% of all sound recordings manufactured and sold in the U.S.. While some artists view the RIAA as the "enemy," representing big money and big business, the company does in fact provide a wealth of information on what's happening in the industry. The RIAA site is regularly updated with information on new technologies, copyright law, freedom of speech, licensing, royalties, market data and more. Hanging out at the RIAA site will definitely give you a different perspective - the business perspective, and that's a perspective you ought to know.

Releasing a Record: A Legal Checklist - http://www.musicbizacademy.com/articles/legalchecklist.htm
For artists who are releasing their own record for the first time, without the involvement or assistance of a label, the process can be a little intimidating. It can be easy to miss some key legal details in the process. Here, therefore, is a very basic checklist of issues to be considered when releasing a record.

Tips for Selecting an Entertainment Attorney - http://musicdish.com/mag/?id=2153
Sooner or later you will need legal counsel as a musician, songwriter, label owner or industry careerist and it's important to know how to select the best counsel for your needs. Here are a few tips to help you with the screening process.

U.S. Copyright Office Homepage - http://www.copyright.gov
The U.S. Copyright Office has recently updated their web site to make it much more user-friendly. You'll find all the forms you need, details on copyright basics, as well as the latest news on copyright law. Get all your forms here.

Quick Reference Guide

Want more? Just can't get enough? Here's a categorized list of some of the many resources I recommend on the Internet. Many of these are mentioned within the pages of this book, and others are provided so that you can do further research on your own. Items in **BOLD** receive my highest recommendations:

Internet Service Providers

Comcast: http://www.comcast.com
Verizon: http://www.verizon.com/dsl
Clear Mobile Internet: http://www.clear.com/
Clearwire Internet: http://www.clearwire.com/
Broadband/DSL Reports: http://www.dslreports.com/search
The List: http://www.thelist.com
How DSL Works: http://computer.howstuffworks.com/dsl.htm

Anti-Virus, Firewall & Spyware Software

AVG Free Antivirus: http://free.avg.com/us-en/homepage
Kaspserky Antivirus: http://usa.kaspersky.com/
McAfee Internet Security: http://home.mcafee.com/Store/PackageDetail.aspx?pkgid=273
WebRoot Spy Sweeper: http://www.webroot.com/En_US/consumer-products.html
Trend Micro Internet Security: http://www.trendmicro.com/en/products/us/personal.htm
ZoneAlarm – Free Firewall: http://download.cnet.com/ZoneAlarm/3000-10435_4-10039884.html

Web Browsers

Mozilla Firefox: http://www.mozilla.com/firefox/
Internet Explorer: http://www.microsoft.com/windows/internet-explorer/default.aspx
Safari (Macintosh):   http://www.apple.com/safari/
Other Browsers: http://browsers.evolt.org

Web Hosting

PowWeb: http://www.powweb.com
GoDaddy: http://www.godaddy.com
Site5   http://www.site5.com
LunarPages   http://www.LunarPages.com
Surpass Hosting   http://surpasshosting.com
How to Choose a Hosting Service: http://www.wilsonweb.com/wmt2/issue27.htm#WebHosting
Top Host Comparison and Search: http://www.tophosts.com
Compare Web Hosts: http://www.comparewebhosts.com/
Free Web Site Hosting Services: http://www.thefreesite.com/Free_Web_Space/
Free Web Hosting: http://www.free-webhosts.com/

Domain Name Registration

DirectNIC: http://www.directnic.com
Go Daddy: http://www.godaddy.com
000domains.com: http://www.000domains.com/
Network Solutions: http://www.networksolutions.com/

FTP Clients and Tutorials

CoreFTP (free FTP tool):   http://www.coreftp.com
CuteFTP: http://www.cuteftp.com/cuteftp/
WS_FTP: http://www.ipswitchft.com/Individual/Products/ws_ftp_home/Index.aspx
FTP Explorer: http://www.ftpx.com/
Fetch (for the Mac):   http://www.fetchsoftworks.com/

Free Email Services

Yahoo Mail: http://mail.yahoo.com
Gmail: http://gmail.google.com
HotMail: http://www.hotmail.com
Free Email Address Directory: http://www.emailaddresses.com/

"Instant" Web Site Builders

HostBaby.com: http://www.hostbaby.com/
BandZoogle: http://www.bandzoogle.com
BandVista: http://www.bandvista.com
ReverbNation: http://www.reverbnation.com
Wix: http://www.wix.com/
Homestead: http://www.homestead.com
Viviti: http://viviti.com
Wordpress: http://www.Wordpress.com and http://www.Wordpress.org

Web Page Editors, Builders, Tools, Tutorials

Namo WebEditor:	http://www.namo.com/products/webeditor.php
TextPad (Text File Editor):	http://www.textpad.com
HTML Tutorial for Beginners:	http://davesite.com/webstation/html/
Site Spinner:	http://www.virtualmechanics.com/products/spinner/
CoffeeCup VisualSite Designer:	http://www.coffeecup.com/designer/
StudioLine Web:	http://www.studioline.net/EN/products/overview-web/default.htm
Nvu:	http://net2.com/nvu/
PageBreeze:	http://www.pagebreeze.com/
SWiSH (Flash made easy):	http://www.swishzone.com/
25 WYSIWYG Editors Reviewed:	http://tinyurl.com/5bwu3v
HTML Editors - Info & Reviews:	http://webdesign.about.com/od/htmleditors/
HTML Clinic:	http://www.htmlclinic.com/
HTML Goodies:	http://www.htmlgoodies.com/tutorials/getting_started/
HTML Center:	http://www.htmlcenter.com/
Web Design from Scratch:	http://www.webdesignfromscratch.com/
Flash Tutorial:	http://www.w3schools.com/Flash/default.asp
Adobe Flash Developer:	http://www.adobe.com/devnet/flash.html

Web Site Templates, Graphics and Images

Free Web Site Templates:	http://www.freewebsitetemplates.com/
Boxed Art:	http://www.boxedart.com/
4Templates.com:	http://www.4templates.com/
Design Galaxy:	http://www.designgalaxy.net/
Deonix Design:	http://www.deonixdesign.com/
Template Monster:	http://www.templatemonster.com/
Free Site Templates:	http://www.freesitetemplates.com/
Elated Pagekits:	http://www.elated.com/pagekits/
Ice Templates:	http://icetemplates.com/
Full Moon Graphics:	http://www.fullmoongraphics.com/
A+ Templates:	http://www.aplustemplates.com/
Basic Templates:	http://www.basictemplates.biz/servlet/StoreFront
The Template Store:	http://www.thetemplatestore.com/

Web Site Graphics, Images and Stock Photography

iStockphoto:	http://www.iStockphoto.com
FreeGraphics.com:	http://www.freegraphics.com
Trout's GIF Optimizer (freeware):	http://www.chemware.co.nz/tgo.htm
GUIStuff:	http://www.guistuff.com/
ButtonGenerator:	http://www.buttongenerator.com/
FlashButtons:	http://www.flashbuttons.com
CoolText:	http://www.cooltext.com/
Flaming Text:	http://www.flamingtext.com/start.html

Web Site Designers for Hire

HostBaby.com Designer Search:	http://www.hostbaby.com/wddb
Freelancer.com:	http://www.freelancer.com/
Elance Agency:	http://www.elance.com/p/websites/index.html
ScriptLance.com	http://www.scriptlance.com
Wix (Flash Design):	http://www.wix.com
Auntie Momo Design:	http://www.auntiemomo.com/

Web Stats and Counters

FastStats:	http://mach5.com/products/analyzer/index.php
GoStats Free Counter:	http://gostats.com/
WebLog Expert:	http://www.weblogexpert.com
Free Web Counters:	http://www.thefreesite.com/freecounters.htm

Scripts, Forms, Site Tools and More

Bravenet Web Services:	http://www.bravenet.com/
The Free Site:	http://www.thefreesite.com/
Web Site Tools:	http://www.webpage-tools.com/
FAQ: SSI:	http://www.andreas.com/faq-ssi.html
The CGI Resource Index (SSI):	http://tinyurl.com/29p2gcd
HotScripts:	http://www.hotscripts.com/
Dynamic Drive DHTML Library:	http://www.dynamicdrive.com/
JavaScript Made Easy:	http://www.jsmadeeasy.com/
JavaScript Kit:	http://www.javascriptkit.com/
JavaScript Search:	http://www.javascript-2.com/
EchoEcho:	http://www.echoecho.com/
Matt's Script Archive:	http://www.scriptarchive.com/
Remotely Hosted Scripts:	http://www.cgi.resourceindex.com/Remotely_Hosted/
Codango (Hosted Applications):	http://www.codango.com/
Email AutoResponders:	http://www.sendfree.com or http://www.getresponse.com
	http://www.freeautobot.com or http://www.aweber.com/
Create Surveys, Registration Forms:	http://www.formsite.com
Privacy Policy Generator:	http://www.the-dma.org/privacy/privacypolicygenerator.shtml
Ace Popup Generator:	http://www.cgiscript.net/site_software.htm
iCoder.com (script installation):	http://installations.icoder.com/
Vworker (programmers for hire):	http://www.vworker.com
ScriptLance.com (for hire)	http://www.scriptlance.com

Protect Your Email

How Spammers Get Your Address:	http://www.private.org.il/harvest.html
Email Protector:	http://www.iconico.com/emailProtector/
Email Address Munger:	http://www.addressmunger.com/
Stop Spam-Bots:	http://www.safeemail.org/
Automatic Email Protection:	http://www.bronze-age.com/nospam/encode.html
MailWasher:	http://www.mailwasher.net

Web Site Maintenance Tools

LinkAlarm:	http://www.linkalarm.com/
Web Site Monitor:	http://tinyurl.com/3y6lco4
LinkScan QuickCheck:	http://www.elsop.com/linkscan/quickcheck.html
Web Link Validator:	http://www.relsoftware.com/wlv/
Web Site Tips and Tools:	http://websitetips.com/tools/

Sound Tools

Audacity:	http://audacity.sourceforge.net/
MP3Gain:	http://mp3gain.sourceforge.net/index.php
MPtrim and WAVtrim:	http://www.mptrim.com/
Wimpy Player:	http://www.wimpyplayer.com/
MP3 Trimmer (for the Mac)	http://www.deepniner.net/mp3trimmer/
Windows Media Technologies:	http://www.microsoft.com/windows/windowsmedia/default.asp
Apple Quicktime:	http://www.apple.com/quicktime/
Web Jukebox:	http://www.coffeecup.com/web-jukebox/
ReverbNation:	http://www.reverbnation.com
Secure TSPlayer:	http://www.tsplayer.com/
DivShare:	http://www.divshare.com/
e-phonic:	http://www.e-phonic.com/mp3player/
A4Desk Music Player:	http://music.a4desk.com/
Royalty Free Music:	http://tinyurl.com/3amwmp
XSPF Music Player:	http://musicplayer.sourceforge.net/
JetAudio:	http://www.cowonamerica.com/products/jetaudio/
CDex:	http://cdexos.sourceforge.net/
dBpoweramp:	http://www.dbpoweramp.com/dmc.htm
Fission:	http://www.rogueamoeba.com/fission/
Blaze Media Pro:	http://www.blazemp.com/
Sound Forge:	http://www.sonymediasoftware.com/products/soundforgefamily.asp
Zamzar (online file converter):	http://www.zamzar.com/
Pro Tools:	http://www.avid.com/US/products/family/Pro-Tools
GoldWave (for editing WAV files):	http://www.goldwave.com
MP3Machine:	http://www.mp3machine.com/
Shareware Music Machine:	http://www.hitsquad.com/smm
Music Software Tutorials & Tips:	http://www.hitsquad.com/smm/tutorials.html

E-Commerce Plug-Ins, Add-ons and Shopping Cart Systems

1AutomationWiz.com: http://www.1automationwiz.com
CD Baby: http://members.cdbaby.com/
Bandcamp: http://www.bandcamp.com
Mal's E-Commerce: http://www.mals-e.com
CCNow: http://www.ccnow.com
E-Junkie: http://www.e-junkie.com/
1ShoppingCart.com http://www.1shoppingcart.com
PayPal: http://www.paypal.com
2CheckOut.com (recurring): http://www.2checkout.com
Nimbit: http://www.nimbit.com
Audiolife: http://www.audiolife.com
ReverbNation: http://www.reverbnation.com
Bandbox: http://www.bandbox.com

Merchant Vendor Solutions

Simplefy: http://www.simplefy.com
Paynet Systems: http://www.paynetsystems.com
PayPal's Website Payments Pro: http://tinyurl.com/akxqs
PayPal Micropayments: https://www.paypal.com/IntegrationCenter/ic_micropayments.html
How to Shop for Merchant Account: http://tinyurl.com/lyq57r

Web Site Promotion Tools

Google Keyword Suggestion Tool: https://adwords.google.com/select/KeywordToolExternal
Trellian's Keyword Suggestion Tool: http://www.keyworddiscovery.com/search.html
12 Keyword Suggestion Tools: http://www.seocompany.ca/tool/8-keyword-suggestion-tools.html
WordTracker (Keywords Report): http://www.wordtracker.com/
Google Trends: http://www.google.com/trends
Yahoo Buzz Index: http://buzz.yahoo.com
Your Web Site on Your Car: http://www.id-plates-for-you.com/
Web Site Ranking Check: http://www.microsoft-watch.org/cgi-bin/ranking.htm
Who's Linking to You?: https://www.google.com/webmasters/tools
Free Keyword Density Analyzer: http://www.keyworddensity.com/

Search Engine News, Tutorials and Services

Search Engine Watch: http://www.searchenginewatch.com
Search Engine Guide: http://www.searchengineguide.com/
HighRankings.com: http://www.highrankings.com/
Wilson Internet Services: http://www.wilsonweb.com
Pandia Search Central: http://www.pandia.com/
Beginners Guide to SEO: http://www.seomoz.org/article/beginners-guide-to-search-engine-optimization
37 Ways to Promote your Web Site: http://www.wilsonweb.com/articles/checklist.htm
Web Sites Every SEO Should Know: http://www.seounique.com/blog/25-websites-every-seo-should-know
Key Site Ranking Factors: http://www.seomoz.org/article/search-ranking-factors
10 Tips to the Top of the Search Engines: http://www.highrankings.com/tentips.htm
Search Engine Submission Tips: http://www.searchenginewatch.com/webmasters/
Bruce Clay Tactics: http://www.bruceclay.com/web_pt.htm
Virtual Promote: http://www.virtualpromote.com/
Google Alert: http://www.google.com/alerts

Search Engine Optimization Specialists

HighRankings.com: http://www.highrankings.com/
Muse's Muse Online Marketing: http://www.internet-marketing-mm.com/
SEO Consultants Directory: http://www.seoconsultants.com/
SEMList.com: http://www.semlist.com
10 Things to Ask a Promo Company: http://www.netpost.com/tentoask.html

How to Find People

Facebook: http://www.facebook.com
MyLife.com (formerly Reunion.com) http://www.mylife.com/
Classmates.com: http://www.classmates.com
USAReunited: http://www.usareunited.com
MySchoolReunited http://www.myschoolreunited.com/
GradFinder: http://www.gradfinder.com/
Alumni.net: http://www.alumni.net
SchoolNews: http://www.schoolnews.com/
CuriousCat Alumni: http://www.curiouscat.net/alumni/
Spokeo: http://www.spokeo.com
ZabaSearch: http://www.zabasearch.com/
Pandia People Search: http://www.pandia.com/people/index.html
PublicRecordsNow: http://web.public-records-now.com/
Intelius: http://find.intelius.com/
Lycos People Search: http://peoplesearch.lycos.com/whitepage/
AnyWho: http://www.anywho.com/
Knowx: http://www.knowx.com/
PhoneNumber: http://www.phonenumber.com/
U.S. Search: http://www.ussearch.com/consumer/index.jsp

Fan Marketing and Communication Tools

Facebook:	http://www.facebook.com
VistaPrint:	http://www.vistaprint.com
FreeConferenceCall.com:	http://www.freeconferencecall.com
Free Phone Conference:	http://www.freephoneconference.com/
Survey Monkey:	http://www.surveymonkey.com
Bravenet Vote Caster:	http://www.bravenet.com/webtools/vote/
AddThis.com:	http://www.addthis.com/
Email Address Validator:	http://tinyurl.com/d35mg
Email Dossier (Address Validator):	http://centralops.net/co/EmailDossier.vbs.asp
Google Alerts:	http://www.google.com/alerts

Groups, Forums, Discussion Groups:

Zhift (forum search tool):	http://www.zhift.com
Hi5:	http://www.hi5.com
Yahoo Groups:	http://groups.yahoo.com
Google Groups	http://groups.google.com
Google Chat & Forums:	http://directory.google.com/Top/Arts/Music/Chats_and_Forums/

Blogging

Wordpress:	http://www.Wordpress.com
Blogger:	http://www.blogger.com
AddThis:	http://www.addthis.com
AddToBookmark:	http://www.addtobookmarks.com/
Blog? Yep, and Here's How:	http://bit.ly/92LtUh
Blogging for Beginners:	http://www.problogger.net/archives/2006/02/14/blogging-for-beginners-2/
Blogs 101:	http://www.searchengineguide.com/ross-dunn/stepforth-tutor.php
Learn How to Blog:	http://www.blogbasics.com/beginner-tutorials.php
25 Blog Optimization Tips:	http://tinyurl.com/5e4qe5
7 Ways to Keep Content Flowing:	http://ow.ly/uI6
Everything About RSS:	http://www.rss-specifications.com
RSS in Plain English:	http://www.commoncraft.com/rss_plain_english
RSS Network:	http://www.rss-network.com/submitrss.php
Feed 101:	http://www.google.com/support/feedburner/bin/answer.py?answer=79408
Google Feed Reader:	http://reader.google.com
FeedBurner:	http://www.feedburner.com
Technorati:	http://www.technorati.com
Google Blogs Search:	http://blogsearch.google.com
How to Promote Your Blog:	http://www.search-this.com/2007/04/23/how-to-promote-your-blog/
25 Paths to an Insanely Popular Blog:	http://tinyurl.com/26buvf
Is Your Mom Your Only Reader?	http://bit.ly/1xW3sb
Free Essential Tools for Bloggers:	http://tinyurl.com/2wwj34

Blog/Article Submission Sites

Digg:	http://www.digg.com
StumbleUpon:	http://www.stumbleupon.com
Articles Factory:	http://www.articlesfactory.com/
Go Articles:	http://www.goarticles.com/
FreeSticky:	http://www.freesticky.com/stickyweb/
EzineArticles.com:	http://www.ezinearticles.com/
IdeaMarketers.com:	http://www.ideamarketers.com/
20 Directories to Submit your Blog to:	http://tinyurl.com/2xf2xz
Top 25 Content Submission Sites:	http://www.wilsonweb.com/linking/wilson-article-marketing-1.htm

Social Media / Social Networking

Facebook:	http://www.facebook.com
Twitter:	http://www.twitter.com
YouTube:	http://www.youtube.com
MySpace:	http://www.myspace.com
Flickr:	http://www.flickr.com
Digg:	http://www.digg.com
StumbleUpon:	http://www.stumbleupon.com
Top 15 Social Bookmarking Sites:	http://www.ebizmba.com/articles/social-bookmarking
Tools for Engaging in Social Media:	http://tinyurl.com/d6kp6e
Branding with Social Media:	http://tinyurl.com/59zhp8
How to Influence Social Media Users:	http://tinyurl.com/yp6ztz
How to Target Social Media Sites:	http://tinyurl.com/6c585s
35 Must-Read Articles:	http://tinyurl.com/6arhjn
Social Media Etiquette Handbook:	http://tinyurl.com/5tuf4s
Categorized List of Social Media Sites:	http://traffikd.com/social-media-websites/
Social Media Networking Sites:	http://bit.ly/SC4l
Social Networking Stats for 2010:	http://tinyurl.com/ydashyr
Twitter Search Tool:	http://search.twitter.com/
15 Ways to Track Twitter Trends:	http://mashable.com/2009/04/04/twitter-trends/
Google Trends:	http://google.com/trends
Yahoo Buzz:	http://buzz.yahoo.com/

Making and Marketing Your Video

Animoto.com:	http://www.animoto.com
Tubemogul Video Distribution:	http://www.tubemogul.com/
How to Make Your Video:	http://www.youtube.com/watch?v=3zFePU1uvtc
Getting a Web Cam:	http://www.youtube.com/watch?v=XLjpZUsFEXo
How to Edit a Video:	http://www.youtube.com/watch?v=gmvjvlOnBYw
How to Create a Video Blog:	http://desktopvideo.about.com/od/videoblogging/ht/howtovlog.htm
Choosing a Video Editing Program:	http://www.youtube.com/watch?v=yiQ6OtLHgX4
Video Marketing Tips & Trends:	http://www.reelseo.com/
YouTube Sharing & Optimization Tips:	http://www.reelseo.com/seo-for-video/#youtube
How to Go Viral on YouTube:	http://arielpublicity.com/blog/archives/how-to-go-viral-on-youtube

Writing Your Press Release:

How to Write Your Press Release:	http://www.publicityinsider.com/release.asp
How to Write a Successful Release:	http://tinyurl.com/2wm36lp
What to Do, What Not to Do:	http://www.rapidpressrelease.com/tips/writing.asp
The Anatomy of a Press Release:	http://www.pressflash.com/resources_anatomy.php
Press Releases 101:	http://tinyurl.com/alwhc6
The Ten Commandments of a PR:	http://www.musicdish.com/mag/?id=12018
Sample Press Release:	http://tinyurl.com/ybphvq4

Press Release Distribution Services

20 Free PR Distribution Sites:	http://tinyurl.com/yl5dbar
PR Web:	http://www.prweb.com/
Mi2N: Music Industry News Net:	http://www.mi2n.com/
Beat Wire:	http://www.beatwire.com
RapidPressRelease.com:	http://www.rapidpressrelease.com/music+band+press+release/
PRLog	http://www.prlog.org
PRLeap	http://www.prleap.com
eReleases:	http://www.ereleases.com/
EWorldWire.com	http://www.eworldwire.com
Pressbox:	http://www.pressbox.co.uk/index.html
Harmony Central:	http://www.harmony-central.com/

Pay-for-Promotion Services

Ariel Publicity:	http://www.arielpublicity.com
Evolution Promotion:	http://www.evolutionpromotion.com/
The Music Dish Network:	http://www.musicdish.net/
SonicBids:	http://www.sonicbids.com/
MusicSubmit:	http://www.musicsubmit.com

Converting Visitors to Customers

Choice Kills Conversion:	http://tinyurl.com/22mmb9d
Too Many Choices = Less Sales:	http://sivers.org/jam
20 Tips to Minimize Abandonment, Pt1:	http://bit.ly/b41P7D
20 Tips to Minimize Abandonment, Pt2:	http://bit.ly/bCcDPO
Constant Contact:	http://www.constantcontact.com
Campaign Monitor:	http://www.campaignmonitor.com
FanBridge.com:	http://www.fanbridge.com
MailChimp:	http://www.mailchimp.com/

Royalties

SoundExchange:	http://www.soundexchange.com
SESAC:	http://www.sesac.com
ASCAP:	http://www.ascap.com
BMI:	http://www.bmi.com
How Music Royalties Work:	http://entertainment.howstuffworks.com/music-royalties7.htm
ASCAP vs. BMI Commentary	http://tinyurl.com/df6oga
BMI vs. ASCAP (CD Baby forums):	http://cdbaby.org/stories/06/08/10/4085523.html
ASCAP vs. BMI (TAXI forums):	http://bit.ly/9K0VPi
Does SoundExchange Have Your Money?:	http://tinyurl.com/29fmdfs

Internet Radio and Podcasting

Live365.com:	http://www.live365.com
Starting a Broadcast on Live365.com:	http://bit.ly/9REwMY
ShoutCast:	http://www.shoutcast.com
SAM Broadcaster:	http://www.spacialaudio.com/
StreamGuys:	http://www.streamguys.com/
Music 1 Software:	http://www.gomusic1.com
Music Alley:	http://www.musicalley.com/
MagnaTune:	http://www.magnatune.com
Podcast Alley:	http://www.podcastalley.com
Podcasting 101:	http://www.podcasting-tools.com/podcasting-101.htm
Podcast Primer for Indies:	http://tinyurl.com/24y25lr
podOmatic:	http://www.podomatic.com/
Make Your First Podcast:	http://podcastingnews.com/articles/How-to-Podcast.html
Create Your Own Podcast:	http://reviews.cnet.com/4520-10163_7-6246557-1.html?tag=nl.e501
How to Podcast:	http://www.how-to-podcast-tutorial.com/
Propaganda:	http://www.download.com/Propaganda/3000-2170_4-10381177.html
FeedForAll:	http://www.feedforall.com/
ePodcast Creator:	http://tinyurl.com/355cl2v
PodProducer:	http://www.podproducer.net/en/index.html
Podcasting Legal Guide:	http://wiki.creativecommons.org/Podcasting_Legal_Guide
Creating Legal Indie Music Podcasts:	http://alchemi.co.uk/archives/mus/creating_legal_.html

Booking, Gigging and Touring

HouseConcerts.com:	http://www.houseconcerts.com/venue.php
Concerts in Your Home:	http://www.concertsinyourhome.com/index.html
Folkmusic.org venue listings:	http://www.folkmusic.org/shows/venues.html
The Choice Privileges Visa Card:	http://www.choicehotels.com

Banner Advertising and Affiliate Programs

Google AdSense:	https://www.google.com/adsense/
ValueClick Media:	http://www.valueclickmedia.com/
Amazon Associates:	https://affiliate-program.amazon.com/
iTunes Affiliates:	http://www.apple.com/itunes/affiliates/
Commission Junction:	http://www.cj.com
Advertising.com:	http://www.advertising.com
BURST!:	http://www.burstmedia.com/
Affiliate First:	http://www.affiliatefirst.com/
Affiliate's Directory:	http://www.affiliatesdirectory.com/
AssociatePrograms.com:	http://www.associateprograms.com/directory/
AffiliateTip.com:	http://www.affiliatetip.com/
How to Set Up Your Own Program:	http://www.associateprograms.com/search/howto.shtml
MyAffiliateProgram:	http://www.myaffiliateprogram.com/
AffiliateShop.com:	http://www.affiliateshop.com/
AffiliateTracking:	http://www.affiliatetracking.com/
SimpleAffiliate:	http://www.simpleaffiliate.com/
Free AdDesigner:	http://www.addesigner.com/
AdButler Banner Rotation Software:	http://www.adbutler.com/
Banner Ad Placement Study:	http://www.webreference.com/dev/banners/
GW Web Design Banner Portfolio:	http://www.gwwebdesign.com/banner_portfolio.html

Copyrighting Your Music, Web Site, and Digital Creations

U.S. Copyright Office:	http://www.copyright.gov/
eCO Online Copyright System:	http://www.copyright.gov/eco/
eCO System Tutorial:	http://www.copyright.gov/eco/eco-tutorial.pdf
Copyright Your Digital Creation:	http://www.myfreecopyright.com
Creative Commons:	http://www.creativecommons.org/
World Intellectual Property Org	http://www.wipo.int/members/en/
Copyright and Fair Use:	http://fairuse.stanford.edu/
Web Site Copyright Protection:	http://www.keytlaw.com/Copyrights/Register.htm
Copyscape: Search for Plagiarism:	http://www.copyscape.com/

Final Words

Making the Intangible Tangible

Up until about five years ago, the occasional artist would email me, scoffing somewhat, because they couldn't see the Internet as something *tangible* that could impact their music career. I remember one artist telling me the Internet was for musician wannabes, while *real* musicians played the stage and toured.

Well, no one is scoffing now. The Internet permeates our daily lives. Today's youth culture doesn't differentiate between music and the Internet. The two are completely intertwined. And with the explosion of portable devices like the iPhone and the Droid, more people are *continuously* connected to the Internet, from *anywhere*, with instant access to virtually *anything*, than ever before. The Internet is as readily accessible as your cell phone and as *wearable* as a watch or a pair of sunglasses.

The Internet is changing not only our culture, but the face of the music business. So much so, that what you do on the Internet *today* may very well determine how successful you are *tomorrow*. Ten years ago I was working behind a desk, managing people and quality control for a computer software company. Today, I'm doing music full time, and it's because I utilized the Internet *then* to change the course of where my music career is *now*.

So where will *your* music career be in five or ten years? That depends on what you do now. If you do nothing, then nothing exceptional will happen. If you work at it for a little while, but then grow weary and give up on it (as most people tend to do), then that's as far as you'll go. To find success, you have to keep going, even though it may take years to accomplish your goals. Remember, I've been promoting my music online for over *fifteen years*, and I still have much to do. Promoting your music online is an ongoing life process, not a six month commitment.

In my life and business as a professional artist, I have come to realize that whether or not you "make it" financially and artistically depends, to a large degree, on your ability to outlast and out-persist almost everyone else. Will you endure the doubts, criticisms, setbacks, and obstacles that cause most everyone else to stumble and finally concede? If you do, and if you outlast most of your competition, you'll soon find that others just starting out in this business will look to you as an example of success. If you truly have *the gift*, but fail to shine with it, it may simply be because you gave up on the dream too soon. Don't give up. Don't stop. Just keep *doing*, and *being* who you are.

If you take the suggestions in this book to heart, you have months, perhaps years, of hard work ahead of you. And while the task may seem a bit overwhelming (it should), just start simple. Begin at the beginning, as they say. If you're just starting out, don't worry about affiliate programs, advertising, targeted web sites and all that yet. Just design a professional-looking web site to present your music, optimize it and get listed on the search engines. Next, get your music on iTunes, Amazon.com, Pandora and CDBaby.com. Then use the social networking, people-targeting, and exposure-creating strategies I've talked about in this book to generate awareness about you and your music to the Internet-browsing world at large. It's a long process, but worth it. You can do it! I did it, and if I can do it, you can, too!

One final piece of advice: Stay focused! It's easy to get distracted. You may find yourself going along just fine and then realize you've spent an entire month working on something that's not going to improve your exposure or your sales! Create a plan and stick to it. Yes, you can be flexible, but with each new task you take on, ask yourself whether that task will really move your career forward... or is it just taking up your time?

I hope that you have found this book to be helpful and useful. I welcome your comments about it. Feel free to email me at dnevue@rainmusic.com and let me know what you think. If I can improve upon it, or there's a topic or subject you think I should cover that I have not, let me know.

Once again, thank you for purchasing this book. I wish you luck, success, and much more music to come.

David Nevue
The Music Biz Academy
http://www.musicbizacademy.com
http://www.davidnevue.com
http://www.twitter.com/musicbizacademy

Be sure to check out our other products:

The Complete Guide to Starting a Record Company
Music Is Your Business
The Guerrilla Music Marketing Handbook
How to Be Your Own Booking Agent
The Indie Bible

Available at the Music Biz Academy Bookstore: http://www.musicbizacademy.com/bookstore .

Made in the USA
Charleston, SC
04 April 2013